Voice of the Tribes

NEW DIRECTIONS IN NATIVE AMERICAN STUDIES

Colin G. Calloway and K. Tsianina Lomawaima, General Editors

NATIONAL TRIBAL CHAIRMEN'S ASSOCIATION

UNITY • STRENGTH • JUSTICE

Voice of the Tribes

A History of the National Tribal
Chairmen's Association

THOMAS A. BRITTEN
Foreword by Charles Trimble

UNIVERSITY OF OKLAHOMA PRESS : NORMAN

Publication of this book is made possible through the generosity of Edith Kinney Gaylord.

Library of Congress Cataloging-in-Publication Data

Names: Britten, Thomas A. (Thomas Anthony), 1964– author. | Trimble, Charles E., writer of foreword.

Title: Voice of the tribes : a history of the National Tribal Chairmen's Association / Thomas A. Britten ; foreword by Charles Trimble.

Other titles: New directions in Native American studies; v. 20.

Description: Norman : University of Oklahoma Press, [2020] | Series: New directions in Native American studies ; volume 20 | Includes bibliographical references and index. | Summary: "A comprehensive history of the National Tribal Chairmen's Association (NTCA) from its inception in 1971 to its 1986 disbandment"—Provided by publisher.

Identifiers: LCCN 2019052242 | ISBN 978-0-8061-6492-2 (hardcover) ISBN 978-0-8061-8390-9 (paper)

Subjects: LCSH: National Tribal Chairmen's Association—History. | Indians of North America—Politics and government—20th century.

Classification: LCC E93 .B865 2020 | DDC 323.1197—dc23

LC record available at https://lccn.loc.gov/2019052242

Voice of the Tribes: A History of the National Tribal Chairmen's Association is Volume 20 in the New Directions in Native American Studies series.

The paper in this book meets the guidelines for permanence and durability of the Committee on Production Guidelines for Book Longevity of the Council on Library Resources, Inc. ∞

Contents

Illustrations

Foreword

Historian Thomas Britten's two most recent books, *Voice of the Tribes: A History of the National Tribal Chairmen's Association* and *The National Council on Indian Opportunity: Quiet Champion of Self-Determination* (2014), are important additions to the history of a pivotal time that might be called the Golden Age of Indian Policy: the Nixon Era in Indian affairs—a truly memorable era that marked the end of termination and the beginning of self-determination as the foundation of national Indian policy.

That period—the 1970s and early 1980s—saw the issuance of the seminal "Indian Message to Congress" by President Richard Nixon, and Congress's enactment of legislation called for in that message. In addition, the Nixon White House made precedent-setting changes in official policy that included actual restoration of, rather than remuneration for, lands illegally taken from tribes without due process or just compensation.

Leading up to that prolific era were presages of what was to come as Presidents John Kennedy and then Lyndon Johnson began to take note as the poverty and abandonment of racial minorities came into focus against a backdrop of the country flourishing in a postwar economic boom. Martin Luther King Jr. wakened the nation to awareness and drew Kennedy into the struggle for an end to segregation and for civil rights. On the West Coast, Cesar Chavez led a new movement to call public attention to working and living conditions of migrant workers by organizing boycotts of targeted produce, leading to a national Chicano rights movement.

These movements inspired younger leaders in the urban Indian communities in the late 1960s, igniting activism manifest in demonstrations and militancy in the takeover and occupation of surplus military facilities to claim them for Indian people; in 1969, Indian militants occupied the out-of-commission federal prison on Alcatraz Island.

Early Indian activism first targeted the white man as a conqueror and exploiter; then turned on the paternalistic federal bureaucracy, especially the Bureau of Indian Affairs, and finally on Indian leadership as intimidated sellouts to the dominant white society and the federal government. The National Congress of American Indians (NCAI), the singular national organization representing Indian Country, became the lightning rod of the growing activism and militancy.

NCAI conventions increasingly came under attack from Indian activists, who often disrupted sessions and took over the stage to rail against the NCAI leaders as "uncle Tomahawks" for not standing up to the federal government and demanding delivery of services and protection guaranteed in the Indian treaties. The NCAI conventions were fully democratic functions, and the floor microphones were generally open to any Indian individual who paid the modest registration fees and membership dues. The new activists saw this as a ready forum to air their radical views. And NCAI, adhering to its tolerant practices, was seen by some tribal leaders as weak, losing control, and surrendering itself to the urban Indian militants.

The first convention that was disrupted was in 1969 in Albuquerque, resulting in considerable damage to the host hotel. At that convention, the militants made inroads when the NCAI Executive Council elected as executive director Bruce Wilkie (Makah), one of the founders of the National Indian Youth Council, the organization that spearheaded the new Indian militancy. And the attitude of the new director and his staff reflected the general attitude among young militants: one of disrespect for the older leaders, whom they characterized as pawns of the federal government.

Following a year of gross mismanagement and profligacy, the organization was in dire financial straits and Wilkie was voted out. But the damage had been done: their arrogance and the near-terminal condition in which they left the organization caused many tribal leaders to pull their tribes out of NCAI, drastically reducing revenue from membership fees.

In addition, the proliferation of new Indian special-interest organizations representing health, education, housing, natural resources, and economic development was luring away NCAI leaders in those areas. Whereas, in the past, the annual NCAI convention was the single major annual event in Indian politics, conferences were now being held throughout the year by the better-funded special-interest Indian organizations.

In Washington, meanwhile, the new National Council on Indian Opportunity, housed in the White House complex and with direct access to higher levels in the federal departments, was replacing NCAI as the base camp for tribal delegations coming to the nation's capital.

In the national media, militant Indian leaders were attracting prime-time coverage with their increasingly violent and destructive demonstrations and rhetoric. With NCAI politically and financially weakened, some tribal leaders and federal agencies saw Indian Country as leaderless, and viewed the National Tribal Chairmen's Association (NTCA) as the answer to the problem of who speaks for the tribes. The prevailing attitude among the core of NTCA founders was that NCAI was no longer viable, and that its seemingly imminent demise would be a merciful end to its suffering and to the problem of who speaks for the tribes.

This all provided impetus for the formation of the National Tribal Chairmen's Association, and a group of its founders—mostly from Northern Plains tribes—lost no time in promoting nationwide tribal support and launching the NTCA. But the organization met with rejection on the part of small tribes and tribes seeking federal recognition, NCAI loyalists particularly from the Northwest, and militant organizations.

Britten's *Voice of the Tribes* is an excellent historic account of the genesis and launching of the NTCA, and the favorable partisan political developments that set the stage for the prolific era of progressive Indian legislation and policy. The background surrounding major issues and developments are described with accuracy and impact that come from thorough research and understanding of both the federal democratic process and the tribal political experience needed to deal with the process.

Especially important is the chapter on exclusivity, which the NTCA claimed as the basis of its existence: if Indians claim sovereignty and nationhood, they must accept the fact that in international affairs, it is the head of state who speaks for the state. Accordingly, the National Tribal Chairmen's Association—made up of chiefs, presidents, governors, and chairs—is, in fact, the voice of the Indian tribes. This, in the minds of NTCA founders, meant that the real Indians are those living on the Indian reservations because they are the only ones recognized by the federal government.

Voice of the Tribes is a book that should be in the library of every college with an Indian studies curriculum, and in the library of all scholars of contemporary Indian history.

Britten told me, "While researching the NCIO I discovered that there was little to nothing written about the NTCA and that I could make a contribution by trying to fill that niche." That makes me hopeful that his work on the NCIO and NTCA books will inspire scholars to chronicle the history of the National Congress of American Indians during that same important historical period. Several books have examined the early history of the NCAI, but none have touched on the period from 1969 forward through the administrations of Richard Nixon through Ronald Reagan; that period saw internal upheaval and near dissolution of the NCAI—and its struggle to stay alive in the face of NTCA's intent, abetted by the NCIO, to euthanize it.

Charles "Chuck" Trimble (Oglala Lakota)
Principal founder of American Indian Press Association
NCAI executive director (1972–1978)

Introduction

On October 26, 1972, the *Navajo Times* ran a story under the headline "Indian Protest Planned during Election Week." The piece detailed efforts by various Indian rights groups to recruit Native Americans from across the country to converge on Washington, D.C., during the first week of November to conduct peaceful demonstrations against the government's historic mistreatment of Native peoples. Participants also intended to hold spiritual ceremonies at Arlington National Cemetery to honor the sacrifices of Native American veterans. The decision to stage the protest on the eve of national elections was a strategic one—to maximize press coverage and to pressure the presidential campaigns of Richard Nixon and George McGovern for commitments of "more enlightened and sensitive performance of treaty responsibilities for American Indians."[1] The first arrivals of the so-called Trail of Broken Treaties Caravan (TBTC) rumbled into the nation's Capitol early in the morning of November 1. Despite organizers' assurances that they had taken care of participants' accommodation needs, the only place that made good on its offer to house the travelers was St. Stephen and the Incarnation Episcopal Church, which caravan participant Woody Kipp (Blackfeet) described as "an old, disemboweled, empty church" with "no amenities, not even running water." When rumors spread that someone had seen rats in the building, the grumbling increased, as did Indian anger and disillusionment. After discussing the depressing situation, caravan leaders tossed out their original itinerary and announced that everyone should go to the Bureau of Indian Affairs (BIA) building on Constitution Avenue.[2]

By late afternoon on Thursday, November 2, several hundred Native Americans were inside the BIA building—some in the auditorium, some in the cafeteria, others roaming the hallways gazing curiously into the offices of the bureaucrats responsible for administering the maze of programs and services that constituted part of the federal government's obligations (or trust responsibilities) to tribal nations. Around five o'clock, caravan leaders convened a press conference where they announced their acceptance of the government's offer of a meeting with high-level Nixon administration officials and the use of the Labor Department's auditorium. Where the Indians would spend the night apparently remained a work in progress—at least until the sounds of screams and breaking glass ended the press conference and signaled the start of a pro-tracted occupation.[3]

For reasons that remain unclear—but apparently due to a rumor that a law enforcement official was trapped inside—police officers in riot helmets entered the building during the press conference and began attempting to "escort" Indi-ans outside. Fighting erupted, and when the dust cleared, the police were back outside and the Indians in control of the building. From the evening of Novem-ber 2 through November 8, a tense standoff ensued. Caravan participants inside the BIA, expecting an all-out police assault at any moment, began erecting bar-ricades and crafting makeshift weapons. Indian women placed buckets of water and wet rags near windows for defenders to hold up to their faces in the event the police attempted to lob tear-gas canisters into the building. At the top of each flight of stairs, men stacked typewriters to drop on anyone storming the stairwells. Cans of gasoline and Molotov cocktails stood ready to transform the BIA into an inferno should an all-out assault take place. In preparation for what some hard-core activists believed would be a fight to the death, a medi-cine man initiated a ceremony to paint the faces of those who intended to give their lives. Other activists seized the opportunity to unleash their anger and frustration on the building itself. Reviewing the devastation (smashed windows and furniture, graffiti, broken toilet fixtures, destroyed office equipment, and an estimated $700,000 in damage to Indian art and artifacts), Rep. Wayne Aspi-nall, the chair of the House Committee on Interior and Insular Affairs, likened the destruction to post–World War II Europe and as an example of "human meanness at its worst."[4]

Tribal leaders from across the nation were quick to disassociate themselves and their constituents from the dramatic scene playing out in Washington. On Saturday, November 4, tribal representatives from nineteen Pueblo tribes, the Jicarilla and Mescalero Apache tribes of New Mexico, and the Southern Ute and Ute Mountain tribes of Colorado issued a joint statement declaring that the occupiers "in no way have the right to imply to the general public that they are speaking in behalf of all Indians" and that the protestors were "casting a bad reflection on all Indians." Joseph Upicksoun (Iñupiat), president of the

Arctic Slope Regional Corporation in Alaska, echoed these sentiments, stating that "responsible Indian and Eskimo leadership is not represented by the fiasco in Washington, D.C." James Henry, tribal chairman of North Dakota's Turtle Mountain Band of Chippewa, described the occupation as "a disgrace to the American Indian."[5]

In hopes of setting the record straight about where elected tribal leaders stood on the occupation, a contingent of tribal spokespersons organized an 11 A.M. press conference on November 6 at the Roger Smith Hotel in Washington, D.C. Shortly after it started, however, an "invasion" of pro-occupation protestors—apparently led by members of the American Indian Movement (AIM), an urban-based Indian rights organization founded in 1968—quickly transformed the gathering into a shouting match pitting tribal leaders against AIM members. Genevieve Hooper, secretary of the Yakama Tribal Council, denounced the "present disruption" under way at the BIA building and criticized the federal government for negotiating with the occupiers without the participation of elected Indian leaders. The BIA had been "literally destroyed" in recent years, she argued, because it "gets deeper and deeper in its involvement with non-reservation Indians who are militant and who do not represent the reservations." Why would the BIA shift its attention to urban Indians, she queried, who "generally do not make responsible demands" and "concern themselves mainly with the hysteria of unrest, militancy, etc.?"[6] On November 9, a day after the occupation ended, twelve tribal leaders inspected the ruins inside the BIA building, and what they saw confirmed their worst suspicions about urban Indian groups such as AIM—or what Webster Two Hawk (Rosebud Sioux) called "a small handful of self-appointed revolutionaries." Of particular concern was the theft or potential destruction of real estate documents, tribal enrollment records, lease agreements, and treaties. "Congress made these programs for people on the reservations," declared Yakama chair Robert Jim. "Now they have been destroyed by a few urban Indians." Roger Jourdain (Red Lake Chippewa) harbored other suspicions. "These Indians must have been under the influence of drugs. No Indian in his right mind would do this. . . . We want them prosecuted." The assembled tribal leaders, who claimed to be the "legitimate voice of the Indian peoples," called for the reconstruction of the BIA building and a resumption of its services to reservations; for an immediate investigation and prosecution of the "ruthless, self-seeking, self-appointed Indian leaders" responsible for the occupation; and for the federal government to cease negotiations with "illegitimate groups" and instead consult exclusively with "recognized and legally elected tribal leaders."[7]

A second press conference on November 10 at the National Press Club likewise degenerated into pandemonium when AIM members in attendance began shouting challenges to the assembled tribal leaders. The AIM protestors seemed particularly incensed about what they perceived as preferential and unwarranted government assistance for reservation-based Indian leadership.[8] "Who paid your way here?" demanded Herbert Powless (Oneida), head of the Milwaukee chapter of AIM. "You are using government funds."[9] Another AIM member, Carter Camp (Ponca), charged the tribal leaders as being "part of the establishment. You flew here first class, wear $200 suits, live in $20,000 houses and don't give a @#!*% who goes to jail." Tribal leaders angrily denied that the government had paid their travel expenses. Wendell Chino (Mescalero Apache) explained that several of them were already in Washington, D.C., to talk about budget affairs while others were on hand to attend a meeting about Indian health care. An emotional Chief Vernon Lane (Lummi) yelled, "I paid my own way. We took up a collection on the reservation to get me here so I could try to get 250 acres of our land back because a navy base was being evacuated." As the bickering continued, Nathan Little Soldier (Sahnish) shook his head in frustration. "This is what the press and TV enjoys," he declared. "We should work together. We will work together. My door and my hand is open to anyone. We should adjourn rather than make fools of ourselves."[10]

As tempers cooled and the press conference drew to a merciful close, those involved in the episode warily shook hands and exchanged pledges of Indian solidarity, but fundamental disagreements lingered. Paramount among them were questions about legitimacy, representation, and authority. In an era of "cacophonous voices" all claiming to speak for the Indians, how would Native Americans articulate a unified vision for tribal sovereignty and self-determination? Who would prioritize their demands for improved health care, education, and protection of their natural resources? Who would determine the strategies most likely to advance these demands? In short, who spoke for Indians?[11]

The tribal chairs who squared off against AIM protestors during the BIA occupation crisis were members of the National Tribal Chairmen's Association (NTCA), an organization established in the spring of 1971 with a very clear focus: to promote and protect the interests of federally recognized tribes. As such, the NTCA did not profess to represent the substantial population of Native Americans residing in urban areas or in off-reservation Indian communities, nor the many indigenous groups seeking federal recognition. Although the association consisted of leaders representing several different tribes, the NTCA was not a pan-Indian organization. The organization's logo featured a war lance holding aloft a feathered headdress with the words "Unity, Strength, and Justice" encircling them (strength comes from unity, which leads to justice); the NTCA, however, was not interested in promoting broad-based Indian solidarity nor in coordinating its efforts with other Indian rights organizations to unite all Native Americans via the promotion of a new identity or to advance universal goals such as Indian welfare and reform. While at times sympathetic to the objectives of such efforts, the NTCA, as we will see, adhered to its disciplined—if at times rigid and divisive—focus on promoting and protecting the interests of federally recognized Indian nations, thereby serving as the voice of the tribes.

The chairs who formed the NTCA made much of the fact that they had been "duly elected" by their respective peoples and were, therefore, legitimate leaders and authorized spokespersons who were accountable to those who had elected them. These arguments may have satisfied political scientists, but not Native Americans who questioned the legitimacy of elected tribal chairs and who longed for a restoration of "traditional" tribal governments. The dilemma here was that "tribes" and "tribal governments" were not "traditional" political structures but legally constructed concepts of relatively recent origin. During the eighteenth and nineteenth centuries, non-Indian negotiators eager to gain access to Indian lands and resources sought to create within diverse Indigenous communities political structures that were similar to those of non-Indians. Most useful to non-Indians was concentrating autonomous bands and villages of Native peoples sharing ethnological traits into tribes with centralized political leadership that could be employed and often manipulated to legalize (or legitimize) resource transfer to non-Indians. Over time, the constant linking by both Congress and the courts of the concept of "tribe" with the idea of "sovereignty" focused Indians' political attention and even loyalty on the tribe—even if that structure had not traditionally been viewed as the locus of legitimacy.[12]

Keeping in mind that thousands of Indian communities once existed each with their own unique histories, traditions, and structures of governance, determining a monolithic Native American perspective on political legitimacy is difficult to say the least. In general, Indians selected leaders for many of the same reasons as any other group of people. They sought individuals with status, who represented and fought for their interests, and who had no ulterior or selfish motives for seeking positions of authority. Ideal Native American leaders achieved status and legitimacy in a variety of ways—through their knowledge and respect for their peoples' values and history, their generosity and courage, their ability and willingness to solve problems diplomatically and via broad consultation and persuasion, their capacity for and experience in working with Euro-American institutions, and their ability to communicate a vision for a viable socioeconomic life for their people. Legitimate Indian leaders were servants who accepted leadership roles when the tribe needed their particular talents. Unlike Euro-American political traditions that emphasized hierarchy and static bureaucracies, tribal leadership was, according to Martha McLeod (Bay Mills Indian Community), a "cultural expression" and "the embodiment of a lifestyle, an expression of learned patterns of thought and behaviors, values, and beliefs."[13]

While tribal chairs of the 1960s–70s most certainly possessed varying degrees of these leadership traits, what delegitimized them in the eyes of some tribal members (the Oglala Lakotas, for example) was that the manner or process by which they gained office did not conform to tribal tradition or, because once elected, tribal chairs lacked the requisite authority to actually lead and make decisions. These delegitimizing factors had roots stretching back roughly two generations. During the latter decades of the nineteenth century, the federal government's relentless pursuit of Indian assimilation and detribalization spawned a multipronged effort to "civilize" and "individualize" Native Americans through education, the extension of the American legal system over reservations, and the passage in 1887 of the Dawes Severalty Act, which Theodore Roosevelt likened to a "great pulverizing machine to break up the tribal mass." By "pulverizing" reservations through the allotment process, the Dawes Act sought to destroy the Indians' land base along with the traditional economic, social, religious, and political relations that sustained Indian identities. To further its domination over tribal communities, the federal government's Office of Indian Affairs (renamed the Bureau of Indian Affairs in 1947) employed what anthropologist Thomas Biolosi terms "administrative technologies of power": the creation of reservation courts and police forces, restrictions on the ability of individual Indians to spend their own money and use their lands, and a ration system for the disbursement of treaty-sanctioned annuities and supplies. As intended, Indian communities soon became dependent upon the critical resources administered by the Office of Indian Affairs (OIA) and had little choice but to comply with the forced colonization of their lands.[14]

The devastation to tribal nations wrought by this assimilation/colonization juggernaut was visible to anyone interested in looking, yet a generation passed before federal officials came to realize that the human costs of forced assimilation were simply too high. In June 1934 Congress enacted a "new deal" in Indian affairs with the passage of the Indian Reorganization Act (IRA). Perceived by its architects as the last chance to halt the elimination and destruction of Indian political structures and cultures, the IRA halted the allotment process, promoted cultural expression, and provided statutory authority for a restoration of Indian home rule by encouraging tribal nations to adopt written constitutions and elect new tribal governments based on those constitutions. Commissioner of Indian Affairs John Collier selected tribes to serve as the act's primary organizational structure because "that was the way Whites saw Indians" as well as for more practical reasons; the federal government refused to recognize and deal with preexisting historical subgroups (bands, villages, clans, families, etc.).[15] Sensitive to the fact that tribes were not the traditional locus of political legitimacy among most Indian communities, Collier nonetheless pushed forward under the belief that tribal unity would be the most successful vehicle in arresting the destruction of Indian communal life. Tribal governments, on the other hand, would be managed via indirect colonial rule and incorporated into the nation's political system through a "watered-down version of American republican democracy."[16]

Often hailed as a landmark piece of legislation that repaired the incalculable damage wrought by the allotment policy and its corollaries, the IRA was nonetheless controversial and responsible for sowing new seeds of division within tribal communities. Many Indian nations viewed the IRA with deep suspicion. The federal government had frequently violated treaty obligations in the past. Why should it be trusted to abide by the IRA? Critics also complained about the law's complexity and the high-pressure tactics and manipulation that the OIA used to coerce tribal members to vote for the measure's implementation. Few Indians, moreover, had been consulted while technical specialists in Washington, D.C., were drafting the bill—an odd omission considering its professed emphasis on tribal self-determination. Other complaints focused on the unfamiliar process of choosing tribal leaders by election and majority rule. According to many traditional value systems, leaders were selected by consensus, and authority was vested in the individual. The IRA, on the other hand, required tribes to select leaders by democratic election and vested authority in the position. Among the Iroquois tribes in New York, the IRA's provision for allowing women to vote was especially troubling. Although Iroquois women had traditionally exercised considerable political influence, it was usually exerted behind the scenes and not in open debate. The IRA "constituted a totally new and unfamiliar level of organization for many Indian groups," writes historian Graham D. Taylor, especially for southwestern tribes such as the Apaches, Navajos, Pueblos, and Pimas, whose traditions stressed local band or village autonomy. Some tribal factions—full-bloods in particular—feared that elections would disadvantage them vis-à-vis mixed-bloods, given their declining demographic strength. Another major concern was the fear that tribal governments elected under IRA rules would continue to be dominated by the OIA and that tribal sovereignty would be weakened given the law's requirements that tribal governments obtain approval of the OIA or interior secretary before acting. Testifying about the IRA in 1940 Seneca activist Alice Lee Jemison insisted, "There was no self-government in the act, all final power and authority remains with the Secretary of the Interior, which is exactly where it has always remained heretofore." Although 161 Native constitutions were written and approved by tribal nations and formally recognized by federal officials within twelve years of the IRA's passage, over seventy tribal nations voted against participation—proof that the act was not unilaterally imposed on all Indian peoples. That said, according to one count, of the approximately ninety-seven thousand Indians who were declared eligible to vote in IRA referendums, thirty-eight thousand (39 percent) voted to approve, twenty-four thousand (25 percent) voted against approval, and thirty-five thousand (36 percent) abstained—hardly a ringing endorsement.[17]

In his 1971 political memoir, titled *The Tortured Americans,* Robert Burnette (Rosebud Sioux) described the Indian Reorganization Act as a "cruel fraud":

The plan looked splendid on paper and had the best of intentions behind it. But, in practice, it was doomed from the beginning. The Indians were given a charade to play. No act of the tribal government, except the taxing of its own people, could be performed without the express approval of the BIA. Far worse than offering the Indian people a system of self-government that was composed merely of shadows, it offered them a system in which the Indians who became leaders, because they lacked real political power, found importance and profit by playing upon the greed, ambition, and desire for influence that existed within and without the reservation. Instead of a tribal government, many tribes discovered to their dismay that they had a tribal gang as their representative.[18]

The men and women elected to serve on IRA-inspired tribal councils were, of course, not all driven by avarice and self-interest (Burnette himself served as chair of the Rosebud Sioux tribe and as a member of the NTCA not long after writing *The Tortured Americans*). Many—if not most—served (and continue to serve) to advance the interests of their people and to rebuild, reunite, reshape, and revitalize their Indigenous nations.[19] To accomplish these goals and to guarantee continued self-governing authority (limited though it was), tribal governments were forced to adhere to non-Indian legal and political forms. They created tribal court systems with appellate review, environmental protection agencies, bills of rights, economic development corporations, and more. From the perspective of traditionalists (whom Biolosi refers to as "old dealers"), however, IRA tribal councils were "culturally alien impositions" that violated treaties and traditional methods of tribal governance. The individuals making up those councils, furthermore, were "artificial elites" who would likely rule in an arbitrary manner.[20]

IRA proponents, on the other hand, argued that the new law would lead the way to self-determination, curtail the further loss of Indian lands and the destruction of cultural uniqueness, and empower tribal governments to protect themselves against the power of their white neighbors. Over time, the law indeed promoted these desirable conditions, but in the short term, it failed to transfer meaningful decision-making and policy-formulating authority to newly created tribal governments. Unable to shake long-standing paternalistic instincts, policymakers had infused the IRA with updated administrative technologies of power. As a result, tribal councils grew increasingly dependent upon government-appointed bureaucrats and lawyers to provide "technical assistance" and advice. The OIA, meanwhile, retained oversight over tribal budgets as well as control over OIA personnel working on reservations. As Alice Lee Jemison noted, the IRA required the secretary of the interior to review and approve practically all tribal government decisions. The result of such an arrangement was predictable. With virtually no control over OIA programs on the reservations, tribal councils could not consistently deliver resources to their constituents. When the delivery of those programs and services faltered (and they often did), complaints to the bureaucrats in charge fell on deaf ears since the Indian Office took its marching orders from Washington, D.C.—not from tribal councils. Elected tribal leaders, consequently, made convenient scapegoats and could be safely vilified. As Biolosi argues in his examination of the IRA on the Pine Ridge and Rosebud reservations, "The hostility, or at least a good part of it, embedded in the ambivalence of the Lakota toward the IRA was thus displaced away from the OIA agencies and directed toward the tribal councils which represented the OIA."[21]

Reminiscent of conditions prior to the Indian New Deal, tribal officials operated from dilapidated office buildings, on meager budgets, amid populations staggering from shockingly low incomes, inadequate housing, and poor health care. Most reservations are in rural areas and, as such, are largely invisible to most Americans. "On multiple dimensions," writes political scientist Laura Evans, "American Indian politics is about isolation from centers of institutional power."[22] A job description published in the February 1970 edition of *The Indian* detailed the arduous responsibilities of tribal chairs at that time: "The job of Tribal Chairman requires a man of considerable administrative ability and experience, of diplomacy, and a keen perception of both the Indian and white mind. He occupies the most powerful liaison position between his people and the white community that still governs much of Indian affairs. Upon the Tribal Chairman is placed the ultimate responsibility for the entire Tribe's welfare."[23] From the perspective of at least some reservation-based Native Americans, however, the legitimacy of "duly elected chairmen" leading IRA-inspired tribal governments was suspect—even though the chairs had been democratically elected in accordance with tribal constitutions. To the hundreds of thousands of Native Americans living off reservation and to members of non–federally recognized tribes and bands excluded from the IRA's provisions, the claims of tribal chairs to be the exclusive voice in Indian affairs was incomprehensible. Finally—and perhaps most importantly—the persistent barriers (geographic isolation, inadequate investment, substandard education, vacillating federal policies) that undercut the ability of reservation communities to achieve economic self-sufficiency in the decades before and following the IRA's passage and their continued dependency on government assistance led to a displacement of blame away from the OIA and widespread dissatisfaction with tribal governments as representatives of the Indian people and their interests.[24]

Assuming they were elected via free and fair elections, the claims of tribal chairs to legitimacy and to possess a proper representative relationship with their constituents appear to rest—at least from an academic perspective—on fairly solid ground. They had been authorized as representatives and spokespersons by their election, they were accountable to their constituents, and they were expected to look after the interests of their tribe. Failure on any of these fronts could, at least in theory, lead to their removal from office.[25] To have their motives impugned and their legitimacy challenged by "outside agitators" who, the tribal chairs believed, lacked concern for or understanding of reservation life was not only an affront to them personally, but posed an existential threat to Native Americans nationwide. Attacks on tribal governments, for starters, weakened and demoralized reservation communities, which in turn undermined their ability to advance tribal sovereignty and protect their lands and resources. Should Native Americans lose their reservation lands, they would forfeit their power base within America as well as the crucial underpinning or prerequisite of tribal histories, identities, and cultures. Without reservations, the dispersal of Native peoples would accelerate, their tribal identities disintegrate, and their assimilation into the majority society become complete.[26] From the perspective of tribal chairs, therefore, the battle over who spoke for Indian peoples was a matter of life or death. In their eyes, urban—and other off-reservation—Indian leaders and protestors lacked any clear constituency, were self-appointed rather than elected, and were accountable to no one. For this reason, they were illegitimate, and the federal government had no business negotiating with them, involving them in policy discussions, nor providing them with financial assistance. To do otherwise would further delegitimize and weaken duly elected tribal governments and begin the process of Native American disintegration described above.

While tribal chairs faced charges of illegitimacy (or worse) from traditionalists seeking a restoration of earlier forms and traditions of tribal governance, the leaders of non-reservation-based Indian reform organizations such as AIM, the National Indian Youth Council, and the Indians of All Tribes faced substantial credibility and legitimacy problems of their own.

Established in Minneapolis, Minnesota, in 1968, AIM's original purpose had been to protect the rights of urban Indians in the Twin Cities who suffered high levels of poverty, discrimination, and police brutality. Within a few years, however, AIM became involved in a much wider array of issues, including religious freedom, the protection of treaty rights, land restoration, environmental protection, and combatting racism and stereotyping. Best known for its outspoken leaders (Dennis Banks, Clyde and Vernon Bellecourt, George Mitchell, Russell Means, Eddie Benton-Banai) and its militancy, AIM was beset by frequent factionalism, financial difficulties, and turbulent relationships with federal authorities and other Indian rights organizations.[27]

In June 1961, delegates representing over two hundred tribes convened in Chicago to draft a Declaration of Indian Purpose, which they hoped would provide the John F. Kennedy administration with recommendations for a new direction in federal Indian policy based on tribal self-determination. College-age students in attendance (the so-called Chicago Conference Youth Council) resolved not to wait for the government to act. In August, they met at the Gallup Indian Community Center in Gallup, New Mexico, and formed what would become the National Indian Youth Council (NIYC). Initially committed to assisting more established organizations such as the National Congress of American Indians, the NIYC's involvement in Indigenous fishing rights protests occurring in Washington state influenced the organization to adopt a more activist bent. Led by the talented and charismatic Mel Thom (Paiute), Clyde Warrior (Ponca), Herb Blatchford (Diné), Joan Noble (Ute), and Shirley Hill Witt (Mohawk), the NIYC became involved in other "grassroots-level" protests which, according to Thom, made the NIYC the best representative of Native peoples' concerns and interests. Other Indian organizations, Thom maintained, "are mostly echoing what their White Brothers tell them." Indian professionals working in the BIA or who had otherwise become part of "the system," Clyde Warrior added, were "bootlickers" and "classic Indian finks" who "stand up and recite" when the bureau snapped its fingers. During the mid-1960s, the NIYC sought to spread its message of self-determination, cultural preservation, sovereignty, and treaty rights by organizing or attending regional councils, conferences, and workshops across the country.[28]

The Indians of All Tribes (IAT) was an ad hoc group of young Indian activists—many from UCLA and San Francisco State University—who landed on Alcatraz Island in San Francisco Bay in November 1969 and laid claim to the former prison complex for all Native peoples. Led by Richard Oakes (Mohawk) and John Trudell (Santee Sioux), the IAT called on all Native peoples to "let youth be the fire of positive action in this new and lasting demand for self-determination." In its 1970 "Manifesto," the IAT declared that the failure of Native Americans to unify would lead to their extinction since the policy of the U.S. government remained one of genocide. In addition to its goal of obtaining title to Alcatraz, the IAT sought government assistance for reservation and urban Indian needs, land restoration, and education reform. While unsuccessful in securing title to "the Rock" or to the decommissioned army installation at Fort Lawton (which IAT members had occupied in March 1970), the IAT was successful in "pushing the Red Power movement into the American conscience" and inspiring subsequent takeovers and occupations such as that by AIM at the BIA headquarters and at Wounded Knee.[29]

Democratic representation generally requires the authorization of a representative by a constituency through election, combined with the capacity of a constituency to hold the representative accountable for their performance in subsequent elections. Since the leaders of non-reservation-based Indian reform organizations such as AIM, the NIYC, and IAT were self-appointed and not popularly elected, they could not be held accountable by the people the leaders claimed to represent. But did this render them (as the tribal chairs frequently charged) illegitimate? According to political scientist Laura Montanaro, self-appointed representatives may not be popularly elected, but they can still play an important role in democracy by providing representation for marginalized groups of people "whose interests are affected by policies but who are not situated within electoral constituencies that can determine those policies." Urban Indians, along with Native peoples belonging to non–federally recognized tribes, would certainly fit into this category. While able to vote in national and statewide elections, off-reservation Indians were increasingly marginalized since they had no representation as Native Americans and were excluded from the opportunity to influence decisions that affected them as Native peoples. The self-appointed or surrogate representatives in organizations such as AIM, consequently, had the potential to make these invisible and inaudible Indian communities politically present and, by identifying and publicizing issues of injustice, to serve as catalysts for reform. From the vantage point of off-reservation Indians, the self-appointed representatives serving in AIM, the NIYC, the IAT, and other groups may have been unelected and unaccountable, but they were likely preferable to having no representation at all.[30]

In his 1974 "Indian declaration of independence" titled *Behind the Trail of Broken Treaties,* Vine Deloria Jr. (Standing Rock Sioux) discussed the gulf separating urban Indian activists such as those involved in the occupation of the BIA building from reservation-based tribal chairs regarding the appropriate strategy to combat the myriad problems facing Native Americans at that time. Each reservation had a number of "traditional Indians," Deloria explained, largely full-bloods who were leaders in tribal religious and cultural ceremonies, who rejected what they perceived as accommodationist tribal governments that permitted gross violations of treaty rights without a fight. What traditionalists sought instead was the "establishment of ancient methods of government by open council instead of elected officials" and "the replacement of white laws with Indian customs." During the late 1960s, the traditionalists forged an informal coalition with urban militants, many of whom had never lived on a reservation but hungered for the deep tribal connection that boarding school, government relocation programs, landlessness, or life's vicissitudes had denied them. Hypersensitive to charges that they were not "grassroots Indians" or maybe not even Indians at all, the urban militants sought coalition with tribal elders to provide them with both a connection to their cultures and a degree of "reservation legitimacy" that they knew they were lacking. Over time, "urban Indian activists seeking an Indian identity and heritage and traditional Indians buttressed by the energies of the young combined forces and made ready to push the Indians who had accommodated the white man off the reservations." Caught between these forces were the elected tribal chairs whom the government recognized as legitimate and a large number of Indian professionals who sought to improve the lives of their people by working within the system. They occupied a "middle ground of progressive ideology" in Indian affairs that Deloria believed was "fast eroding, and desperate confrontation was in the air over the issue of the nature of the modern Indian community."[31]

Deloria's warning proved prescient, and during the decade of the 1970s, Indian leaders and organizations confronted the federal government, and at times each other, in an effort to shape a future for "the modern Indian community." In this book, I endeavor to deepen our understanding of this "desperate confrontation" and its important results. Trapped in a no-man's-land or "in between status" as sovereign peoples and as colonized dependents, some Indian organizations sought to define their own paths as political agents in the modern era—to create what political theorist Kevin Bruyneel terms a "third space of sovereignty" that resided neither inside nor outside the American political system.[32] The tribal chairs who made up the NTCA, on the other hand, elected to pursue an insider strategy based on the establishment of a stable network of relationships with policymakers and serving as intermediaries or "brokers" between the government and federally recognized tribes. The ensuing conflict within the Indian rights movement over goals, strategies, and tactics wrought the "desperate confrontation" to which Deloria alluded.

Scholars of contemporary Native American history have produced an impressive body of work surveying the major twists and turns in federal Indian policy in the post-WWII era.[33] The Red Power movement, in particular, generated a wave

Attorney, scholar, and activist Vine Deloria Jr. (Standing Rock Sioux) held an ambivalent attitude about elected tribal chairs and their role in federal-Indian relations. Courtesy of the Center of Southwest Studies, Fort Lewis College, Durango, Colo.

of contemporary writing and spun a wide array of scholarship chronicling the efforts of extra-tribal Indian rights groups (such as the American Indian Movement) and their much celebrated and publicized "resistance model" of occupations and confrontations with local, state, and federal governments.[34] While they were significant contributors to the evolution of federal Indian policy, Red Power groups constituted only one side of a multifaceted movement seeking to advance Indian rights, sovereignty, and self-determination. In their edited compilation *Beyond Red Power,* scholars Daniel M. Cobb and Loretta Fowler argued that the popular fixation on the Red Power movement as the "quintessence of Indian activism" obscures the significant reform efforts of Indigenous peoples going back to the late nineteenth century.[35] Cobb's subsequent monograph *Native Activism in Cold War America* likewise sought to reconceptualize "activism" to acknowledge the reformative goals and conventional tactics pursued by Native peoples from the end of the Second World War to the advent of AIM.[36] While the rhetoric and tactics employed by these proto–Red Power activists may have failed to capture the imagination of the media or dominant society, their contributions were no less important to the cause of Indian policy reform. The same can be said of "mainstream" national Indian organizations such as the National Congress of American Indians (NCAI), which had been a dominant player in the Indian rights movement since its inception in 1944. Thomas W. Cowger's *The National Congress of American Indians: The Founding Years* provided the first detailed study of the NCAI's first two decades, but a companion volume tracing its history from the 1960s to the present remains to be written.[37]

There has been very little—if any—scholarly attention paid to the goals and activities of the elected tribal chairs and Indian professionals occupying the "middle ground of progressive ideology." While often denigrated as puppets and sellouts manipulated by the BIA or as "Uncle Tomahawks" unwilling to take a strong stand against an oppressive and exploitive federal government, their vision of a confederation of tribal leaders as the appropriate and most viable option to challenge the federal government's imposition of political and cultural boundaries on tribal nations was quite different from that of the much-heralded and celebrated Red Power groups.[38] To counter what they saw as a dangerous shift in federal government attention and resources away from reservations, elected tribal leaders established the National Tribal Chairmen's Association (NTCA). Convinced that Indian sovereignty and self-determination could only be realized through conformity (or adaptability) to the forms and processes of their federal government counterparts, the tribal chairs adopted a conventional "insider" or relationship-oriented advocacy strategy (as opposed to militancy) to promote change.

For a time, the NTCA played a significant role in the formation and implementation of federal Indian policies and advancing a vision of tribal sovereignty and self-determination that sought the re-creation of strong viable tribal governments capable of deciding what was in their peoples' best interests, of protecting their lands and resources, and of negotiating on a government-to-government basis with federal officials. Without the active participation of tribal leaders, the important reforms of the late 1960s and 1970s never would have been achieved. NTCA representatives met frequently with top decision makers in the executive and legislative branches, and for a while at least, Native American communities nationwide recognized the NTCA as an important, if not the most important, voice in Indian affairs. During the 1980s, the association responded aggressively to changing conditions ushered in by the so-called Reagan revolution. Those responses were consequential—both for the direction of federal Indian policy and for the NTCA's future.

That said, there have been no published studies of the NTCA and its place in contemporary Native American history. With this book I seek to fill this void by placing the association within its historical context and explaining the complex reasons for its establishment. Subsequent chapters explore the organization's stance on critical issues such as tribal sovereignty, self-determination, cultural preservation, and resource protection; the association's persistent claim to be the exclusive voice of federally recognized tribes; its occasionally tumultuous relationship with other Indian rights organizations; and its efforts to combat the backlash against Native Americans during the mid-1970s and into the 1980s. Concluding chapters examine the NTCA's responses to Reagan-era budget cuts and administration proposals to promote the development of reservation economies, the NTCA's demise in the mid-1980s, and the association's effectiveness as an interest group as well as its legacy for Native Americans today. My intent here has not been an NTCA rehabilitation project but to offer a balanced and nuanced understanding of its role in contemporary Native American history from its creation in 1971 to its dissolution in 1987. By giving voice to the elected tribal leaders who formed the NTCA, I hope to provide a more comprehensive understanding of the people and events that shaped the so-called era of Indian self-determination: what many scholars believe was the most significant period in contemporary Native American history.

Chapter 1

Genesis

To better understand the goals of the National Tribal Chairmen's Association (NTCA) and the strategies it pursued to achieve them, a review of its origins and the historical context in which it was founded is necessary. The NTCA did not simply appear out of the blue; it was the product of several converging forces that culminated in the spring of 1971 in, of all places, the state capitol in Pierre, South Dakota. Federal officials welcomed the establishment of a tribal chairmen's organization and hoped the NTCA would bring clarity to the widely divergent hopes and expectations of the national Indian community. Policy-makers in the Bureau of Indian Affairs (BIA) and its Interior Department parent, in particular, sought a "voice for the tribes" with whom they could consult. An association of tribal chairs, they reasoned, would simplify the consultative process and bring obvious efficiencies to the formulation and implementation of federal Indian policy. That said, the Nixon administration assisted but did not create the NTCA. Tribal chairs, as we will see, had compelling reasons of their own for doing so.

The NTCA was an interest group that served a variety of functions and engaged in political activities aimed at advancing the interests of federally recognized tribes. It was created at a time of relatively intense interest-group proliferation in the United States. While public interest groups (PIGS, as some people referred to them) have always been active in American politics, during the 1960s and 1970s the number of nationally active interest groups in the country more than tripled. The reasons for this explosion of interest group formation are complex. The great diversity (racial, economic, religious, etc.) of the U.S. population not surprisingly breeds different goals and desires, while our constitutional freedoms enable people to voice these goals and desires in a variety of ways. The nation's federal organization, meanwhile, has by one estimate created over ninety thousand different governments (national, state, county, municipal) for people to access and lobby. If an interest group fails to influence the political decisions of one branch of government, the separation of powers allows the group to take its concerns or complaints to two others.[1]

During the 1960s and 1970s the expansion of Great Society programs, policies, and regulations; the modern civil rights movement; the election of Richard Nixon; and the Vietnam War provided new impetuses for interest group formation. According to political scientist Norman J. Ornstein, political decentralization brought about by congressional reforms during this period led to an increase in the power and influence of subcommittee chairs and rank-and-file members of Congress, which in turn brought about a vast expansion of staffs on Capitol Hill. More people wielding power (and thus more people who needed to be contacted and persuaded to support a lobbyist's point of view) spurred a corresponding increase in the number and size of interest groups and the use of "more sophisticated methods for communicating group opinions and exerting group influence." As the number of interest groups mushroomed during this time, so did their solicitations for government assistance. By the late 1970s, federal support to nonprofit organizations outpaced private charitable support by a factor of two to one.[2]

When placed within this context of interest group proliferation in the 1960s–70s, the creation of a body comprising elected tribal leaders seeking to protect and advance the interests of the nation's reservation-based Indian population (approximately 450,000 people in 1970) was hardly an anomaly. In addition, tribal chairs faced a unique set of pressures and concerns that explain the genesis of the NTCA in the spring of 1971. The dispersion of Indian-related programs and services that occurred in the late 1960s ended the BIA's long monopoly over Indian affairs and forced tribal leaders to make important adjustments to ensure that their peoples received the assistance promised them in treaties. Personnel and policy changes in the BIA and within the influential National Congress of American Indians likewise prompted widespread anxiety and frustration among many leaders of federally recognized tribes who viewed these changes as potentially threatening to the interests of their constituents. The efforts of Canadian Indian (First Nations) leaders to unite and work together in defense of tribal rights and sovereignty provided an additional impetus for tribal chairs in the United States to expand their own intertribal collaboration. The efforts of an ailing tribal chairman from the Standing Rock reservation to begin the process also proved critical. A common concern casting a shadow over virtually all of these issues was the growing schism between federally recognized tribes residing on reservations and urban and rural Indians who did not possess federal recognition or who resided off-reservation. Their differing visions about federal assistance, tribal sovereignty, self-determination, and how best to secure the well-being of Native Americans, Vine Deloria had cautioned, was reaching its climax, and "desperate confrontation was in the air over the issue of the nature of the modern Indian community."[3]

The Dispersion of Programs and Services for Native Americans

In January 1964 President Lyndon B. Johnson announced that he had directed the Office of Economic Opportunity (OEO)—the engine driving his Great Society antipoverty efforts—to "put our Indian people in the forefront" and pledged "a continued effort to eradicate poverty and to provide new opportunity for the first citizens of America." Title IIA of the Economic Opportunity Act of 1964 established the Community Action Program (CAP), the cornerstone of which was "maximum feasible participation" of the poor in the planning and implementation of antipoverty initiatives. Its primary objective was ambitious: to "effect a permanent increase in the capacity of individuals, groups, and communities afflicted by poverty to deal effectively with their own problems so that they need no further assistance." The vehicle that the government used to shift the delivery of antipoverty-related human services from itself to communities was contracting. Simply put, the government negotiated contracts with for-profit and not-for- profit entities for the provision of specific goods and services to impoverished communities, in essence becoming the customer rather than the provider. The new arrangement proved to be a mixed blessing in many cases, difficult to evaluate and often altering the providers' structures and goals (see chapter 2).[4]

As applied to Native Americans, the Indian Community Action Program (ICAP) permitted tribal governments to form Community Action Agencies (CAAs), which prepared and submitted plans for local antipoverty projects. Once approved, the OEO contracted with tribal organizations to administer the programs themselves. By June 1967, tribal CAAs had implemented 625 programs at a cost of $45.8 million, affecting an estimated 80 percent of the reservation population. They included Head Start programs, remedial education classes, community betterment and beautification projects, counseling services, credit unions, and health and home improvement initiatives.[5]

Johnson's decision to have the OEO become directly involved in Indian affairs became part of a larger trend in federal Indian policy that sought to improve the government's provision of services to Indian communities. Instead of near-exclusive reliance on the BIA to oversee the implementation of the government's trust responsibilities to Native Americans, the Johnson administration decided to expand opportunities for Indians by instructing other federal departments and agencies (such as OEO) to consider how their various programs might benefit them. By the time Johnson left office in 1969, "the BIA's traditional role as the Big Daddy of the reservations" had been greatly altered as other federal agencies channeled millions of dollars to tribal communities to fund programs and services administered by tribal governments.

This diffusion of federal responsibilities—and dollars—to reservations proved divisive. The Snyder Act of 1921 (25 USC 13) had given the Commissioner of Indian Affairs broad latitude in spending appropriations and developing programs to meet Indians' needs. The legislation stated simply that appropriations were to be used for "Indians across the United States." The BIA, however, chose to restrict its services to only members of federally recognized tribes residing on or near reservations, establishing a precedent that "the Government's special responsibility to the Indian people stops at the reservation gate." The highly acclaimed Meriam Report of 1928 supported (and perhaps explains) the BIA's decision. In its chapter on "Migrated Indians," the Meriam Report recommended that "the efforts of the national government in the larger cities to which the Indians will naturally migrate should be directed *not* toward building up an independent organization in such cities for aiding the migrated Indians, but rather toward establishing cooperative relations with existing agencies which serve the population as a whole."[6] The BIA, in other words, should not serve the needs of off-reservation Indians but instead encourage them to seek assistance from agencies serving non-Indians.

As the diffusion of government programs and services to Native Americans expanded during the late 1960s, tribal leaders insisted that the government extend this restriction to all federal funding for Indians so that federal outlays would remain directed exclusively to members of federally recognized tribes living on or near reservations. Federal dollars directed toward off-reservation Indian peoples, tribal leaders feared, would come at the expense of federally recognized tribes and threaten the existence of reservations. Without a strong reservation power base, the tribal leaders warned, all Indians—including urban Indians—would suffer.[7] The problem here was that the off-reservation population was growing rapidly—and many of those individuals needed help too. During the 1950s, the BIA's Voluntary Relocation Program exacerbated the crisis by enticing thousands of Native Americans to leave reservations for what they were led to believe would be attractive jobs in cities. The reality proved much different. Relocatees were not adequately screened for ability to adjust to city life, and they were placed in menial, low-paying occupations in cities as far from their homes as possible to prevent easy return. Before long, a sizeable population of destitute and stranded urban Indians took root in urban America.[8] Next to the Navajo reservation, with a population of about 120,000 persons, the next largest concentrations of Native Americans during the early 1970s were in large metropolitan centers such as Los Angeles (23,908), Tulsa (15,183), Oklahoma City (12,951), San Francisco (12,041), Phoenix (10,127), Minneapolis–Saint Paul (9,911), and Chicago (8,203).

A related problem concerned the substantial number of landless communities that claimed to be Native American but were not federally recognized. These groups faced many of the same social and economic problems afflicting their on-reservation counterparts. According to the 1970 U.S. Census, of the 763,594 people identified as American Indians, 340,367 individuals (nearly 45 percent of the total) resided off reservations.[9] While these estimates are imperfect, they generally support the widely published contention that about half the Indian population resided off reservation by the end of the 1960s. Not surprisingly, this burgeoning off-reservation Indian population demanded access to federal programs and services and rejected the arguments of the BIA, the Meriam Report, and reservation-based tribal governments that they obtain assistance instead from the same local, state, and federal agencies as non-Indians.[10]

The dispersion of federal programs and services for Native Americans inspired by the Great Society community action programs of the 1960s promoted self-determination by giving tribal governments the self-confidence that came with executive and administrative experience, thereby loosening the onerous grip of BIA paternalism and meddling.[11] Tribal governments now began to actively assert their control in other areas—over reservation lands, resources, and individuals (tribal members and nonmembers)—by right of their own inherent sovereignty. They also began competing with states and other tribes for access to finite federal funds.[12] From the perspective of elected tribal leaders, the efforts of urban-based Indian rights organizations such as AIM to challenge their authority and to redirect federal dollars to cities and rural areas far away from reservations were worrisome developments—as was their willingness to use inflammatory rhetoric and militant tactics to bring attention to their cause.

By 1970, elected tribal leaders looked on these developments with growing concern.

The BIA in Crisis

Despite being one of the most criticized and ridiculed bureaucracies in the federal government, the Bureau of Indian Affairs' response has often been all talk and no action—to give a superficial appearance of supporting change while simultaneously moving to preserve its existing structure. President Nixon was well aware of this ploy and attributed many of the problems facing Native Americans to "the fact that the [BIA] bureaucracy feeds on itself, defends itself, fights for the status quo, and does very little, in my opinion, for progress in the field." During the 1960s, studies conducted on the BIA's endemic problems led to recommendations for major structural reorganization and/or moving the bureau in toto to the Department of Health, Education, and Welfare. Interior Department officials succeeded in quashing such a transfer, and for the time being, BIA bureaucrats rested easy with the knowledge that the status quo remained intact. In the months leading up to the establishment of the National Tribal Chairmen's Association, however, the BIA's "militant disinclination toward change" sparked an intrabureau civil war unmatched in its history.[13] The turmoil and uncertainty that ensued led some tribal leaders to conclude that a national association of tribal chairs was necessary to keep a closer eye on BIA activities to better protect the interests of federally recognized tribes.

Following Nixon's inauguration in 1969, Native Americans awaited the appointment of a new commissioner of Indian affairs. Many tribes and Indian organizations held out hope that Nixon would retain Johnson administration appointee Robert L. Bennett (Oneida), the first Native American to be appointed to the post in over a century, but Bennett was asked to submit his resignation, which he did on May 31, 1969. Two and a half months later, Nixon appointed sixty-three-year-old Louis Rooks Bruce (Mohawk-Sioux), a soft-spoken businessman and dairy farmer from New York who had served in the Public Housing Administration and earlier as executive secretary of the National Congress of American Indians. A liberal Republican who eschewed the limelight, Bruce seemed a safe choice. Upon accepting the appointment from President Nixon in August 1969, Bruce likened his new position to that of a tightrope walker. To be a successful commissioner, he reflected, one had to "look clearly at the goal of improving the conditions of Indian people" while operating simultaneously as "part of the governmental process bouncing on the tightrope." Like

Louis Bruce (Mohawk-Sioux) served as commissioner of Indian affairs from 1969 to 1973. His efforts to reorganize the BIA and to consider assisting urban Indians help explain the creation of the NTCA. Courtesy of the Center of Southwest Studies, Fort Lewis College, Durango, Colo.

his immediate predecessors, Bruce supported policies that advanced tribal self-determination and called for greater Indian involvement in managing their own affairs. He encouraged other federal agencies and departments to expand their programs and offerings to Indian communities—both on and off reservation. "I didn't accept the job as commissioner because I wanted to be a big chief," Bruce declared in a speech delivered on his fortieth day in office. "I accepted the job because there is a desperate need for something to be done and because I want to see to it that it is done the way Indians want it done." Disavowing any desire to engage or participate in power struggles, Bruce called for a united front. "If Indians are divided," he warned, "Indian aspirations will be defeated."[14]

Heeding Interior Secretary Walter Hickel's instructions to put into effect a restructuring of the BIA (and Nixon's admonition to "shake it up, and shake it up good") to make it more fully responsive to the needs of Native Americans, Commissioner Bruce initiated a series of personnel changes—what he characterized as a "realignment"—by demoting or reassigning many of the bureau's conservative or old-line bureaucrats who served as area directors in one of the BIA's twelve administrative areas. These efforts were in keeping with historian Alvin Josephy Jr.'s February 1969 report to President Nixon, which had singled out conservatives in the BIA (along with officials in the Congressional Budget Office and members of Congress sitting on the Committee of Interior and Insular Affairs) as potential obstacles to tribal self-determination. As commissioner of Indian affairs, Bruce sought to resuscitate internal BIA reform efforts and to liberate reformers by removing the logjam of bureaucrats opposing the policy. To assist him, he hired a group of young reform-minded advisers—many of them Native Americans—whom Bruce called the "New Team" but whom critics dubbed the "young Turks," the "fabulous fourteen," or the "Katzenjammer Kids"—a reference to the comic-strip twins who famously rebelled against authority. Enthusiastic about the prospect of tribes assuming greater control over their own affairs, the New Teamers—some of whom had prior experience in tribal community action programs—energetically pushed tribal contracting and worked to accelerate the day when tribes directly administered the programs and services formerly parceled out by BIA bureaucrats. Perfectly comfortable bypassing regulations, making creative use of old statutes, and moving outside the traditional bureaucratic ladder, Bruce's team of reformers quickly drew the ire of career bureaucrats and their congressional sponsors who opposed Bruce's attempts to implement contracting in the absence of "normal" statutory authority. This latter group set out on a campaign to undermine Bruce and his New Team and recruited conservative tribal leaders to join them.[15]

The support of some tribal chairs for a retention of the status quo in regard to the power and influence of area directors seems counterintuitive given the many criticisms leveled against them. "The Area Directorships," read one internal government memorandum, "have become fiefdoms run by career civil servants who need not be and are not responsive to Indian needs and initiative." Efforts by the tribes to exert pressure on the area directors, however, "are cut short because of the extraordinary powers directors have to reward cooperative tribes and punish the uncooperative. Under this kind of set-up, it is nearly impossible for tribes to assert themselves to improve the quality of reservation life."[16]

Why then would tribal chairs seek to retain the seemingly omnipotent area offices, which according, to the National Indian Youth Council's (NIYC) Gerald Wilkinson, had "debilitated and emasculated generations of tribal leadership"?[17] For some tribal chairs, fear likely explains their decision. If an area director discovered that a tribal chair supported any type of initiative that reduced his power, he might very well seek to punish the "disloyal" chair by shifting opportunities and resources to "loyal" chairs of other tribal nations.[18] Given the constant reorganizations and realignments of the recent past, tribal chairs must have understood that today's weakened area director could become tomorrow's powerful and vindictive area director. The safest course of action, therefore, was to support the existing (albeit imperfect) system or simply keep quiet.

A related concern centered around the lingering threat of termination—the policy that sought to destroy tribal communities by terminating the government's trust responsibilities to Native Americans and forcing their assimilation into the majority society. Many tribal leaders believed that criticizing the BIA would weaken their best insurance against that horrific possibility. Since the bureau was primarily concerned with its own self-preservation, so the thinking went, it would always strive to perpetuate its reservation-based clients. Some scholars, consequently, have likened the BIA–tribal government relationship to a protection racket. "The less tribes invest in supporting it, the more likely it is that Congress will terminate their political existence."[19]

A second possible explanation was opportunity. Like it or not, tribal chairs had grown accustomed to the BIA's twenty-five-year-old policy that had led to the creation of area directors and had worked to curry their support. Some may have been true believers that the existing system was working, and that increased decentralization was preferable to maintaining power and authority in a distant and out-of-touch central office. While not quite victims of the Stockholm Syndrome, the tribal chairs may have calculated that stronger area directors—even if paternalistic and manipulative—could bring additional resources to their reservation constituents, thereby solidifying their own position as duly elected officials.

In November 1970 the movement to reform the BIA suffered a setback when Nixon fired Secretary Hickel over negative comments he had made about the administration's treatment of American youth in the aftermath of the Kent State massacre. Two months later, Nixon appointed Rogers C. B. Morton, the former chair of the Republican National Committee, to head the Department of the Interior. While Hickel had proven to be flexible and willing to innovate, the six-feet-eight Morton (whom some Indians nicknamed the Jolly Green Giant) seemed much more interested in restoring order and administrative normalcy in the BIA. When Morton appointed long-serving bureaucrats John O. Crow (Cherokee) and Wilma Victor (Choctaw) to "assist" Bruce in the BIA, an intense

Commissioner Louis Bruce and Secretary of the Interior Rogers C. B. Morton accepted the NTCA as its principal consultant in federal-Indian affairs during the early 1970s.
NARA Photo Archive, College Park, Md.

power struggle commenced that pitted Morton and his appointees against Commissioner Bruce and the New Team. Morton's subsequent decision to empower Crow to countermand any of Commissioner Bruce's decisions led to the transfer or demotion of many of these reform-minded individuals. Crow demoted Leon F. Cook (Red Lake Chippewa), for example, whom Commissioner Bruce had appointed director of economic development, and replaced him with a non-Indian—a decision that some Indian leaders interpreted as new evidence of BIA "regression" into "old patterns of paternalism and stagnation." Angry with Bruce for not stepping up to save his position, Cook resigned from the BIA altogether and lashed out that the commissioner "has never taken a stand. Whenever there's a hassle he's under the bed, and when the smoke clears he's up like a hero. Bruce has lied to the Indian people so much he doesn't know when he's telling the truth." Played out amid widespread press coverage, the self-inflicted dysfunction in the BIA contributed to the sense of alienation and betrayal evinced by Red Power activists and to renewed protests across the country. In September 1971, for example, a small group of Indians from the National Indian Youth Council and the American Indian Movement seized the BIA's information office in Washington, D.C., and announced their intention to conduct a citizens' arrest of John Crow for "gross misconduct and criminal injustice against the Native American People." When security arrived at the scene, a fistfight ensued, and twenty-six Indians were arrested.[20]

The drama and bureaucratic chaos within the BIA deeply troubled tribal leaders. While some tribes supported the commissioner's decision to reassign long-serving reservation superintendents, area directors, and other BIA appointees, they criticized Bruce and his New Team for failing to consult with tribal leaders before announcing the policy. This alleged breakdown in the consultation process was a recurring problem that tribal chairs complained about repeatedly. According to Philip S. "Sam" Deloria (Standing Rock Sioux), "consultation" is a code word in the often dysfunctional relationship that exists between tribal and federal governments. "The sense of being aggrieved is part of the nature of the relationship, and it manifests itself in complaints about consultation."[21] Tribal leaders consequently interpreted inadequate consultation as a sign of disrespect and deliberate humiliation, a signal that their federal counterparts disvalued their opinions and questioned their competence. This was especially frustrating when applied to areas where tribal leaders had vast experience and expertise. Transferring area directors every two or three years, chairs argued, risked increased inefficiency since it took at least two years for an individual to learn about the problems and needs of a reservation. To then arbitrarily transfer area directors to a new position made little sense. From the perspective of William Youpee, the chair of the Fort Peck Sioux and Assiniboine Tribal Council, Bruce's directive was deeply frustrating and "just another case where the administration is acting without first getting input from the Indians."[22]

The New Team's enthusiastic support for tribal contracting was also a source of concern. While tribal leaders sought greater control over government programs and services, there was always a lingering fear that "more Indian control is just one step down the road towards an end to the trust relationship" and was little more than "self-termination" in disguise. A related concern was that once tribes had taken over a certain program, the government would cut its budget and then blame Native Americans for managerial incompetence. In an editorial titled "BIA Policies Worry Tribes" published in the *Northwest Indian Times,* members of the Northwest Affiliated Tribes charged that the New Team was "being stampeded into radical changes in the relationship between the tribes and the BIA before the tribes had had a chance to think over the changes."

Contracting, in particular, was seen as a pretext for termination as federal officials sought to "contract away" all the essential federal trust responsibilities.[23]

Some tribal leaders expressed concern about the New Team's qualifications and their loyalties to Indians residing on reservations. Apparently buying in to the popular portrayal of the New Team as the Katzenjammer Kids and as "OEO graduates" (since some had experience working on community action projects sponsored by the Office of Economic Opportunity), critics of Bruce's assistants charged that they were outsiders with little knowledge or experience about reservation life. According to Edison Real Bird (Crow), the New Teamers "shadowed" Commissioner Bruce. After making a commitment to tribal leaders, for example, the commissioner would be immediately hounded by the New Team and the commitment promptly abandoned. Still angry about what he perceived as inadequate BIA consultation over contracting and personnel changes, William Youpee commented that, after hearing some of Bruce's staff testify, he left with the impression that "most of these guys were Indians who had lost contact with the reservation." Commissioner Bruce, Youpee maintained, "has surrounded himself with a staff of militant, off-reservation people and he is listening to these people rather than the reservation Indian."[24]

Commissioner Bruce's modest efforts to placate urban Indian concerns also drew the ire of tribal leaders. During a Tribal Economic and Social Development Seminar held in Albuquerque in July 1970 Bruce outlined changes in BIA policies that included meeting the needs of reservation Indians while simultaneously recognizing the BIA's "obligation to be a strong advocate of urban Indian interest" and to "actively help coordinate State, local, and private resources for the benefit of urban Indians."[25] From the perspective of the tribal chairs, the BIA's obligations stopped at the borders of reservations, and the bureau's limited time and resources should not be redirected to assisting urban Indians. "Some of our Indian people have been integrated into urban areas, and we sympathize with their causes and problems," Youpee maintained, but "elected tribal leaders have an obligation to the reservation people; and we intend to uphold that responsibility." Unlike the self-appointed Indian leaders in AIM and other Indian rights organizations, Youpee continued, "We will not resort to the use of four-letter words to attract attention. We do not have to wear long hair and beaded headbands to prove we are Indian, nor do we have to capture islands or storm forts. We have an inherent and historical right [and will not accept any diversion of funds for] programs that subvert the intent of the Congress when it appropriated money for reservation use." BIA collaboration with unelected urban militants, furthermore, was inappropriate and potentially threatening to reservation-based tribes. The "urbans" had no official standing, they were not representative of reservation Indians, they were only concerned with their own personal welfare and not the good of all, and by their provocative actions, they threatened to undermine federal support and assistance for Native Americans nationwide. The creation of a national organization of duly elected tribal chairs, consequently, was necessary to bring oversight to and help stabilize the BIA so that it could better fulfill the nation's trust responsibilities.[26]

The National Congress of American Indians in Crisis

While the civil war within the BIA raged throughout the late 1960s and early 1970s, internal rifts within the National Congress of American Indians (NCAI) threatened to destroy what had for nearly three decades been the dominant national Indian rights organization.[27] Established in 1944 the NCAI was the first organization that truly represented tribes.[28] As constituted by its founders, the organization consisted of tribal delegates, each carrying credentials issued by the governing body of the tribe(s) he or she represented. The traditional thrust of the NCAI had been to strengthen tribal governments by enhancing and facilitating their government-to-government relations with the United States and to convince federal officials that they were responsible enough to handle their own affairs. The NCAI served as the eyes, ears, and voice of Indian peoples through its presence in Washington, D.C., and as a watchdog against violations of tribal sovereignty and individual Indian rights. During the late 1960s and early 1970s, however, the NCAI's dominant position weakened as new, specialized Indian-related interest groups formed around federal programs in housing and education; around professions such as journalism, law, and medicine; and around natural resources including minerals, timber, fisheries, and agriculture. Urban Indians, students, and autonomous Indian communities likewise formed nontribally defined organizations. Before long, few Indians were left unrepresented by some national organization.[29]

In addition to the competition that accompanied the proliferation of Indian-related interest groups, the NCAI was shaken by political movements that were developing in urban Indian communities and on college campuses in the wake of the civil rights movement. Militancy was coming into Indian affairs, and NCAI leaders reacted with caution during the 1960s as activist Native American college students and urban Indians stepped up their challenges to tribal officials, whom they accused of being "apples" (red on the outside but white on the inside) and accommodating Uncle Tomahawks. The path to strengthening Indian ideals and the Indian community, they argued, was not by "Indianizing the BIA" or by the efforts of a tribal chairs' meeting or an NCAI convention, but through acts of resistance such as the occupation of Alcatraz and the takeover of the BIA building. At its 1969 annual convention in Albuquerque, Indian activists took the stage to rail against NCAI leaders as "sellouts" for not taking a more forceful stand against the federal government. The election of Bruce Wilkie (Makah) as NCAI executive director ushered in an especially tumultuous period in the organization's history. As one of the NIYC founders, Wilkie reflected the general attitude among militants of suspicion and disrespect for the older leaders. His mismanagement of NCAI funds left the organization deeply in debt, and his alienation of tribal leaders led to plummeting memberships. Weakened financially and divided over how to reconcile the needs and interests of an increasingly diverse Native American population, the NCAI struggled to keep up with the flurry of Indian-related initiatives introduced during the early Nixon administration.[30]

At its twenty-eighth annual convention, held in Reno in November 1971, the growing power and influence of the Indian activists led some NCAI leaders to consider revising the organization's constitution and expand its membership to include urban Indian organizations. By "opening up" for all Indian participation rather than "tightening up" around federally recognized tribes, they argued, the NCAI could rightfully claim to speak "for all the nearly one million Indians, Eskimos, and Aleuts and not just the estimated 440,000 Indians who live in reservations." The NCAI's selection of former BIA administrator Leon F. Cook to serve as president was a watershed event in the organization's often-acrimonious debate about permitting urban Indians to become full voting members. The thirty-one-year-old Cook was a strong proponent of enfranchisement. "There's no big hassle between the NCAI, the American Indian Movement, and the National Indian Youth Council," Cook declared shortly after the convention. "Their prejudice and jealousy about each other, in my mind, is more apparent than real."[31]

But not all NCAI members agreed. Many reservation Indians viewed their urban brethren with varying degrees of contempt. Urban Indian groups such as the Indians of All Tribes (IAT), AIM, and the NIYC, they argued, were too radical, too militant, and all too willing to employ controversial tactics, like the Alcatraz occupation, that were "not the Indian way." Urban Indian leaders, they insisted, were publicity hounds and "usurpers who carried no credentials to speak for the tribes." Their blatant attempts to "out-Indian" tribal leaders by eschewing suit and tie and instead wearing leather vests, headbands, and fringed jackets, and braiding their hair was especially irritating. Some reservation leaders suspected that urban Indians simply sought a share of the federal assistance given to reservations or, even worse, to "liquidate the reservations and divide the money." The raucous behavior of AIM and NIYC representatives at the NCAI's Albuquerque and Reno conventions confirmed such suspicions. When the urban Indians refused to pay the twenty-dollar membership fee to gain admission into the convention, an estimated thirty or forty Indian youths managed to slip in and disrupt the proceedings. Shouting slogans and charging that the NCAI was little more than a government pawn, the militants accused conference organizers of using the admission fees to gamble in one of Reno's many casinos. Meanwhile, AIM coordinator Russell Means (Oglala Lakota) declared that the question of whether or not the NCAI would admit urban Indian groups as equals "would mark the funeral or the rebirth of the N.C.A.I."[32]

While opposing the admittance of urban Indian groups as well as tribal organizations that were not federally recognized, many reservation-based tribal chairs likely agreed with Means's assertion that the answer to his question would have serious repercussions for the NCAI—and for their future role in the organization. As we will see, before that important issue was decided, the tribal chairs were already making preparations to form a new organization that catered exclusively to federally recognized tribes.

Nixon's "Indian Message" and Legislation

On July 8, 1970, President Nixon issued a special message to Congress on Indian affairs declaring that "the time has come to break decisively with the past and to create the conditions for a new era in which the Indian future is determined by Indian acts and Indian decisions." Rejecting previous federal Indian policies that had advocated either termination or paternalism, what Nixon described as "equally harsh and unacceptable extremes," the president asked Congress to pass a resolution that would "expressly renounce, repudiate, and repeal the termination policy" along with eight bills that would promote tribal autonomy. In simple terms, the bills called for the right of Indians to contract for the control or operation of federal programs (what tribal leaders referred to as "the takeover bill"), the restoration of lands around Blue Lake to the Taos Pueblos, greater Indian control over the education of their children, and increased funding for reservation economic development and Indian health services. Nixon also called for the provision of funding to OEO and the Department of Health, Education, and Welfare (HEW) to support urban Indian centers, the creation of an independent Trust Counsel Authority to protect Indian lands and resources, and the appointment of an assistant secretary of the interior for Indian and territorial affairs to oversee the BIA rather than the assistant secretary for public land management, whose responsibilities in the natural resources area often conflicted with his responsibilities toward Indians.[33]

Despite receiving fairly widespread acclaim for proposing such an ambitious agenda, Nixon failed to obtain congressional approval for any of it, save the restoration of Blue Lake to the Taos Pueblos. During 1970 and 1971 the Senate Interior Committee held hearings on just two of the bills (the Indian Trust Counsel Authority and appointing an assistant secretary for Indian and territorial affairs), but the Senate passed only the latter proposal. The House of Representatives, meanwhile, had not acted at all, and during 1971 neither chamber scheduled hearings on the president's other requested reforms.[34]

Blame for these setbacks, not surprisingly, was widespread. In addition to the opposition of conservatives serving on the House and Senate Interior Committees, Democrats were in no mood to hand Nixon many legislative victories. As Nixon aide Daniel P. Moynihan later recalled, "Nixon was barely elected, and carried almost no one into office with him. Congress remained solidly in control of the opposition Democrats. The leaders of this party, and those of much influence within it, disliked or detested the incoming President in a degree that had few counterparts in American history. The prospects seemed hardly favorable for radical social change." According to historian Dean Kotlowski, Secretary Morton showed little interest in Indian legislation and testified poorly on behalf of the Indian Trust Counsel bill. William Timmons, who headed Nixon's congressional liaison office, also ignored the president's Indian agenda. "With no adviser choreographing Indian policy, confusion reigned at the White House."[35]

Indian leaders were also wary about parts of the administration's legislative package. At the Kansas City Conference on Indian Self-Determination held in mid March 1971, the agenda indicated that attendees would give final consideration to Nixon's proposals, but the legislation "received little attention and little support." Instead, Native Americans reminisced about the Johnson administration's unsuccessful attempt four years earlier to gain Indian support for an "omnibus bill" package of Indian-related reforms that had been inadequately vetted by tribal leaders before their introduction. Ironically, the final round of meetings for that doomed effort also took place in Kansas City, a venue that Indian leaders referred to as the "burial grounds for pre-packaged Indian legislation."[36]

The tribal chairs attending the Kansas City conference would have certainly disapproved of any process that involved the government's prepackaging of Indian-related legislation without their input. That said, the tribal chairs were supportive of tribal contracting, increased government funding for Indian health care and education, the creation of an independent Indian Trust Counsel Authority, and a congressional resolution that repealed termination. The Nixon administration's failure to follow up and press forcefully for their passage was a cause for concern. The policy window to gain approval for these far-reaching measures could close with the stroke of a pen. To ensure that eventuality did not take place, the duly elected leaders of federally recognized tribes had to get organized.

Douglas Skye and the National Tribal Leaders Conference

From the mid-1940s through the 1960s, the U.S. government pursued a policy designed to "liberate" Native Americans from their dependence on the federal government by ending (terminating) its trust responsibilities and requiring Indians to assume full responsibility for managing their own economic interests. By placing Native Americans on equal footing with non-Indians, proponents argued, they might at last be empowered to free themselves from poverty and assimilate into the majority society. Codified in House Concurrent Resolution 108 and Public Law 280, the "termination" policy led to the withdrawal of federal assistance to over one hundred tribes and permitted states to assume civil and criminal jurisdiction over several reservations. The policy quickly proved an unmitigated disaster. Fragile reservation economies collapsed without federal assistance, and the overwhelming majority of Native peoples were disinterested in assimilation and in seeking their fortunes in the white man's competitive world. In response to virtually unanimous Indian opposition to the policy as well as stark evidence that the abrogation of treaty-sanctioned promises was not emancipating tribal communities from poverty, termination was halted in the late 1960s.[37]

As government officials in the United States were coming to realize that termination was a bad idea and a calamitous policy, Canadian policymakers introduced termination-like policies of their own. In 1969 the administration of Prime Minister Pierre Trudeau (1968–79, 1980–84) introduced a White Paper on Indian policy titled "Statement of the Government of Canada on Indian Policy," which sought to reduce the economic and social stagnation of Canadian Indians (First Nations) by eliminating "Indian" as a distinct legal status—thereby making First Nations "equal" to other Canadians. The White Paper also proposed dismantling the Department of Indian Affairs and eradicating all treaties between First Nations and Canada. Finally, the White Paper advocated converting reservation lands to private property owned by bands or their members, and like Public Law 280, to transfer legal responsibilities to provincial governments.[38]

Trudeau's White Paper met with fierce resistance from tribal communities across Canada, which viewed the proposed policy as "tantamount to committing cultural genocide." The Indian Association of Alberta drew up a "Red Paper" in response, and after meeting with tribal leaders from other provinces, they gained the backing of the National Indian Brotherhood (a prominent Indian rights organization in Canada similar to the NCAI in the United States). Protests, meanwhile, took place across the country. Following a B'nai B'rith dinner held in Montreal on February 9, 1970, for example, the prime minister was confronted by thirty-five Indian protestors who presented him with an "award" for being "the most unjust man of the year." The protestors went on to thank him for his new Indian policy, which "promises to us a place in the slums of his Just Society in return for the surrender of our lands, our treaty rights, our culture and our identification as people."[39]

As these dramatic events played out in Canada, a Canadian Chippewa (Ojibwa) activist named Peter Kelly (Tobasonakwut Kaagagewanakweb) traveled to the United States to investigate how Canada's Native American neighbors responded to unpopular government policies. In the fall of 1969, Kelly met with Douglas Skye, the sixty-four-year-old chairman of the Standing Rock Sioux tribe of North and South Dakota. Born on the Standing Rock Reservation in 1905 Skye had attended schools at Fort Yates and Flandreau and later majored in business at Haskell Institute in Kansas. A thirty-year veteran of the BIA and a World War II veteran, the stocky, broad-shouldered, soft-spoken Skye was the epitome of a progressive Indian leader. Well educated and adept in federal Indian policy and procedures, he went to work each day wearing dress slacks, a button-down shirt, and a tie. Despite failing health and, as a father of seven children, various family responsibilities, Skye agreed to run for tribal chairman of the Standing Rock Sioux in 1969 and was elected by a resounding majority. As one tribal spokesman explained, "he was badly needed and he knew it." Promising to make the tribal council more responsive to the people and determined to craft a long-term plan for reservation development, Skye's philosophy of leadership was straightforward: "If you help a man get a job, and a decent house for his family to live in, you go a long way in solving his social as well as economic problems." Although understandably reluctant to criticize the BIA, Skye believed that the federal government had failed to meet its obligation to assist tribal governments in the performance of their many responsibilities. The way to address these failures, he argued, was by strengthening tribal governments and encouraging the federal officials to live up to their trust responsibilities.[40]

During his discussion with Peter Kelly, Skye learned about what was happening in Canada with the unpopular White Paper on Indian affairs and how tribal leaders had collaborated to draw up a Red Paper that asserted Indigenous rights and the importance of a genuine government-to-government relationship between Canadian tribes and the Canadian government. Skye was intrigued about the idea of heads of government coming together to talk about this relationship and was convinced that a confederation of Indian leaders and Indian nations—a body he likened to a clenched fist—could be a powerful tool to advance tribal sovereignty and self-determination. In pursuance of that idea, Skye invited tribal leaders from across the northern plains to a National Tribal Leaders Conference in Denver during the latter part of May 1970. At a meeting attended by forty tribal chairs on the morning of May 20, Skye promoted his idea about creating an organization of tribal leaders that would "act as a single voice for all the tribes" and the possibility of the NCAI acting in that capacity. Skye also railed against the growing popularity of militant urban Indian organizations and other "self-appointed leaders" who were seeking to formulate policy. "Only elected heads of Indian governments," he argued, "had the authority to consult on an equal basis with heads of non-Indian governments."[41]

Tribal Chairs Get Organized

Douglas Skye passed away on October 9, 1970, but calls for the establishment of an organization to provide one voice for all the tribes continued. At the twenty-seventh annual convention of the NCAI held in Anchorage just a couple weeks after Skye's death and again at the NCAI's executive session held in Washington, D.C., in January 1971, the tribal chairs renewed their discussions about creating an organization to represent reservation-based Indian nations. According to an article appearing in the *Northwest Indian Times,* a catalyst for these discussions came from a group calling itself the Small Tribes Organization of Western Washington (STOWW), which had demanded that the NCAI apportion votes to delegates representing its fifteen tribes—some of whom were not reservation-based or federally recognized—on an equal basis as larger federally recognized tribes. STOWW leader Roy George Sr. (Nooksack) heightened anxieties further by insisting that "the federal government give equal consideration to urban, landless, and non-federally recognized tribes."[42]

One of the leading voices at this time for the creation of an association of tribal chairs was Douglas Skye's thirty-year-old son, Clarence. A graduate of Black Hills State College, Clarence W. Skye was the executive director of the United Sioux Tribes of South Dakota Development Corporation in Pierre, South Dakota. In February 1971 Skye worked with tribal leaders Wendell Chino (Mescalero Apache), Roger Jourdain (Red Lake Band of Chippewa), Edison Real Bird (Crow), Benny Atencio (Pueblo), and William Youpee (Fort Peck Sioux) to organize a Reservation Tribal Chairmen's Conference at Eastern Montana College in Billings.[43] Over fifty tribal chairs from eleven western states attended the event, as did Commissioner Bruce, former commissioner Bob Bennett, and Bob Robertson, the executive director of the National Council on Indian Opportunity.[44] Local newspapers publicized the event as the largest Indian conference in Montana since Custer's Last Stand in 1876. Although reservation economic development was the ostensible theme of the gathering, most of the press coverage focused on the chairmen's complaints about the BIA, their concerns about the financial solvency of the National Congress of American Indians, and demands that federal officials reorient their attention and focus on reservation communities rather than on urban Indians. Newspaper accounts of the conference also reported that the assembled leaders had agreed to establish a "council of tribal chairmen"—the "kind of organization that the NCAI used to be" before it opened its membership to urban and non-reservation Indians. Self-appointed spokespersons of these latter groups, the gathered chairs charged, "travel around the cities on credit cards, hold meetings, use four-letter words, protest, make trouble, and still nobody represents the real Indian, the reservation Indian." Creating a new interest group that focused on reservation Indians, they believed, would correct this omission.[45]

Clarence Skye provided a different rationale for organizing an association of tribal chairs. Echoing his father's vision of a national tribal government, Skye called for an extension of federal recognition of Indian government beyond the tribe to the recognition of regional and national Indian government. Doing so, Skye argued, would permit tribes "to capitalize on their collective strength instead of struggling along in the fragmented manner of the past century." The creation of an association of tribal chairs was an important step in this direction, proponents maintained, since it could provide a structure for this national Indian government and render it impossible for federal officials to promise consultation and then complain that they had no formal body with whom to consult. "A tribal chairman is a head of state and should be treated as such," Wendell Chino, a former president of the NCAI, noted in his Billings speech, "for our respective reservations do represent sovereign states."[46]

Bob Bennett gave an interesting speech on the second day of the conference, parts of which likely resonated well with the assembled tribal leaders. To his credit, Bennett touched briefly on the controversial issue of the federal government's responsibilities toward urban Indians. As commissioner of Indian affairs in the Johnson administration, Bennett was well aware of the desperate plight facing urban Indians and in August 1968 asked his staff to prepare a report on the subject. That report, "Study of Urban Indian Problems," was delivered to Bennett on December 31, 1968. "An Indian does not cease being an Indian simply by moving from the reservation," the study declared, and the urban Indian, isolated among the many urban ethnic groups, "lacks an effective voice and commands no advocate for its interest."[47] Bennett did not have an opportunity to act on the report before departing the BIA, but before his audience of tribal chairs, Bennett advocated "meaningful discussions" between reservation Indians and their nonreservation counterparts to foster unity and mutual assistance. He then proceeded to blast the federal government for its dealings with "individual Indians and self-styled Indian leaders" in urban areas who were "receiving more than their share of attention." The provision of private— and in some cases government—financial assistance to off-reservation Indians was acceptable, Bennett continued, "but when it comes at the expense of the tribes where lies the Federal government's first responsibility, then something needs to be done."[48]

Bennett also took his successor Louis Bruce and the New Team to task for their efforts to reorganize (or realign) the BIA bureaucracy by rotating reservation superintendents and area directors to new positions every two to three years. "All reorganization is what you do when you want to avoid dealing with the issues and the problems," Bennett derisively noted, saying, "I don't know what rotation is supposed to do, but I think it means to go round and round and round on your axis."[49]

Of particular interest to the assembled tribal chairs was Bennett's confession that it had always been his hope "that in addition to an Indian organization like the National Congress of American Indians . . . that there should be a National Association of Tribal Chairmen." A unified voice and position by such an organization, he believed, "would have more impact than all of the loud mouths going about the country trying to curse their way into positions of Indian leadership" and who "show their disrespect to those whose guests they are by having temper tantrums and wreck[ing] the place." An association of tribal chairs, conversely, would "be a source of support to Indians everywhere and the means so desperately needed of bringing us back together as one people."[50]

Attending the Billings conference and listening to the stream of criticisms and complaints about the BIA and his New Team's reform efforts must have been an uncomfortable experience for Louis Bruce. He had promised upon accepting the commissioner's post that he would not be an accessory to power struggles or factional disputes, but he had little choice but to defend the BIA against the charges leveled both at him and his agency. The tribal chairs' accusations that the BIA was giving urban Indians preferential treatment were simply not true, Bruce declared: "We are reservation centered, and our programs are coming along real well." The BIA was "not to blame for the reservation vs. urban Indian squabble," Bruce insisted, and he advised tribal leaders to focus their attention on reservation development and to "go out and push programs on [their] reservations" or they would "miss out." The commissioner professed to being "impressed" by what he'd heard at the Billings conference and that he "liked the concept of a united reservation front to get at the sources of problems." That said, the tribal chairs needed to "get down to the nitty gritty, and try to work out answers for their problems" rather than just talking about them.[51]

Several of the tribal leaders attending the Billings conference expressed understandable concerns about how a new tribal chairs' organization would affect the NCAI. Virtually all the leaders in attendance, after all, were members of the NCAI and some had served in leadership positions.[52] Given the NCAI's weak financial condition and ongoing controversies over admitting non–federally recognized tribes and off-reservation Indians as voting members, the creation of a new organization would likely erode tribal support for the NCAI even further. Emotions boiled to the surface when Robert Dellwo, an attorney representing the Spokane, Coeur d'Alene, and Kalispel tribes (all strong supporters of the NCAI), pressed tribal leaders to comment on the new organization's potential impact on the NCAI. Clarence Skye reportedly responded by questioning why the non-Indian lawyer was involved in the discussion in the first place. There was talk about a possible compromise such as amending the NCAI's constitution to give reservation tribes a stronger voice and replacing its executive council with a council of tribal chairs, but in the end, tribal leaders voted to leave the work of amending the NCAI's constitution to the NCAI itself and to move forward with an independent tribal chairmen's association. Bill Youpee assured the assembled leaders that any new organization would supplement the NCAI—not weaken or destroy it—and he announced that the Fort Peck tribal council had authorized a donation of twenty-five hundred dollars to the NCAI to help it through its financial crisis.[53]

As noted previously, from March 8–12, 1971, the NCAI and the National Council on Indian Opportunity cohosted a Conference on Indian Self-Determination in Kansas City. Nearly four hundred Indian leaders representing 150 tribes attended (travel costs were reportedly covered by the Office of Economic Opportunity) to provide feedback on the Nixon administration's Indian policies and to assess the president's commitment to self-determination. Speaking on the opening day of the conference, Vice President Spiro Agnew drew strong applause with his promise to "oppose any doctrine of termination, no matter under what name it masquerades" and to promote tribal administration of government programs and services. Later that day, Navajo tribal chair Peter MacDonald provided an impassioned defense of Commissioner Bruce and his efforts to promote tribal self-determination via contracting and by reassigning long-serving BIA administrators who opposed meaningful reform. He also rebuked tribal chairs who criticized those efforts on the grounds that they had not been adequately consulted and suggested that they were being used by BIA administrators to sow intertribal dissension and cripple self-determination. Lastly, MacDonald urged tribal leaders to set aside their dissatisfaction with the urban Indian situation and to unify in support of self-determination—what he described as a "feast of freedom."[54]

While not on the agenda, the formation of an association consisting of tribal chairs emerged as the major point of discussion and controversy during the conference, and a resolution supporting the formation of a "National Indian Chairmen's Association" was narrowly defeated by a vote of 85-83. Similar to the Billings conference, opponents expressed concern that the creation of a new organization would kill the NCAI and undermine Indian unity; there was again talk of revising the NCAI's constitution to strengthen the role of tribal chairs so that a new organization was no longer necessary. Concentrated opposition to the creation of a tribal chairs' association came from small tribes located in the Pacific Northwest, California, the Great Lakes, and from the eastern part of the country that viewed the effort as a "power play" by large tribes. At one of five press conferences held by AIM representatives, Russell Means blasted the Indian self-determination gathering as "a last gasp at playing at white man's politics" and called the conference leaders "apples" who were "holding on for their last bit of prestige and power." Means denied that urban Indian groups were seeking "a piece of the reservation pie" but instead a portion of the federal government's assistance that other disadvantaged groups (blacks, Chicanos, rural Appalachians, and Puerto Ricans) were receiving. Urban Indians needed the assistance of reservation leaders to secure this assistance, Means maintained, but were being thwarted by "old line tribal leaders" who were "hanging on with finger tips to little vestiges of power."[55]

True to his pledge not to embroil himself in power struggles, Commissioner Bruce insisted that during his tenure in the BIA he had not been afraid to speak out on behalf of all Native Americans, and he reiterated his previous calls for unity and an end to divisiveness. In his address to the assembled delegates, Bruce was a bit cryptic in his plea for assistance. "I ask which of your many voices I should listen to. It is you who should determine who I listen to. I need to know your total needs, not hear just the loudest voices. We are prepared to follow a unified voice."[56]

Despite the close—but ultimately failed—vote to win support in Kansas City for the creation of a chairmen's association, tribal leaders pressed ahead with an organizational meeting slated to take place April 22–24, 1971, at the South Dakota capitol in Pierre. Webster Two Hawk, Rosebud Sioux chair and head of the United Sioux Tribes of South Dakota, served as the conference chair and predicted that more than eighty chairs from across the nation would attend. Clarence Skye, director of the United Sioux Tribes of South Dakota Development Corporation, also played a significant—albeit honorary—role, given his father's part in inspiring the effort. The general mood at the conference was upbeat. The event's theme, "Unity through New Horizons," bespoke the general sense among attendees that the timing was right for meaningful change but that immediate action was necessary on the part of tribal chairs to capitalize on the favorable political climate by moving on the creation of the NTCA. That said, actual attendance at the Pierre conference fell short of expectations. Only thirty tribal chairs attended the conference (others sent representatives), and reaching consensus even among that small group was at times difficult. Some chairs argued that only reservation (or land) tribes be represented in the organization, while others supported the inclusion of nonreservation tribes as long as they were federally recognized. The issue of the new organization's possible effect on the NCAI also remained a sensitive one. At one point in the conference, for example, Elmer Hunt (Zuni) declared that he still had faith in the NCAI and had "always believed that it was the voice of the American Indians. No matter how you look at it—this new organization will compete with the NCAI." Seeking to reassure concerned NCAI members such as Hunt that the new organization would complement—not replace—the older organization, Two Hawk declared that the tribal chairs—like other Indian leaders—were "working for the same goals of justice, equality, freedom and a higher standard of living. The young and the old, rich and poor, activists and those who remain silent all believe that something must be done."[57]

Perhaps in response to the advanced age of some of the tribal chairs (or out of concern that the meeting might get out of hand), conference organizers announced that a complete first-aid station had been set up and that a full-time nurse would be on duty. There was even a dentist on call for emergency work should the need arise. While tempers flared periodically over mundane issues such as committee assignments and substantive issues such as the credentials necessary to join the association (e.g., were tribal chairs from federally recognized tribes without reservations, such as the Comanches of Oklahoma, welcome in the association?), there were no reports that the medical personnel had been necessary.[58]

The three-day conference was divided into morning and afternoon breakout sessions interwoven with guest speakers (politicians, BIA administrators, tribal chairs). Webster Two Hawk managed the agenda and nudged participants to keep working on their assigned tasks. Fort Peck tribal chair Bill Youpee and Navajo tribal chair Peter MacDonald gave especially memorable talks. Youpee, who had served on the Fort Peck Tribal Council for nearly two decades and as chairman since 1961, spoke on the opening day. An outspoken critic of the BIA and urban Indians, and a staunch advocate of the prerogative of elected tribal chairs to be the sole spokespersons for reservation-based tribes, Youpee was unambiguous about his concerns that urban Indians were "the wrong Indian voices" and were garnering unmerited attention from the BIA. In a veiled swipe at Commissioner Bruce's New Team, Youpee insisted that it was "time that we had Indians in Washington who are reservation oriented, Indians who share our thinking, our hopes, and our aspirations." The federal government, he insisted, must "return priorities to where they belong—to the reservations." Creating an association of tribal chairs would not only benefit reservation communities, Youpee continued, but would empower the BIA to do a better job since it could "now consult with real Indian leaders who represent the real Indians, the reservation Indians." In regard to funding the new organization, Youpee recommended "having the government fund our activities, so that consultation fees that each agency spends [on outsiders] can now be applied to an area where there are more genuine Indian experts than anywhere else in the country—the reservations."[59]

Peter MacDonald's address marked a stark contrast to that of his Fort Peck colleague. In an impassioned call for unity and for action, MacDonald insisted that the Nixon administration's movement toward tribal self-determination was an unprecedented opportunity for positive change. "We have never had more to gain. But also, we have never had more to lose. And if we do not act now, for years to come, we will be told: See. We offered the Indians the opportunity to be heard, to shape their own destiny, to control their own affairs. They just aren't ready yet. They just don't want self-determination." He then went on to enumerate several proposals that he believed would lay the groundwork for the successful implementation of tribal self-determination:

1. Establishment of an official all-Indian commission on BIA reorganization to monitor bureau activities and serve as the eyes, ears, and voice of Native Americans in Washington
2. Immediate implementation of all Commissioner Bruce's realignment plans
3. Finalizing a constitution and by-laws for the NTCA
4. An immediate provision for government revenue sharing to tribal governments so that chairs could focus their time and energies on being tribal leaders and not just on weekends

"No one," MacDonald maintained, "can conduct tribal business on a part-time volunteer, one-day-a-week basis and do the job effectively as possible."[60]

Contrary to Youpee, MacDonald declared his opposition to a "Tribal Chairmen's Organization which delegates urban Indians as second-class citizens or which pretends to be the sole spokesman of all Indian interests on all

Indian matters." Instead, the NTCA should strive "to strengthen all the other groups and organizations and form a confederacy through which all problems can be discussed and presented in Washington."[61]

In conclusion, MacDonald offered a compelling and amusing statement in support of immediate and increased funding for Native Americans. "I noted the other day that the Department of the Interior has brought back the buffalo as its official sign. But the government of the United States has not put the Indian back on the nickel. Well, I don't want us to be put back on the nickel. I am tired, and I'm sure you are, very tired of nickels. I want the government to put the Indian on the dollar and then I want the government to put the dollar on the Indian and I do not want to wait until inflation makes the dollar worth a nickel."[62]

After three days of meetings, debates, and speeches, a draft constitution passed on April 24 by a vote of 18–2 with nine abstentions from attendees who wanted feedback from their tribes before signing. The next step was to have the document ratified by individual tribal councils within sixty days and then to hold a second convention to reaffirm the constitution and consider amendments. Heeding Peter MacDonald's recommendation, the chairs also adopted a resolution calling on Commissioner Bruce to establish a fifteen-member "All Indian Commission on Bureau of Indian Affairs Reorganization" to ensure that tribal leaders were consulted about any new plans for restructuring or realigning the BIA. Speaking on the second day of the conference, Commissioner Bruce commented that the new organization would be "a fine start toward Indian involvement in the affairs of the national Indian people at all levels" and expressed his desire to meet with the new fifteen-member commission "not in a few months but within two weeks" to discuss critical issues including land, water, natural resources, revenue sharing, "and all the issues that will face our Indian people in the future."[63]

———

Roughly two years after Douglas Skye met with Peter Kelly to strategize about ways to enhance the government-to-government relationship that existed between Indigenous nations and federal governments, the National Tribal Chairmen's Association was formally conceived in Pierre, South Dakota. The context for its creation, as I have attempted to show, was rather complex.

As the NCAI struggled with the issue of whether to "open up" its membership to off-reservation and non–federally recognized tribes or to "tighten up" around reservation-based Indian nations, conservative tribal leaders who were put off by the NCAI's financial morass and what they perceived as the organization's leftward shift and potential "radicalization" decided to go their own way. Some NTCA members went so far as to argue that the NCAI's many problems had rendered it invalid and claimed the NTCA was now "the only Indian organization which represents the population, tribes and reservations for which the government has a special responsibility." Tribal chairs and the NTCA bore this special responsibility, William Youpee had declared, "because they are the elected leaders and spokesmen for these particular tribes of Indians whom are federally-recognized. No other Indian organization is organized in this way and cannot claim to share the responsibility with the United States government *nor can any other Indian organization claim to be the bona-fide [representative of] federally-recognized Indians.*"[64]

While sympathetic to the problems facing urban Indians, the NTCA was convinced that any new federal programs or services directed toward off-reservation Indians or landless tribes would invariably come at the expense of federally recognized tribes. The controversial tactics and rhetoric of urban Indian groups such as AIM, the NIYC, and the IAT, furthermore, did more harm than good—particularly when they threatened to disrupt the special relationship that existed between tribes and the federal government by making unrealistic demands and undermining the efforts of elected tribal leaders. Many tribal chairs remained suspicious of Commissioner Bruce's realignment efforts and concerned about the reform-minded New Team, who, the chairs believed, had little idea about what was happening on reservations. The policy changes under way in the BIA, tribal chairs charged, had not been adequately vetted by tribal councils and were likely an overreaction to the demands of young urban militants.

The point here is that there were legitimate reasons for tribal chairs to be anxious about the direction of federal Indian policy and the increasingly powerful forces seeking to alter the federal trust relationship that had heretofore catered almost exclusively to reservation-based tribes. The creation of the NTCA was a rational response based on the self-interest of federally recognized tribes and in keeping with the deluge of special-interest groups proliferating across the country at the time. That said, scholars of Native American history as well as some contemporary Native American leaders have interpreted the NTCA's creation as some sort of Machiavellian plot hatched by Commissioner Bruce and the BIA, the Interior Department, and/or the executive branch to manage or co-opt the Indian reform movement by creating a "puppet group" of compliant tribal chairs who would serve as useful mouthpieces for the Nixon administration.[65] The BIA-NTCA collusion theory is certainly understandable. Federal officials undoubtedly preferred working with people they knew and trusted, and it was likewise desirable to work with a small group of Indian leaders rather than negotiating with hundreds of tribal governments. Various federal agencies helped finance assemblies of tribal leaders in the months leading up to the NTCA's constitutional convention and provided substantial funding afterward. That said, there are several reasons to question the BIA-NTCA collusion theory. First, there has been no documentary evidence offered to substantiate the claim that the BIA created the NTCA. Second, tribal leaders were harsh critics of the BIA at the time. Why would the bureau seek to further empower them? Third, just because an organization receives funding from the federal government does not mean the government created it; several national Indian organizations of the period, in fact, received funding from the federal government (see chapter 2). Fourth, tribal chairs strongly denied suggestions that the BIA had created the NTCA. Finally, there were several valid and compelling alternative reasons for tribal chairs to found a new Indian rights organization. As discussed in this chapter, the chairs' frustration with Commissioner Bruce's policies, the unwillingness of Congress to even consider President Nixon's legislative reform package, the perceived weakness of the NCAI, the growing challenge of urban Indian reform groups, and Douglas Skye's vision of a national tribal government explain the creation of the National Tribal Chairmen's Association.

Chapter 2

Early Years

Roger Jourdain (Red Lake Chippewa) and Wendell Chino (Mescalero Apache) were giants in the modern Indian rights movement. Aggressive, flamboyant, and often controversial, the two men are remembered both as "benevolent dictators" on their respective reservations and as champions of tribal sovereignty and self-determination. From the perspective of at least some Red Power activists, however, their leadership in the National Tribal Chairmen's Association (NTCA) rendered them as sellouts, empty suits, and compliant Uncle Tomahawks who had been co-opted by the federal government. How is one to make sense of such glaring disparities of judgment?

A heavy equipment operator by training, Roger Jourdain's entry into tribal politics began in the late 1950s when he led a group of younger tribal leaders to change the Red Lake Chippewas' system of governance by hereditary chiefs and adopt a new democratic constitution.[1] Elected chair in 1959 Jourdain served in that capacity for over three decades—a remarkable feat given the diversity of interests and factionalism prevalent within many tribes. He was instrumental in getting the Indian Health Service hospital reopened, and was widely praised with bringing running water, housing, and good roads to the Red Lake reservation. In a nod to tribal sovereignty, Jourdain demanded that visitors to Red Lake first secure a passport and that tribal courts admit only those defense attorneys who lived on the reservation and could speak Ojibwa.

When General Electric ran an ad for its new photo flashbulbs with a picture of children dressed up as Indians under the headline "When you shoot wild Indians you can't afford to miss," Jourdain dispatched an indignant telegram to GE, informing them, "You should be able to sell your product without resorting to this type of advertising." The company's response that "wild Indians" was meant as a "term of endearment" made matters worse. "It wasn't too endearing to us!" Jourdain declared. "We are trying to coexist, and we take exception to this advertisement." A chastened GE promptly pulled the ad. A frequent critic of the Bureau of Indian Affairs (BIA) ("I tried my damnedest to help them" but "they have never improved"), Jourdain sought to work instead with higher-ups in the Interior Department on a "nation-to-nation level." Reflecting on Jourdain's impact on the evolution of Native American rights, Vine Deloria Jr. commented that "50 clones of Roger Jourdain needed to be turned loose in Indian Country."[2]

Like his Chippewa contemporary, Wendell Chino led an effort to draft a new constitution for his people to replace the Indian Reorganization Act (IRA) model in effect since 1936. In 1965 the ordained Dutch Reformed minister was elected president of the Mescalero Apaches—a post he held for the next thirty-three years. Described as "casting a towering shadow" over Indian affairs in the Southwest and as a "Martin Luther King and Malcolm X wrapped up into one man," Wendell Chino transformed the Mescalero Apache reservation into an economic powerhouse. Intent on providing or improving housing, jobs, and education on the reservation, Chino hired non-Indian specialists to manage a particular project—for example, the Inn of the Mountain Gods resort—but told them up front, "You're here to train your replacements. Your replacements will be Apache." A forceful speaker with a gruff exterior, Chino was convinced that the path to Mescalero sovereignty and self-determination lay in economic development. To that end, he instructed his staff to pursue grant opportunities; he also pushed for the creation of a tribal cattle company and began laying the groundwork for a chalet-style resort with a golf course, restaurant, and casino. "You have to have capital to make progress," Chino maintained. "Navajos make rugs, Pueblos make pottery, but Apaches make money." His leadership did not go unrecognized. In 1967 and 1968 Chino was elected president of the National Congress of American Indians (NCAI), where he encouraged member tribes to more forcefully take the reins of self-determination.[3]

As long-serving leaders of their respective Indian nations, Roger Jourdain and Wendell Chino faced periodic charges of financial irregularities, tyrannical rule, and usurpation of power from their respective tribal councils. Few would have characterized them, however, as sellouts or compliant rubber stamps who had been co-opted by a federal government intent on managing Indian opposition and clamping down on the burgeoning Indian rights movement. Yet those are precisely the allegations Red Power advocates constantly leveled against the NTCA and its membership. According to Charles Wilkinson, on the matter of tactics, Indian leaders had a different style. Tribal council members tended to be

Roger Jourdain (Red Lake Chippewa) and Wendell Chino (Mescalero Apache) helped found the NTCA and held leadership positions throughout its existence. Courtesy of Bob Robertson.

conservative and sought to preserve age-old practices based on diplomacy and negotiation. Some tribal leaders, especially the older ones, wanted nothing to do with activist strategies. For the leaders of federally recognized tribes, adopting an insider or relationship-based advocacy strategy offered the most realistic chance of advancing their agenda without endangering the special relationship that existed between federal and Indian governments. But does this indicate co-optation or the acceptance of symbolic representation over substantive change? Did the NTCA soft-pedal its demands for reform to protect itself and placate its government "handlers"? This chapter seeks to address these questions by reviewing the association's role as an interest group, its quest for financing, and its initial interactions with the federal government.

The primary functions of interest groups like the NTCA are to influence government decisions in a manner that benefits their particular membership and to advance their specific agenda and goals. Most interest groups likewise perform several secondary functions that carry additional awards for their members. Some of these functions are largely symbolic and designed to give groups an opportunity to express their specific interests or values. Whenever the NTCA convened a meeting of tribal leaders, for example, the gathering provided an important symbolic expression of support for Douglas Skye's vision of Native American leaders forming a national tribal government; an NTCA meeting with Department of the Interior officials, meanwhile, gave expression to the association's oft-touted notion that elected tribal chairs were the legitimate representatives of federally recognized tribes. Closely related to these symbolic functions were ideological ones that gave voice to the group's specific ideological goals. For the NTCA, this meant providing an articulate and amplified voice for tribal sovereignty, self-determination, cultural preservation, and justice. Interest groups like the NTCA also perform an information function: collecting, analyzing, and disseminating information or data to the federal government or to the broader public while bringing back information about pending legislation, newly enacted laws, and the attitudes and behaviors of relevant government organizations and the officials who run them. This information function requires the group to closely monitor government activities that might affect them, which in turn entails securing access to information and to decision makers. To be effective, most interest groups need a full-time staff working in Washington, D.C., and perhaps branch offices across the nation. Finally, interest groups perform economic functions—raising money to press the fight for their particular causes or, like the NTCA, to fund lobbying efforts to ensure the uninterrupted flow of government programs and services for their constituents, and perhaps to expand those programs and services further.[4]

The Constitutional Ratification Convention. July 12–14, 1971

To identify the tribal chairs' goals and the raisons d'être for the NTCA's creation, a brief review of the association's constitution is a good place to start. On June 8, 1971, convention organizers sent out a mailing advising tribal leaders that the NTCA Constitutional Ratification Convention would be held July 12–14 at the Hilton Hotel in Albuquerque. The tentative agenda called for a series of workshops and speakers with a ratification vote on day one, the election of officers on day two, and the NTCA's first executive session on day three. A thirty-thousand-dollar grant from the Office of Economic Opportunity (OEO) covered the travel and per-diem expenses of tribal chairs attending the convention. By all accounts, the event went smoothly. Peter MacDonald (Navajo) welcomed the tribal leaders on the morning of July 12 and urged them to consider the proposed NTCA constitution and bylaws that had been drawn up in Pierre, South Dakota, a couple months earlier. "The Constitution and Bylaws we adopt here should be a tool to assist us in improving the opportunities of our Indian people," MacDonald declared, and with the NTCA, "we have the opportunity to achieve the rights of Indian self-determination which we've sought for many, many years as tribal leaders." Dr. Alonso Spang (Northern Cheyenne) gave the keynote address later that day, which stressed the need for intertribal unity, the desirability of self-determination, balancing reservation economic development with environmental sensitivity, and the need for Native Americans to be involved in the selection of personnel working for government agencies that served tribal communities.[5]

The preamble of the NTCA constitution (see appendix 1) evinced several ideological and symbolic goals: to establish unity, justice, respect for treaty rights, cultural preservation, and the promotion of social, educational, economic, and political progress. Not surprisingly, the preamble also included language asserting that "the elected or appointed tribal chairmen of all Indian reservations and federally recognized tribes" were to serve as the "official voice of Indian leaders" in the country. Article II of the constitution provided an enumerated list of its purposes. In general, these focused on the NTCA's desire for consultation between federal officials and federally recognized tribes but specified that the consultation be "direct" and "meaningful" as befitting genuine government-to-government relationships. Article II also declared that tribal governments should play a more expansive role in directing and administering federal programs on reservations, in keeping with the government's promise of self-determination. As the representatives of sovereign Indian nations, tribal governments would employ treaty rights and privileges for the promotion and protection of human and natural resources, to ensure that Indian peoples received their rightful share of federally funded programs and services, and to guard against any unilateral modification or termination of the trust relationship between the U.S. government and federally recognized tribes. To satisfy the concerns of tribal leaders about the relationship between the NTCA and the NCAI, the final enumerated purpose was "to continue to support, promote and complement the National Congress of American Indians."[6]

The NTCA constitution restricted membership to "duly elected or appointed chairmen, presidents, governors or chiefs of reservation Indians or of federally recognized tribes with federal trust land or whose members live on or nearby federal reservations." The association would be led by elected officers—a president and vice president who served one-year terms and a secretary and treasurer who served two-year terms. A twelve-member NTCA Board

Table 1
NTCA Officers and Board Members, 1971

Office	Name	Tribal Organization
President	William Youpee	Fort Peck Tribal Executive Board
Vice President	Lee Motah	Comanche Business Committee
Treasurer	Odrick Baker	Lac Courte Oreilles Governing Board
Secretary	Nathan Little Soldier	Fort Berthold Tribal Council
Aberdeen Area Representative	Edward Cline	Omaha Tribal Council
Albuquerque Area Representative	Wendell Chino	Mescalero Apache Tribal Council
Anadarko Area Representative	Gerald Reid	Kiowa Business Committee
Billings Area Representative	Allen Rowland	Northern Cheyenne Tribal Council
Juneau Area Representative	Don Wright	Alaska Federation of Natives
Minneapolis Representative	Norbert S. Hill	Oneida Executive Committee
Muskogee Representative	B. Bob Stopp	Cherokee Executive Committee
Navajo Area Representative	Peter MacDonald	Navajo Tribal Council
Phoenix Area Representative	Ted James	Pyramid Lake Tribal Council
Portland Area Representative	Edward Claplanhoo	Makah Tribal Council
Sacramento Area Representative	Peter Masten Jr.	Hoopa Valley Business Council
Washington Office Representative	Buffalo Tiger	Miccosukee Business Committee

of Directors representing the twelve BIA administrative areas would also provide oversight to the association's activities. Like the president and vice president,
the directors were elected by the NTCA membership and served one-year terms
(see table 1).[7] The inaugural elections yielded few surprises. William Youpee,
Fort Peck's chair, narrowly defeated Mescalero Apache chair Wendell Chino for
the presidency. Long-serving Comanche chair Lee Motah from Oklahoma was

elected vice president; Nathan Little Soldier (Sahanish), who chaired the Fort Berthold Tribal Council of North Dakota, was elected secretary; and Odrick (Rick) Baker, chairman, Lac Courte Oreilles Tribal Governing Board in Minnesota, was elected treasurer. Other notable election results included Wendell Chino, who, after being passed over for both the presidency and vice presidency, won election as the Albuquerque area representative on the NTCA board. Peter MacDonald, chair of the influential Navajo Tribal Council, was elected representative from the Navajo Area; Don Wright, president of the Alaska Federation of Natives, was elected to represent the Juneau area.[8]

There was little in Bill Youpee's personal background to explain his strong interest in tribal politics or his path to NTCA leadership. Born in humble surroundings at Fort Kipp on the Fort Peck reservation of Montana in 1914 (according to one account, he was born in a tent), Youpee's main interest as a youth was sports. He attended school in Poplar and was a member of his high school's state basketball championship team and a Golden Gloves boxing champion. During the Great Depression, Youpee left Fort Peck and moved to Portland, where he found work in construction. Living off reservation, he later recalled, is "something everyone should do" because "you get an objective outlook and you're able to put yourself on both sides of a question or a problem." A self-made farmer and rancher, Youpee played in a country-and-western band and hosted a radio show. If those activities did not keep him busy enough, Youpee was the father of twelve children. After spending nearly fifteen years in Portland, Youpee returned home and was elected to the Fort Peck Tribal Council in the early 1950s and as chair in 1961. One of Youpee's first orders of business was to deal with the National Park Service's decision to cut off shipments of elk meat to the reservation without first consulting the tribal council. Park Service officials imposed the ban after one of the helpers on the delivery truck—a nineteen-year-old Indian—became intoxicated en route to Fort Peck. In response to Youpee's condemnation of the decision, Park Service officials promised in the future to consult more closely with the Fort Peck Tribal Council. Like other tribal chairs, Youpee worked to bring economic development opportunities to the reservation. In the spring of 1969 Fort Peck Tribal Industries was formally dedicated to "provide an opportunity for the tribes to engage in business under their own management and control." Within a year's time, Fort Peck Tribal Industries employed 118 tribal members to repair M-1 rifles for the U.S. military. In August, the Small Business Administration awarded it an additional $1.5 million in federal supply contracts. An active but not a leading member of the NCAI, Youpee also presided

A strong advocate of elected tribal chairs, William Youpee (Fort Peck Sioux) maintained that the only "real Indians" were members of federally recognized tribes. Courtesy of the Center of Southwest Studies, Fort Lewis College, Durango, Colorado.

over the Montana Intertribal Policy Board, which provided him a bully pulpit of sorts to criticize the reform agenda of Commissioner Bruce and the New Team. A talented individual and a hard worker, Youpee was uncompromising in his belief that the path to tribal sovereignty and self-determination lay with elected tribal governments. As such, he was a virulent and often blunt critic of urban Indian activists and what he believed was the inordinate amount of attention they received both from the national press and from the federal government.[9]

On the afternoon of July 12, more than 160 Indian leaders from across the nation voted overwhelmingly to ratify the proposed constitution, and the NTCA formally came into being.[10] At the request of convention organizers, Louis Bruce and a delegation of BIA staffers attended the convention and participated in the workshops that followed the ratification vote. Although the entire proceeding, one should recall, was at least partially a response to some tribal chairs' rejection of Bruce and his New Team—a fact that the commissioner undoubtedly understood—Bruce nonetheless described the creation of the NTCA as an "intelligent, satisfying and marvelous accomplishment" and predicted that the "good work" of tribal chairs would be remembered as one of the "major accomplishments of Indian history and as one of the major accomplishments of Indian leadership of the 20th century." To his credit, Bruce reiterated his support for the National Congress of American Indians before commenting unconvincingly that "I'm sure the people who joined this organization did not intend for it to replace the NCAI." The establishment of the NTCA—at least in principle—promised to make consulting with tribes easier and more efficient since Bruce would now have a single entity to negotiate with rather than hundreds of sovereign Indian nations. This simplification held understandable appeal to the commissioner, and he no doubt wanted to start off on the right foot with his new "partner" in Indian affairs. He may also have believed that an association of tribal chairs might very well assist him in his efforts to advance the new self-determination policy. That said, it's hard to reconcile Bruce's glowing praise for the NTCA with the many criticisms tribal chairs had leveled against the BIA during his tenure as commissioner.[11]

At the NTCA's first executive session held on Wednesday, July 14, the association's leadership discussed various "technicalities" with the recently adopted constitution. One issue was that some tribal chairs had sent representatives instead of attending in person. Going forward, would that arrangement be accepted? After considerable discussion, the consensus was that tribal representatives could attend meetings, but they would have no vote, nor would proxy voting be permitted for chairs not in attendance. From Wendell Chino's perspective, the practice of sending representatives defeated the purpose of the association, and if chairs were not going to attend in person, the group may as well disband. There were also lingering questions about who was in charge of the NTCA—the officers or the board of directors—and how NTCA members were to be replaced should they be defeated in their bids for reelection as tribal chairs. Buffalo Tiger (Miccosukee) muddied the waters further by mentioning that Emmet York, chair of the Mississippi Choctaw Tribal Council, had recently been defeated for reelection but was still chair of the intertribal organization United South and Eastern Tribes Inc. (USET). Should York be required to resign his membership in NTCA? After lengthy discussions about these significant issues, the NTCA leadership decided to table the debate pending the creation of an Amendment Committee to draft changes to the constitution.[12]

Financing

The matter of NTCA financing is especially critical to assessing its role in Indian affairs during its decade-and-a-half-long existence. How did the NTCA raise the funding necessary to perform its stated functions? How did its funding sources compare with those of other Native American interest groups, such as the NCAI or AIM? If the NTCA was largely dependent upon government financing, does this prove the frequent criticism that tribal chairs were sellouts and the NTCA little more than a puppet or echo board of the BIA, the Interior Department, and the particular administration running the executive branch? In short, had the federal government co-opted the tribal chairs running the NTCA? Were they so worried about biting the hand that fed them that they watered down their advocacy efforts and muted their criticisms of federal Indian policy?

According to Charles "Chuck" Trimble (Oglala Lakota), the executive director of the National Congress of American Indians from 1972 to 1978, the NCAI depended on a wide array of financial sources to fund its activities. As a membership organization, the NCAI sold memberships to tribes and to individuals and charged registration fees for members attending annual conventions. The NCAI also received financial support from churches, private foundations, and contracts with federal agencies such as the BIA; the OEO; and the Department of Health, Education, and Welfare (HEW). The NCAI cosponsored the Kansas City Indian Self-Determination Conference, for example, through a contract with OEO; the NCAI also received funds from HEW on one occasion, for instance, to develop a textbook on tribal governance. Because the NCAI was a political interest group, it could not be a 501(c)(3) nonprofit, which limited its ability to solicit donations since donors could not write off their financial gifts.[13] Consequently, in 1949 the NCAI established a nonprofit corporation called the National Congress of American Indians Fund (later renamed Americans for Restitution and Righting of Old Wrongs, or ARROW Inc.), which worked closely with the NCAI on a variety of charitable and educational activities. While ostensibly separate entities, cooperation between the NCAI and ARROW remained close and continued for several years.[14]

The American Indian Movement (AIM) likewise raised funds in a variety of ways. It received grants from various church organizations, such as the American Lutheran Church, the Roman Catholic Church's Christian Sharing Fund, and the World Council of Churches. It also received grants from corporations such as Harper and Row Publishers via its Native American Publishing

Program. Despite its often-scathing criticisms of the federal government, AIM was the recipient of grants from HEW and the OEO—the most famous of which was the OEO's payment of $66,650 to participants in the AIM-inspired Trail of Broken Treaties Caravan. Like the NCAI, AIM sought to facilitate donations by establishing 501(c)(3) nonprofit corporations such as the American Indian Movement Interpretive Center and the American Indian Opportunities Industrialization Center, both headquartered in Minneapolis.[15]

While the NCAI charged membership fees for tribes and individuals, the founders of the NTCA only belatedly considered charging chairs to become members. To be relevant, credible, and effective, the association needed strong buy-in among tribal governments, many of which were cash-strapped. To charge them, or to expect individual chairs to pay out of pocket, at the outset for an unproven and somewhat controversial association would likely suppress membership.[16] Another fundraising idea was to solicit small contributions from the general public. With a proposed theme of "Contribute a dollar to the American Indian Future," the campaign could potentially net over $1 million. Along with student scholarships and aid to tribal governments, the campaign would provide "operational money for the NTCA so that it can be a strong, effective advocate of the Indian interest without having to be dependent on federal dollars." The catch was that the NTCA would need free television and radio spots to broadcast the appeal, along with professional advertising and public relations help. The funds to secure this assistance would require financial backing from a major American corporation. For the time being, therefore, the "Contribute a dollar to the American Indian Future" initiative would have to wait for another day.[17]

In an undated NTCA proposal "to make consultation and Indian self-determination a reality," the chairs laid out an ambitious plan to create an NTCA national office that would serve as the "full-time communication link" connecting federally recognized tribes and the U.S. government. To create such a structure, the NTCA envisioned a full-time staff of six, an additional six research specialists, and a legal consultant. Periodic meetings (either biannually or quarterly) of the general association, the board of directors, area representatives, and various committees would "develop input to the Federal government which would reflect the thinking of the broadest possible consensus of the Indian population." The total price tag for this proposed "communication link" exceeded $1.1 million a year.[18]

During the association's second year in operation, annual budget estimates were far more modest, ranging from $150,000 up to $300,000: $25,000 for political consultants' fees, $25,000 for a lawyer, $25,000 for an executive director, $20,000 for a deputy director, $12,000 for a secretary, $40,000 for association meetings, and the remaining $3,000 for office supplies and postage. At some point in time, the association would need its own office space, which did not come cheap in the nation's capital. One funding proposal included the addition of six NTCA field representatives at a cost of nearly $80,000. Don Wright indicated that the Alaska Federation of Natives (AFN) would put up $3,000 to help get an office organized if other tribes also agreed to contribute. Buffalo Tiger thought the Miccosukees would approve $2,000 to $3,000 a year, but the Comanches' Lee Motah and other chairs expressed doubts that their tribal councils would approve annual contributions. Instead, the NTCA counted almost exclusively on federal government support—specifically from the BIA, the Indian Health Service, the OEO, and the Economic Development Agency. During the tribal chairs' April 1971 convention in Pierre, Bill Youpee had argued that the government contract with the NTCA for consulting work since tribal chairs were the "genuine Indian experts" for their respective reservations. Why pay outsiders when there were "more genuine Indian experts than anywhere else in the country" residing on reservations? Not all convention participants agreed. A small group of dissenters from Youpee's own Fort Peck contingent, in fact, made an interesting observation about the NTCA's professed ability to deliver on its promises of Indian unity, expanded tribal sovereignty, and a stronger Indian voice on Capitol Hill. Led by former Fort Peck Tribal Council chair Dolly Akers (Youpee, incidentally, had participated in the successful effort in 1958 to remove her from office), the dissenters argued that self-determination among the Indian people was a myth "as long as we accept money from the BIA and from foundations and other hand-out groups. He who controls the purse," Akers intoned, "controls the policy, and unless Indian people begin to control their own funds, they will never control their destiny."[19]

A little over a month later, a group of tribal chairs met with Commissioner Bruce in Denver. During that meeting, the chairs—apparently oblivious to the arguments proffered by Dolly Akers, inquired about possible BIA funding of the NTCA—perhaps via contracts for consultation services. Bruce reportedly demurred at the request but held out the possibility of BIA assistance in covering travel and subsistence expenses if and when he requested a meeting with the group. The commissioner emphasized that in order for the NTCA to remain independent and "not a rubber-stamp organization of the Bureau of Indian Affairs," private financing opportunities needed to be explored, and he promised BIA assistance in developing funding proposals for submission to foundations. BIA public information specialist Hanay Geigamah (Kiowa/Delaware) was assigned this task while a finance committee comprising Peter MacDonald, Bob Stopp, and Don Wright would be his contacts in the NTCA.[20]

Like the NCAI and AIM, the NTCA had to incorporate a nonprofit auxiliary and secure a nontaxable rating from the Internal Revenue Service before inroads could be made with foundations. To help in this endeavor, the NTCA reached out to Marvin Franklin (Iowa), the director of corporate projects at Phillips Petroleum, who had considerable experience drafting charters of incorporation. On July 29, 1971, the NTCA received a certificate of incorporation in Washington, D.C., for the National Tribal Chairmen's Fund Inc. (NTC Fund), a nonprofit corporation "organized exclusively for charitable, educational, and scientific purposes to advance the social, cultural, and economic welfare of the American Indian, their tribal governments, bodies, and organizations of tribal members." The corporation had two classes of membership: regular membership and associate membership. Regular members had voting rights but had to be tribal chairs in the NTCA; associate membership was open to anyone (individual Indians, tribes, the general public) interested in advancing the goals of the corporation, but associate members had no vote. This would give the new corporation the appearance of having a broader membership than the NTCA, a maneuver intended to satisfy the IRS that the NTCA and the NTC Fund were indeed distinct entities. The corporation's board of directors included Odric Baker (Lac Courte Oreilles), Allen Rowland (Northern Cheyenne), and Edward Claplanhoo (Makah). A few weeks later, the three-member NTC Fund held its first meeting at Southwestern Indian Polytechnic Institute in Albuquerque. After voting to add Norbert Hill (Oneida) and Buffalo Tiger (Miccosukee) to the board, they unanimously approved the corporation's bylaws and ratified their election to the NTC Fund's board of directors.[21]

While the NTC Fund board worked on getting the new nonprofit corporation up and running, NTCA leaders held concurrent meetings (also at Southwestern Indian Polytechnic Institute) where they discussed a wide variety of topics, foremost of which was interim funding for the association. The NTCA's bank account held a balance of twenty-five hundred dollars, money left over from the OEO's earlier grant to finance the July ratification convention in Albuquerque. The BIA remained noncommittal in providing help. Contracting with the NTCA for consultation was off the table for the time being, although the bureau promised to help with travel and per-diem expenses when meeting with NTCA officials. On August 19 Bill Youpee submitted a request for a twenty-five-thousand-dollar OEO "administrative assistance" grant to fund the association's activities until it could acquire funding from private sources. Submitting grant requests to foundations, however, required expenditures. According to Hanay Geiogamah, the BIA official appointed to help the NTCA apply for private funding, grant applications needed to be delivered in person since mailed proposals were apparently often ignored. The boards of foundations, furthermore, met only a few times a year to consider funding requests. Delays were consequently the norm, and there was no guarantee their proposals would be approved for funding. Lacking a dependable revenue stream, not to mention an office, staffing, and supplies, the NTCA was in a serious bind. Additional tribes were inquiring about joining the association but could change their minds if the association appeared incapable or unable to function. At this point, an important new ally offered assistance.

The National Council on Indian Opportunity (NCIO) was established on March 6, 1968, during the final year of the Lyndon B. Johnson administration. Comprising eight cabinet members with Indian-related responsibilities and eight Native American leaders appointed by the president, the council was both a symbolic and potentially dynamic effort to include Native Americans in the decision-making processes that affected them. The NCIO gave Native peoples unprecedented access to some of the highest-ranking decision makers in the federal government, including the vice president, who served as the council's nominal chair. The council's primary responsibilities included coordinating the federal government's services to Native Americans, promoting interagency cooperation to maximize the delivery of those services, and encouraging Indian communities to take full advantage of the programs available. In addition to Indian and executive department members, the NCIO employed a small staff led by an executive director appointed by the vice president. With offices located in the White House annex building on Jackson Place, N.W., the NCIO was well positioned, at least geographically, to promote a more expansive and efficient utilization of federal programs and services by tribal communities.[22]

Given the NCIO's responsibilities as a coordinator of services to reservations and as a liaison between tribes and federal agencies, the council welcomed the establishment of the NTCA as an important ally in fulfilling its mission. Tribal chairs, after all, were the NCIO's most important clients. According to NCIO executive director Bob Robertson, the NCIO's "prime purpose in existing" was "to give maximal support to the elected leaders in Indian country and to do everything possible to strengthen tribal governments." Although the NCIO operated on a meager annual budget of $300,000, when Robertson heard about the NTCA's financial problems, he offered it office space, telephones, office supplies, and mail service, declaring that he was "delighted" to be able to assist "a new organization which will become the most significant group with whom the federal government will deal in meeting the needs of reservation people."[23]

The BIA, meanwhile, loaned clerical staff to the tribal chairs until they were able to secure private funding, and in a magnanimous gesture, the NCAI provided accommodations for an NTCA contingent to attend its Industrial Conference in Chicago. Over the course of the next two years, the NTCA was the recipient of nine contracts or grants from four different federal agencies. After considerable delay, the BIA secured the legal authority to contract with the NTCA for consultation services. Between January 31, 1971, and June 30, 1974, the BIA paid over $550,000 to the NTCA for consultation services, travel reimbursements, and per-diem expenses. During the same time period, HEW contracted with the NTCA for an additional $246,000 in consulting services, and OEO added another $45,000 "to help NTCA become operational and function effectively." In June 1973 the NCIO contracted with the tribal chairs to conduct a study of federally funded programs on Indian reservations at a cost of $30,000. All told, the NTCA received in excess of $875,000 from federal agencies during its first few years in operation. This heavy reliance on government support continued for the duration of its existence.[24]

Before moving on to the NTCA's efforts as an interest group seeking to advance the needs of federally recognized tribes, a word is in order about the possible consequences of its near-exclusive reliance on government financial support. The most obvious issue is the chairs' potential loss of autonomy or independence and the dilution of their advocacy role. How can an organization profess to be a watchdog when the entity it purports to watch is paying its wages? A related concern is public (and, in the NTCA's case, Native American) perceptions of such an arrangement and the accompanying skepticism that the integrity of the group in question has been compromised by its dependence on government funding. Tribal chairs were clearly aware of this problem and, in a draft position paper dated December 5, 1973, acknowledged that the association "is like all other organizations in that it receives money from the government." In spite of this, "The NTCA retains its autonomy and its independence and it is still working hard to maintain that tribal sovereignty which Indians have always cherished." Just how the association was able to accomplish this was not specifically addressed.[25]

Social and political theorists have examined the effects of government support for nonprofit organizations at considerable length and, not surprisingly, arrived at different conclusions about how government funding affects a nonprofit's political activities. Gauging these effects with any precision is difficult to say the least, given the myriad factors that govern what an organization is advocating for or how it carries out its advocacy. According to its constitution, the NTCA was advocating for more frequent and meaningful consultation with the federal government, for the authority to direct and administer federal programs on reservations, and for the promotion and protection of the human and natural resources of federally recognized tribes. To these ends, tribal chairs adopted collaborative and cooperative forms of advocacy (as opposed to militancy and confrontation) with the goal of building personal relationships and trust with federal officials, to enhance their status as the "legitimate" spokespersons for sovereign Indian nations, and to establish the interdependence that (in theory at least) accompanies genuine government-to-government relationships. In an October 1971 press conference NTCA president William Youpee explained the chairs' strategy as follows: "We believe there are different methods to realize our common goals. There is room for innovation and individualism and we welcome this. Some of our leaders sound the war cry to get the attention of the government to tell them of discontent. Others of us are more concerned with keeping that attention and having it directed to our needs through cool and continuous consultation." This insider or relationship-oriented advocacy strategy, the tribal chairs' believed, offered the best prospects for ensuring the stability of government funding for federally recognized tribes—and for the NTCA. Their adoption of this strategy, as we will see, came with costs.[26]

Virtually all scholars agree that the most obvious and direct mechanism by which government funding might suppress a nonprofit's political activities is straightforward resource dependence and the attendant don't-bite-the-hand-that-feeds-you syndrome. According to this argument, organizations that depend on government funding for their livelihood refrain from oppositional political activities frowned upon by that funding source, and as public funding becomes more central to an organization's survival, the potential for co-optation increases. Even if the likelihood of government "punishment" is remote, the mere threat of retribution (e.g., losing funding) causes anxiety, which can modify an organization's behavior.[27]

A second way that government funding can suppress a nonprofit's political activities is by redirecting the organization's attention, energy, and resources away from its core mission and toward the administrative activities necessary to maintain the funding. This could include grant writing, record keeping, receiving training to remain in compliance with regulations, and so on. Government funding—contracting in particular—also brings about several sorts of changes in a nonprofit's organizational structure and often leads to increased formalization, complexity, professionalization, and bureaucratization. These factors in turn can influence the qualifications necessary to lead a nonprofit organization and thus impact the individuals selected to executive boards and management positions. Over time, this shift from community norms to government norms can blur the role of nonprofits as entities separate from the government that funds them.[28]

While nonprofits may succumb to the aforementioned pressures and respond by muting criticisms of their government benefactors or morphing into an altogether different type of organization than originally envisioned, mitigating influences exist that can empower government-funded nonprofits to continue—if not enhance—their political activities. In some cases, for instance, organizations' dependence on the government is a two-way street. When a particular nonprofit is the only or best-qualified entity to provide a particular service, the government is hard-pressed to cease its funding. In cases such as this—where mutual dependence exists—neither can dominate the other, and government agencies and nonprofit organizations approach each other on more equal terms. Like most public or private organizations, governments—and politicians especially—are sensitive to maintaining favorable public relations. Cutting a nonprofit's funding for challenging a particular policy can lead to unflattering press coverage, thereby liberating a nonprofit to pursue more aggressive political activities to advance its mission. With this theoretical framework in mind, we can begin assessing the NTCA's activities as an advocate for federally recognized tribes.

BIA Reorganization

Shortly upon accepting President Nixon's appointment as the fortieth commissioner of Indian affairs, Louis Bruce had commented that the position required him to "look clearly at the goal of improving the conditions of Indian people" while operating simultaneously as "part of the governmental process bouncing on the tightrope." During the spring and summer of 1971, gale-force winds emanating from Red Power activists, reactionaries within the Bureau of Indian Affairs, anxious tribal chairs, and Bruce's supervisors in the Interior Department combined to give the tightrope several vigorous shakes. Heeding Nixon's instructions to address the BIA's notoriously stubborn bureaucracy, Bruce hired his New Team of reformers, who initiated a series of policy and personnel changes that reflected the administration's professed support for self-determination and the transfer of BIA functions to tribes. As stated in the previous chapter, some of these changes, such as the rotation of area directors, brought howls of protest from long-serving old-line bureaucrats as well as from several tribal chairs who argued that Bruce had failed to adequately consult with them before making these changes. In January 1971 Secretary of the Interior Walter Hickel, who had up to this point supported Bruce's policies, was replaced by Rogers C. B. Morton, who "regarded Bruce's staff of activists as long on zeal and short on managerial experience."[29]

In order to get an "independent view of the status of the BIA," Morton convened a Management Assistance Survey Team—comprising individuals from the IRS, the Inspector General's Office, the Civil Service Commission, and the Office of Management and Budget—who spent several weeks conducting a review of the BIA with the goal of making recommendations to improve implementation of the self-determination policy. The survey team found several major problems in bureau operations, such as inadequate planning and preparation for the policy—both among tribes and within the BIA—inadequate mechanisms for consulting with tribal leaders, and managerial and organizational turmoil. To address the first problem, the survey team recommended the creation of "policy strategy staffs" to consider how best to implement self-determination and to "help tribes to prepare themselves" for its enactment. In a recommendation that sounded quite like an organization such as the NTCA, the survey team "felt very strongly some device should exist at the national level for regular consultation with tribal leaders." In a thinly veiled and condescending swipe at Commissioner Bruce's assistants, the survey team found that "some of the new officials did not have as much experience as would have been desirable in running a big complicated federal organization."[30]

With the NTCA already nearly organized, Morton focused his energies on slowing the pace of Bruce's reforms and bringing in experienced administrators to address the perceived "managerial and organizational turmoil" within the

BIA. To that end, he appointed career bureaucrats Wilma Victor and John O. Crow to oversee bureau policy and to reign in Commissioner Bruce and his New Team. When Crow ordered the transfer of William H. Veeder, Indian water rights expert and frequent BIA critic, away from bureau headquarters in Washington, D.C., the response within the sixteen-thousand-member BIA was predictable: renewed managerial and organizational turmoil. Aggravated and discouraged by what they interpreted as Morton's administrative high-handedness and blatant disregard for self-determination, Native Americans from across the political and policy spectrum demanded that Veeder remain in his position and Bruce be allowed to continue his work.[31]

At the NTCA Constitutional Convention held in Pierre, South Dakota, in April 1971, the tribal chairs had passed a resolution creating a fifteen-member All Indian Commission on BIA Reorganization.[32] A month later, the commission held its one and only series of meetings with Interior and BIA officials, including Harrison Loesch, assistant secretary for land management; William Rogers, deputy undersecretary; Commissioner Bruce; and Secretary Morton. While perhaps symbolically important that the administration was taking the commission seriously, the meetings were largely inconsequential, with the Indian participants enumerating a list of issues that concerned them followed by Secretary Morton responding with prepared remarks evincing his support for self-determination, education, reservation economic development, water rights, and the development of reservation road systems.[33]

On July 28, 1971, Commissioner Bruce and White House staffer Bradley Patterson met with NTCA leaders in a wide-ranging and at times contentious discussion of federal Indian policy. Patterson urged the chairs to get behind the Nixon administration's Indian-related legislative initiatives and establish an office (or "a little cubby hole with a staff and a mimeograph machine") in Washington, D.C. While some chairs appeared more interested in pressing issues specific to their particular tribe (e.g., Ted James [Paiute] sought Patterson's assistance to defeat a water compact bill concerning Pyramid Lake in Nevada), considerable discussion focused on broader issues, for example, empowering Commissioner Bruce to distribute grants or low-interest loans to Indian entre-preneurs seeking to start businesses on reservations. Benny Atencio (Pueblo) broached the delicate subject of Bruce's rotation policy, whereby area directors and superintendents would be rotated every two years, by suggesting that "occasional rotations" be implemented following consultation with the tribes. Odrick Baker stressed the need for funding tribal councils. "The way it works right now on most reservations, you find that the tribal councilmen are out working eight or ten hours a day trying to support their families in areas that are depressed to begin with [and] after hours we are trying to run the business of tribal government." On Baker's Lac Courte Oreilles reservation in Wisconsin, for example, the tribal council had over twenty projects to oversee on a part-time basis. At times, the chairs put Patterson on the defensive. Gerald Reid (Kiowa) questioned the sincerity of government officials who made promises they did not keep and expressed frustration with constant meetings followed by inaction. "I would like all men to feel that the time is coming when we just can't sit down and talk—that we must move to make things move" or "we will give up caring." When Patterson replied that "I do not think we waste each other's time when talking," he was interrupted by Nathan Little Soldier, who declared, "Excuse me, you are wasting our time right now. I hate to be rude, but I am gifted that way."[34]

During their August board meeting in Albuquerque, NTCA leaders addressed head-on the ongoing dysfunction in the BIA, particularly the performance of Deputy Commissioner John Crow. Appearing before the NTCA executive board on August 20, Crow defended his conduct and declared that instead of making inflammatory remarks and crying to the press, BIA employees unhappy with his decisions "should be getting [their] shoulders down and really try to protect the Indians." In regard to William Veeder, Crow maintained that he harbored no animosity toward the water specialist, and that if he had not transferred him, "something more drastic would have happened." When the chairs indicated that Indian peoples were concerned that Crow's appointment signaled a return to old-line bureaucratic policies within the BIA and that most were not supportive of this reversion to old ways, Crow retorted that he did not know what people mean when they referred to "old-line bureaucrats" and that his relationship with Commissioner Bruce was a positive one. "The Commissioner is in the saddle," Crow declared, "and recommendations will be made to him." In the end, the chairs drafted a resolution condemning Crow's "power play" in the Bureau of Indian Affairs, along with "any moves to abandon the concept of involvement of Indians and Indian Tribes" in BIA decision making.[35]

Up to this point, the NTCA had certainly been successful in its professed goal of expanded consultation with government officials involved in the drafting and implementation of federal Indian policy. Translating the consultation into concrete results for their reservation-based constituents was another matter. As Nathan Little Soldier had wryly observed, all the talking seemed to have been a waste of his time. By this time, the association had established several committees, each with a specific focus or charge (water rights, education, health care, fundraising, etc.). On September 10, 1971, the tribal chairs convened yet another meeting, this one in Window Rock, Arizona. After an update by one of the committees on the association's dismal finances, Peter MacDonald briefed members on the many consultation sessions that the NTCA leadership had been involved in since the association's founding. To his credit, MacDonald did not try to sugarcoat matters, admitting that government officials had "taken no action on the recommendations that have been made by the Association." When tribal leaders asked questions, they were not given direct answers; when the tribal leaders stated their objections to certain policies or actions, the objections were ignored, and the policy or action implemented anyway. William Veeder's transfer had not been rescinded; John Crow remained in his position at the BIA. "The time has come now," MacDonald declared, to decide "where we should go from this point on to make sure that our voices are not only heard but something is done about our needs—meeting the needs that we have expressed to our people."[36]

Two items of interest occurred on the second day of the Window Rock conference. Lucy Covington (Colville), representing the Northwest Affiliated Tribes and the NCAI, appeared before the chairs, seeking the NTCA's support for a resolution opposing the transfer and reassignment of William Veeder. After Covington read the resolution, she informed the chairs that she had been asked to hand-deliver the document to the NTCA in hopes that Indian leaders "could stand united regardless of what organization" they belonged to. "If we make one strong stand," she added, "we must be heard." Without discussion, Wendell Chino made a motion for acceptance, which passed unanimously.[37]

The second significant event was the introduction of what Chino labeled a "new war plan" for the NTCA drafted by Peter MacDonald. A World War II veteran who had served with the renowned Navajo Code Talkers, MacDonald held a degree in electrical engineering and had attended grad school at UCLA. In 1963 he returned home to take a management position with the tribe. From 1965 to 1970 MacDonald directed the Office of Navajo Economic Opportunity, where his ability to find employment for needy Navajos provided him with considerable political capital. In 1970 the forty-two-year-old was elected chair of the Navajo Tribal Council, promising to expand Navajo control over education and natural resources. A self-described pragmatist who sought "incremental progress based on achievable goals," MacDonald represented a new generation of Indian leadership who "approached traditional Indian problems with political and economic tactics geared to the twentieth century."[38] That said, the Navajo leader was something of an anomaly. While a founding member of the NTCA and its Navajo area representative, MacDonald was not in sympathy with a number of the association's stated positions.

MacDonald had opposed restricting membership to federally recognized tribes, and as we will see, he was more than willing to reach out to and work with urban Indian organizations. Why he agreed to join the NTCA in the first place remains a mystery. The association offered him a national stage, which is always attractive to politicians, and he may have sought to hedge his bets by joining the NTCA in the off chance it became a significant force in Indian Country. Like other tribal chairs, MacDonald may have hoped to use the NTCA for the benefit of his particular constituency. Whatever the reason, MacDonald kept it close to the vest, but his stated positions on hot-button issues such as allying with urban Indian activists must have been vexing to colleagues like Bill Youpee. When reminiscing about MacDonald's political inclinations and willingness to challenge the positions of organizations in which he held membership, NCAI executive director Chuck Trimble put it this way: "Peter was like a non-aligned nation between NATO and the Warsaw Pact."[39]

The Navajo chair began his talk by declaring that Native Americans "are on a collision course with the Department of the Interior," which was seeking to thwart the self-determination policy by creating a "super BIA operating out of the Secretary of the Interior's office" staffed by Wilma Victor, John Crow, and Morton's undersecretary, William Rogers. The only way to combat this development, MacDonald declared, was by moving the BIA out of the Interior Department and placing it as an independent agency within the Executive Office of the President. He then enumerated several arguments to support his description of the Interior Department as a "hostile department" that was seeking to prevent Commissioner Bruce from protecting Indian rights and achieving self-determination. In addition to William Veeder's banishment to the Phoenix office and Secretary Morton's promotion of "reactionaries" John Crow and Wilma Victor to prominent positions in the BIA, MacDonald pointed to the slow pace of tribal contracting and the Interior Department's failure to implement the Indian Preference Act—which sought to increase the number of Native Americans in government leadership positions—as evidence of Interior Department hostility. The Office of Management and Budget, meanwhile, continued to fund the so-called Employment Assistance Program, which relocated (or "drained") talented young Indians off reservations to urban centers. MacDonald then laid out a bold plan of action to bring about change in Indian Country. Instead of letter writing and endless consultation, Native Americans should build on their strengths. The strength he had in mind was an unusual one—the physical dispersion of Indians across the country—on reservations, off reservations, and in cities. "Our troops are everywhere," Mac-Donald exclaimed, and they could be harnessed into a "Truth Network" that could be activated anyplace, anywhere, and at any time. Indian leaders would designate ten federal officials and make sure that wherever they went, members of the Truth Network would be there to tell audiences the truth about how the administration was breaking its promises. Travel costs would be minimal since Native Americans were already there. Establishing the Truth Network would require forging alliances with other Indian rights organizations—including "urban youths" who had been "shipped to the cities" as part of the BIA's failed relocation policies. "We can use our youth, our geographic dispersion and above all, we can use the truth," MacDonald concluded, "to create a new style of Indian fighting that will make the Interior wish that the BIA had never been transferred from the old War Department."[40]

The NTCA members responded with strong applause and voted to approve a resolution moving the BIA out of the Interior Department as MacDonald had recommended,[41] but some tribal chairs—conservatives like Bill Youpee in particular—remained unconvinced that doing so was a good idea. Youpee argued that moving the BIA from the Interior Department would "make the BIA an orphan," while Don Wright questioned the competency of tribes to immediately take over their own administration. "They don't understand the resolution," Wright opined, and "they don't want to jeopardize what they have now. They don't know what it would be like under the White House."[42] Some tribal chairs also felt uneasy about the proposed Truth Network's strategy of forging alliances with urban Indian youth. Developing a "new style of Indian fighting" sounded ominously like the advocacy strategy of AIM and the NIYC and a distant cry from the cooperative, insider-oriented strategy heretofore pursued by the NTCA executive board. According to Jack Forbes, the Truth Network idea failed to garner acceptance among various Indian groups that "were too parochial, too short-sighted, or too prone to seek crisis-oriented 'direct action.'"[43] Regardless of its reasoning, the NTCA's failure to seriously consider the Truth Network initiative was a missed opportunity. Leading such an endeavor would have encouraged a united Indian front with tribal chairs in the driver's seat. Instead, the tribal chairs yielded that symbolic position to AIM, which was only too willing to embrace "a new style of Indian fighting."

Less than two weeks after the Window Rock conference, the NTCA executive committee was back in Washington, D.C., consulting with Secretary Morton, Assistant Secretary Harrison Loesch, and Rep. Sam Steiger (R-Ariz.). No doubt aware of Peter MacDonald's resolution and Truth Network proposal, Morton's team struck a conciliatory tone. When Bill Youpee again stressed the need for better consultation and Indian involvement in decision making, Loesch responded by asking, "Who speaks for the Indians? I hope NTCA will become the voice." Barney Old Coyote (Crow) counseled that everyone involved in federal Indian policy should focus on the issues and "shy away from personalities"; then he informed the group, "We don't see any backup in the Secretary's statements" about being supportive of Native American interests. Changing the subject, Loesch asked about Nixon's legislative package and which parts should be prioritized. To this, Youpee responded that the top priorities were tribal contracting and government loans for reservation economic development. Before departing, the tribal chairs succeeded in extracting promises for a more robust defense of Indian water rights, restarting tribal contracting, improved communication with the BIA, and funding for the NTCA to hire a full-time staff.[44]

By November 1971 there was cause for cautious optimism that the winds of change were blowing in a favorable direction, but Bill Youpee remained skeptical. When it came to new directions and fresh starts in government-tribal relations, the Indians were invariably disappointed when reality failed to match the rhetoric. "We hear that the Commissioner is now again the Commissioner," Youpee declared, but "let us not return to the 'Jammer' Era but let us see the Commissioner really calling the plays . . . and I mean in the entire BIA."[45] In a phone conversation with Youpee, Commissioner Bruce related the details of a late-night meeting with Secretary Morton and members of the White House staff to put an end to the internecine warfare that had raged within the BIA for close to a year. Morton apparently informed the commissioner that "the NTCA was going to give the Department and BIA directions, which they wanted to follow." These included the creation of an Indian water office, a resumption of contracting, and funding for road construction on reservations. The meeting was briefly interrupted, Bruce continued, by a call from President Nixon, who "told the commissioner he was on the right track and asked that he work out the BIA internal situation."[46]

At the thirty-eighth annual NCAI convention in Reno that took place in mid-November, Bruce exuded confidence and demonstrated that he was "back in the saddle" by announcing the reinstatement of New Team members Ernie Stevens (Oneida) and Alexander "Sandy" McNabb (Micmac) to prominent positions in the BIA. What made the appointments—which the *Northwest Indian Times* characterized as a "daring end run"—especially noteworthy was that the commissioner had announced the moves without prior approval from the Interior Department. As assistant commissioner for economic development, Stevens would oversee the $40 million Employment Assistance Program that had previously been used to train young Native Americans who had left reservations and relocated to urban areas. Under Stevens, the funds would instead be used to provide job training to Indians living on or near reservations so that they could take jobs at home.[47]

The Reno convention was also memorable for the drama brought about by AIM and NIYC activists who disrupted the opening sessions of the convention with demands that they not only be admitted as delegates but that the twenty-dollar admission fee be waived. The NCAI executive board had, in fact, scheduled a possible change to the organization's constitution to admit urban Indian groups, but that vote was not planned until later in the week. The delay did not appease the activists, however, who predicted that the convention "will either mark the funeral or the rebirth of the N.C.A.I." Commenting on rumors about a possible NCAI-NIYC merger, whereby the latter would become the NCAI's "youth group," the youth council's Gerald Wilkinson declared, "I'm particular about the horses I ride. I have too much pride as a warrior to ride a sick horse into battle." Although the activists were unsuccessful in their efforts to gain full admission into the NCAI, the election of thirty-two-year-old Leon Cook (Ojibwa) as president provided them cause for hope. A former New Team member who had quit the BIA just prior to the convention, Cook argued that his election implied acceptance of a coalition consisting of "small and large tribes, the young and old, urban and reservation Indians" (or COINS—Coalition of Organized Indians and Natives). That coalition never materialized, however—a casualty of the ongoing divisions within the national Indian community.[48]

A sullen Bill Youpee attended the Reno convention and watched with disdain as AIM and NIYC activists disrupted the proceedings while hurling insults at the NCAI executive board (likening the NCAI to a sick horse and accusing Indian leaders of spending the twenty-dollar admission fees in casinos and saloons). Leon Cook's subsequent call for a coalition with urban activists, in Youpee's opinion, was absurd, although when interviewed, Youpee "made a mild call for unity without asking for specific changes to the NCAI structure." Additional issues also weighed heavily on the NTCA president. There were newspaper reports of financial irregularities at Fort Peck involving "misused or embezzled tribal funds," and a federal grand jury had been empaneled to hear evidence on the matter.[49] Just two weeks earlier, Youpee had been defeated for reelection as chair of the Fort Peck Tribal Council, losing to Joseph Red Thunder by 174 votes out of 1,012 ballots cast. His opponent had made much of the fact that Youpee spent so much time off the reservation attending to his concurrent duties leading Montana's Intertribal Policy Board and as president of the NTCA—positions he would likely have to forfeit now that he was no longer a "duly elected tribal chairman."[50] From his perspective, the timing couldn't have been worse. With the NCAI drifting to the left and the BIA expressing what appeared to be genuine willingness to collaborate with the tribal chairs, the NTCA was needed now more than ever.

The chairs of federally recognized tribes played a significant role in the BIA reorganization crisis of 1971. While supporters of the movement toward tribal self-determination, some had been vocal critics of Commissioner Bruce for not consulting with them before making personnel changes and were suspicious of the New Team for their apparent lack of knowledge or experience dealing with reservations. Tribal chairs also remained convinced that the BIA was shifting its priorities away from federally recognized tribes to urban Indian groups, which not only lacked democratic legitimacy but, according to Bill Youpee, were not "real Indians" anyway. This attitude, along with the fear and uncertainty of dealing with a BIA under White House rather than Interior Department control, led to the NTCA's failure to support Peter MacDonald's Truth Network strategy, a "war plan" that undoubtedly required substantial collaboration with other Indian organizations, logistical preparation, and a more confrontational style of advocacy. Even if the strategy was only partially successful, the NTCA would have reaped the rewards of fashioning and leading the effort. Instead, the NCAI ultimately took the bold step of reaching out to urban and other off-reservation Indian groups in hopes of creating a broad coalition that much more closely reflected the diversity of Indian experiences at the time.

The NTCA's insider strategy of relationship building, influencing policy by assuming the role of "reservation experts" to foster interdependence, and ensuring they were included in Interior Department discussions was partially responsible for the positive changes in BIA operations toward the end of 1971. In meeting after meeting, the NTCA executive board pressed for better protections of Indian water rights, for a renewal of contracting, for improved consultation, and of course, for funding of the NTCA. As the oldest and largest Indian interest group in the country, the NCAI played an integral role as well. It also drafted resolutions and consulted with policymakers to reinstate Commissioner Bruce and to empower him to advance his reform agenda. Peter MacDonald's speech in Window Rock caught Interior officials by surprise. The Navajo leader was an area representative of the NTCA, and his call for direct action placed added pressure on Secretary Morton to get his house in order. The Red Power activists in AIM and the NIYC, meanwhile, sought to place John Crow under house arrest for his role in undermining Commissioner Bruce and the New Team. By serving as the radical fringe of the Indian reform movement, the activists unwittingly pushed Morton, Loesch, and Rogers to seek middle ground with the NTCA and the NCAI. In short, it took the collective effort of all Indian organizations to nudge the federal government to live up to President Nixon's July 1970 Indian message calling for a new policy of self-determination. It is not clear, however, that the NTCA quite understood this reality. If the chiefs did, they were not yet prepared to accept it.

Were the tribal chairs who organized the NTCA sellouts, apples, and compliant Uncle Tomahawks who had been co-opted by the Interior Department to do its bidding?[51] There is certainly an abundance of evidence to show that the NTCA played a significant role in the policy-determining structure of the Interior Department and the BIA and that it was dependent on government assistance for its survival. Not only did the association receive hundreds of thousands of taxpayer dollars to fund its operations, but it also was the recipient of office space, staffing assistance, and travel reimbursements when the chairs came to consult with their federal counterparts. Dependence on government funding, however, does not in itself prove co-optation. The NTCA enjoyed a monopoly of sorts in the provision of reservation-related intelligence to the Interior Department. This may not have made them indispensable, but it likely gave them a degree of self-confidence, if not independence. While Louis Bruce was happy to sit down with AIM's Russell Means and Dennis Banks to discuss their concerns, it's hard to envision Rogers Morton or Harrison Loesch doing so. The NCAI certainly had an abundance of experienced and capable leaders, but their flirtation with urban activists rendered their counsel suspect as well. A review of the meeting transcripts between the NTCA executive board and

Interior Department officials indicate that the chairs were, on occasion, willing to challenge and even criticize Morton and his team. They also show government officials adept at deflecting questions, answering questions with questions of their own, or simply not responding to questions at all. As the Window Rock conference revealed, the chairs were at a loss at how to respond to such political chicanery. Meeting transcripts also reveal the chairs requesting government financing for the NTCA at the end of virtually every consultation session.

Reliance on government grants and contracts also distracted the chairs from focusing on their mission. Time that could or should have been spent strategizing and honing arguments for the next round of consultations instead went into the arduous task of researching and writing up grant proposals. NTCA officials recognized this problem early on. "A common trait of [national and regional Indian organizations] is that they become bogged down in minutia because they are forced to become program operators. The feeble attempts to carry out original missions are impeded by their having to rob Peter to pay Paul—filch operating monies from the program areas to keep the organization afloat."[52] While the NTCA was not a program agency, chairs served as consultants, grant writers, and fundraisers to keep the association afloat. These preoccupations drained time, talent, and energy from their primary mission to advance the interests of federally recognized tribes.

Political scientists Patrick Coy and Timothy Hedeen maintain that government officials seldom possess a "grand scheme" for co-optation, but when power imbalances exist—such as that between tribal governments and the federal government—cooperation and co-optation become virtually indistinguishable.[53] When "challenger movements" such as the NTCA chose to institutionalize and adopt an advocacy strategy based on building a close relationship with the Interior Department and making themselves indispensable as the "voice" of federally recognized tribes, its members surrendered the use of other strategies such as direct confrontation that, at least in some instances, might have yielded quicker, more profound, or at least different results. That said, there was a price for co-optation that the federal government also bore. As Peter Selznick notes, a co-opting force must commit itself to "avenues of activity and lines of policy enforced by the character of the co-opted elements."[54] In other words, the price to pay for the "accommodation" of the NTCA's tribal leaders was for the federal government to commit itself—albeit reluctantly and with a good deal of foot dragging and half-measures—to the demands of federally recognized tribes for advances in critical "avenues of activity," such as tribal sovereignty, treaty rights, and self-determination.

While the degree of their co-optation remains debatable, the perception of Red Power activists and certain segments of the reservation-based Indian population was that the NTCA had sold out and was being used by the Interior Department to manage Indian opposition and preserve the BIA's old-line system of domination. Although tribal chairs were working to improve this system by employing a relatively cautious strategy that promised not to upset the crucial flow of federal assistance to impoverished reservation communities, their efforts were insufficient to satisfy the demands of Native Americans anxious to realize the promise of self-determination. "We didn't appreciate them because they tolerated so many injustices," recalled Della Warrior (Otoe-Missouria). "Now I look at it and I think that they were probably doing what they should be doing, but when you're young you're really impatient. You want things to happen a lot more quickly."[55] Like the New Deal–era Lakota communities examined in Thomas Biolosi's *Organizing the Lakota,* tribal governments of the 1970s—and, by extension, the tribal chairs constituting the NTCA—continued to serve as convenient scapegoats for the actions and policies of BIA and Interior Department officials intent on maintaining their paternalistic control. This displacement of blame helps explain the association's relatively brief existence as an interest group and its mixed legacy as a productive player in the era of self-determination.

Chapter 3

Foundational Issues

Eunice Larrabee lived on the Cheyenne River Sioux Reservation in South Dakota for practically her entire life. A pioneer in Indian community health, a long-serving member of the Cheyenne River tribal council, and one of the founding members of the Lakota Women's Organization, Larrabee was both a witness to and a participant in the dramatic changes in federal-Indian relations that occurred during the twentieth century. In the face of a horrific tuberculosis outbreak in the 1950s, Larrabee helped establish the Lakota TB and Health Association, which organized culturally sensitive workshops to educate tribes about tuberculosis and lobbied tribal governments to issue ordinances to combat communicable diseases. Indian-operated and -planned, the association was a tremendous success. "The people felt it was their organization," Larrabee recalled, "because they had started it."[1]

A practitioner of traditional healing methods, especially in the medicinal use of local roots and herbs, Larrabee was passionate about the need to educate the next generation about Native American cultures and philosophies so that her people could better understand themselves. To this end, she was also an advocate of improving life on the reservation. "To the Indian," she observed, "the reservation is the last frontier," the guarantor of freedom, and the place where "Indian values of generosity, sharing, respect, and compassion" were learned. The protection of Indian lands, consequently, was crucial, since Indian spirituality was centered on traditional homelands (Larrabee was especially interested in the restoration of the Black Hills). Cultural preservation and land protection, in Larrabee's opinion, required strong tribal governments. "We realize that our traditional governments before European contact were beautiful," Larrabee explained, "but various forces have altered our lives to such a degree that we cannot honestly draw together all of the threads of these traditional governmental systems. So now we are adapting and are committed to making these adaptations blend with our traditional forms of government." The activities of Red Power activists who challenged the authority of tribal government were particularly alarming. In response to that perceived threat, Larrabee helped organize the Lakota Women's Organization (LWO) in the fall of 1972—an unofficial National Tribal Chairmen's Association (NTCA) auxiliary that pledged to "stand by the tribal governments because we know that tribal governments in their relationship to the United States are the essence of our survival as a people. Without that status, we would be only minority citizens in the eyes of the federal government."[2]

While not official members of the NTCA, Eunice Larrabee and the LWO nonetheless reflected many of the association's positions as well as the concerns of Native Americans involved in the modern Indian rights movement. While often disagreeing on tactics and at times about goals, Indian leaders from diverse backgrounds and with equally diverse constituencies shared a common interest in certain foundational issues. These issues—tribal sovereignty, self-determination, cultural preservation, and land/resource protection—were indelibly connected and codependent; to sacrifice one was to sacrifice all. What were the NTCA's specific positions on these critical issues, and how did they compare with those held by Red Power activists? How successful was the NTCA in advancing these positions? What implications did they have for modern Native American communities?

Tribal Sovereignty

Scholars from a wide array of social science and humanities disciplines continue to wrestle with the term "sovereignty" and its precise meaning. The significance of the word, as Amanda J. Cobb (Chickasaw) has written, cannot be underestimated. "It is a contested term, carrying with it multiple meanings and multiple implications for Native nations." When defined within a legal and political context, sovereignty refers to "supreme authority within a territory." The source of that authority varies (natural law, divine right, a constitution) but is significant because it conveys legitimacy; a sovereign power has the acknowledged right to exercise authority. That authority, at least in theory, is superior to all others. In the United States, for example, the Constitution is the supreme law of the land and conveys the nation's sovereignty over states, counties, and municipalities. The final ingredient of sovereignty is territoriality—the geographic boundaries within which sovereign power is exercised. People living within those boundaries are considered members of a community who fall under the authority of the sovereign.[3]

Sovereignty is the lifeblood of Indian nations. Without it, tribes would cease to exist as distinct political entities. Should that occur, Indian control over their lands and resources would rapidly dissolve. With no tribal organization or land base, the social, cultural, and economic viability of Indian communities would become untenable. In short, absent sovereignty, the very identities of Native Americans would likely cease to exist.[4]

As U.S. history has shown, during the late eighteenth and early nineteenth centuries, the federal government had sought to make tribes the repository of sovereignty to more efficiently negotiate with Indigenous communities and exploit their resources. The act of treaty making imparted a European version of nationhood to Native peoples that recognized them as coequal sovereigns. In theory at least, this status did not diminish when the relative power balance between the two sides shifted, nor with the passage of time.[5] That said, federal officials dating back to the George Washington administration often sought to limit tribal sovereignty in myriad ways—through legislation, the courts, the expropriation of Indian lands, bureaucratic oversight of reservations, and what Scott Lyons (Leech Lake Ojibwe) has termed "rhetorical imperialism"— the assertion of control over others by setting the terms of debate (for example, shifting the classification of Native nations from "sovereigns" to "wards" or replacing "treaty" with "agreement").[6]

Between 1887 and 1934, the assault on tribal sovereignty escalated following passage of the Dawes Act, which empowered the president to unilaterally break treaties and to allot reservation lands "in severalty" to individual members of the tribe. Designed to "emancipate" Native peoples from their "debilitating tribal relations" so that they could more rapidly assimilate into the majority society, the devastation wrought by allotment on tribal governments, economies, and cultures remains very much in evidence to the present day. Scholars continue to debate the merits of the Indian New Deal, but there is no question that the Indian Reorganization Act halted allotment, protected cultural expression, created semiautonomous tribal governments, and laid the groundwork for the eventual application of self-determination policies. During the post–World War II era, however, the federal government's assault on Indian sovereignty reignited, as evidenced by policies designed to terminate its trust responsibilities to Native nations, to allow states to extend their legal jurisdiction over reservations, and to aggressively exploit the resources of the Indian land base. While the Johnson administration's War on Poverty and deployment of community action programs helped kickstart a process to modestly empower tribal communities (or, according to critics, to shift the burden of social service delivery from the government to the tribes), much remained to be done to realize the goal of self-governing Indian nations whose sovereignty was recognized and respected by state and federal governments.

In October 1972, Indian rights activists leading the Trail of Broken Treaties Caravan assembled in Minneapolis, where they drafted a Twenty Point Position Paper that called for both "reconstruction of Indian communities and securing an Indian future in America."[7] A wide-ranging and extraordinarily ambitious document, the Twenty Points laid out what historian Charles Wilkinson described as "the earnest dreams of modern Indian country."[8] With regard to the promotion of tribal sovereignty, the document called for the restoration of constitutional treaty making (a practice that had ceased a century earlier with the passage of the Indian Appropriation Act [25 USC 71]) and the resubmission of unratified treaties, and that federal-Indian relations be governed once again by treaty relations as befitting sovereign nations. When issues arose over perceived violations of treaty rights, Indian interpretations of those violations would carry significant weight and have a fast track to the Supreme Court for final judgment. The position paper called for an expanded and inalienable Indian land base, tribal control over the determination of their membership, the nullification of state laws imposed over Indian lands and peoples, and the elimination of immunity for non-Indians who committed crimes within reservation boundaries. The position paper also called for the abolition of the Bureau of Indian Affairs (BIA) and its replacement by an Office of Federal-Indian Relations and Community Reconstruction with responsibility shared equally between the president, Congress, and Indian nations. The new office would serve as a clearinghouse for all Indian-related programs and services, oversee the guardianship of Indian property rights, and possess broad powers to review and revise aspects of federal Indian policy that undermined "local tribal sovereignty and self-governing control." To discern the needs and desires of the many Native nations, the position paper called for national Indian referendums to be conducted. This mechanism of decision making was hardly traditional, but preferable to the current system of relying on "a few Indians" who seemed more interested in "little personal power and political games" than in the well-being of their people. The National Council on Indian Opportunity (NCIO), the Association on American Indian

Affairs, and the NTCA, according to the document, were examples of "government, non-Indian directed, and Indian organizations" that "could and should be eliminated"—or at least have their federal funding cut.[9]

The Twenty Point Position Paper's vision for tribal sovereignty, Kevin Bruyneel has argued, made a bold claim for a "third space of sovereignty" that was "neither defined by American colonial rule nor completely separated from the practice and influence of the American liberal democratic settler-state." While many Native Americans—including the tribal chairs—supported the document's demands for expanded sovereignty, federal resources and support, and autonomy, the Twenty Points were, as Wilkinson noted, "an earnest dream" and went a good deal further than the present system of federal-Indian relations could accommodate.[10] In his January 1973 response to the demands enumerated in the Twenty Point Position Paper, Nixon aide Leonard Garment offered a rebuttal to each, pointing out their lack of realism and advising that the administration continue its policy of self-determination.[11]

Roughly a year after the Trail of Broken Treaties Caravan, the tribal chairs of the NTCA responded with their own blueprint for the promotion of tribal sovereignty. Titled *The American Indian World,* the document began with an oblique reference to Red Power activism and the Twenty Point Position Paper:

> These are exciting but critical times for Indians in the United States in terms of the present and the future. Identification of Indian situations and expressions of what Indians want their life to be have become enmeshed in popular movements of contemporary America. This frequently obscures what Indians really want, what they really want their future to be, and how this is to be accomplished.[12]

Laying out a vision for what "elected Indian leadership" believed was needed to "consummate the longstanding relationship" between the United States and federally recognized tribal governments, *The American Indian World* called on the federal government to live up to its commitments to provide "normal community services" to tribal members and to do so via contracting or other delivery systems sanctioned by tribal governments. The assumption of tribal control over the administration of service provision would enable the BIA to focus its full attention on the protection of Indian lands and resources, which tribal chairs believed constituted the "main thrust" of the federal government's trust responsibility. Reminiscent of the Twenty Point Position Paper, tribal chairs professed their belief in the inherent sovereignty of tribes, but in a decidedly different way. While the former document argued for a robust and expansive version of sovereignty as evidenced, for example, by a resumption of bilateral treaty making between sovereigns, the chairs likened tribal sovereignty to "the powers of other local governments" and declared that tribal councils be empowered to govern reservations "just as states govern the territory over which they have jurisdiction." Similar to the Twenty Point Position Paper, the tribal chairs maintained that tribal governments would no longer accept "administrative restrictions" with regard to their jurisdiction over all people within reservation boundaries but conceded that Congress could restrict these powers. This was a departure from the Twenty Point Position Paper's call for the establishment of an Office of Federal- Indian Relations that would require even Congress to recognize limits on its authority to intervene in Indian communities. As far as the BIA was concerned, the tribal chairs called for the federal government to recognize that the agency's current bureaucratic structure (the so-called line-staff concept) was "well accepted" in Indian Country and that federal officials stop "horsing around" with realignment and other reform schemes. That said, the tribal chairs recommended a somewhat novel idea: that BIA regulations be revised on a reservation-by-reservation basis so that procedures were "tailor-made to fit the needs of the particular reservation." The tribe could then adopt them as a tribal code that would be implemented under the sovereignty of the tribe—although the code would also require Interior Department approval to ensure government financial support.[13]

The American Indian World concluded with additional platitudes regarding the importance of sovereignty ("the tribal governmental role must be exercised through processes which ensure continuous assertion of tribal sovereignty") but was—at least compared to the Twenty Points document—short on specifics. In a subtle dig at the militant tactics employed by some Red Power activists, the chairs declared that "Tribal Government must be prepared to face the reality of the future and to deal with these realities in a practical and statesmanlike manner."[14]

The NTCA's relatively moderate stance on sovereignty is not surprising given its composition and its oft-stated strategy of operating "in a practical and statesmanlike manner" to promote incremental progress of its agenda. The dependency of tribal governments—and, by extension, the NTCA—on the federal dollar exerted incredible pressures on Indian leaders to choose their words carefully and to advance sovereignty not by militancy but through court decisions, federal legislation, and negotiated settlements. Convinced that the best or perhaps only practical way to defend tribal sovereignty was, ironically, by adapting or conforming to the non-Indian legal and political examples of their federal government counterparts, the NTCA drew understandable criticism from traditionalists and others who equated "adaptation" and "conformation" with "co-optation" and questioned the extent to which tribal governments reflected their aspirations.[15] The NTCA's Robert E. Lewis epitomized the chairs' approach. A World War II veteran (a submarine torpedo specialist) and governor of Zuni Pueblo for over twenty years, Lewis was the architect of a comprehensive development plan that promoted Zuni sovereignty via creation of the Zunis' own school district, an Indian Health Service Hospital, an airport, and a tribal fish and game program. In a piece appearing in the *Gallup Independent* praising his election as NTCA president in December 1973, Lewis was described as a voice for "steady, deliberate progress amidst cries for revolution, calm where there is confusion, and cool debate where there is a heated argument." A "gradualist in every sense of the word," his "step-by-step" approach to sovereignty and self-determination was "more progressive than the quick turnovers and overnight solutions advocated by some others."[16] That gradualist strategy was obviously unacceptable to other Indian activists who believed that confrontational tactics might bring about more profound and immediate change. As French philosopher Michel Foucault had warned, placing limits on resistance should be avoided "lest those who are engaged become trapped in the very system of power they are trying to overcome—since any limits will be derived from ideals supported by modern power."[17]

No fight for tribal sovereignty would be complete without a frontal assault on HCR 108 and PL 280, the foundation stones of the much-despised termination policy. The weapons the chairs deployed in the assault were political ones—speeches, resolutions, and appearances before Congress—but such is the nature of warfare on Capitol Hill. At its inaugural convention in Albuquerque held in July 1971, the NTCA had passed a resolution calling for the repeal of HCR 108, a measure that the chairs rather meekly declared had resulted in "feelings of mistrust and ill-will" between the Indian people and the federal government. Testifying before the Senate Committee on Interior and Insular Affairs, Bill Youpee reminded policymakers of the disastrous effects of termination on the Klamaths and Menominees and warned that termination "must be resisted at all cost." Youpee endorsed the efforts of Senator Henry Jackson (D-Wash.) to gain passage of Senate Concurrent Resolution 26, a measure that sought to replace termination with a new Indian policy premised on the principles of "maximum Indian control and self-determination."[18]

Appearing before the same committee four years later, Wendell Chino laid out a compelling case for the repeal of PL 280. Declaring that history had proven "the moral, theoretical, and practical bankruptcy and emptiness" of the termination policy, Chino detailed the many instances where termination had so blurred jurisdictional boundaries between federal, state, and tribal governments that "Indians are being denied due process and equal protection of the law." The fact that PL 280 had been enacted without the consent of tribes only compounded the problem and demonstrated "an unlawful and immoral repudiation of tribal sovereignty." In January 1975, NTCA leaders convened in Albuquerque to plot out a strategy to enhance tribal sovereignty and to overturn termination, what Chino described at the time as "the most damnable public law ever enacted." Attended by BIA commissioner Morris Thompson (Koyukon Athabascan) and Senate Interior Committee staffer Forrest Gerard (Blackfeet), the meeting was apparently a warm-up to a gathering held a month later in Denver of representatives from all of the major national Indian organizations. While usually reticent about attending such gatherings, given their claim to be the exclusive voice of federally recognized tribes, association members attended and signed on to a position paper calling for the repeal of PL 280 and a process (or "stable mechanism") for the transfer of sovereignty back to tribes.[19]

In addition to its efforts to roll back termination, the NTCA sought to advance tribal sovereignty by amending the Indian Civil Rights Act of 1968 (ICRA), a measure that the chairs claimed "does violence to the principles of self-government." Passed during the final year of the Johnson administration, the ICRA was an Indian "bill of rights" (also with ten provisions) that limited the power of tribal governments to interfere with certain fundamental individual rights such as freedom of speech, equal protection under the law, and due process. It also required tribal consent to states' assertions of jurisdiction, a positive step in combatting termination. Of considerable concern to many tribal governments, however, was the law's inclusion of a habeas corpus provision that allowed review of tribal action in federal court. To many Indians, this provision constituted an assault on tribal sovereignty since it interposed federal courts between tribal governments, Indian citizens, and non-Indian residents, a problem that became apparent almost immediately. In *Dodge v. Nakai*, Theodore Mitchell, a white man who worked for a nonprofit legal service corporation financed by the Office of Economic Opportunity (OEO), was permanently banned from the Navajo reservation after laughing during a meeting of the Navajo Tribal Council's Advisory Committee. Tribal leaders viewed Mitchell's obnoxious behavior as disrespectful and passed a resolution removing him from the reservation. In an appeal to the U.S. District Court in Arizona, Mitchell sued the tribal chairman to set aside the order on the grounds that the tribe had denied him free speech and due process. After reviewing the matter, the district court found the tribal council's actions "wholly unreasonable" in its interpretation of Mitchell's laughter and invalidated the exclusion order, finding it lacking in due process and in violation of his freedom of speech.[20]

In 1973 and again in 1976, the NTCA passed resolutions challenging the ICRA on three grounds. First, the imposition of "the full body of constitutional law" on tribal judiciaries would lead to "a complete waiver of tribal immunity" from lawsuits and expose tribes to monetary judgments they were in no position to pay. Second, the ICRA's provision that allowed for appeals to federal courts was "contrary to the preservation and continuation of the Indian tribes as sovereign independent nations" and imposed rules and restrictions "contrary to the customs and laws of the tribes." Finally, the ICRA and its attendant erosion of tribal rights to self-government had been implemented without adequate Indian consultation and consent. Consequently, the NTCA resolved that the ICRA be amended by adding a consent provision requiring "an affirmative vote of the adult members of the tribe" before the law could take effect on a particular Indian nation.[21]

A final example of the NTCA's position on tribal sovereignty can be gleaned from its response (or lack thereof) to yet another dramatic episode of Red Power activism. Between February 27 and May 8, 1973, the American Indian Movement (AIM) conducted a seventy-one-day occupation of Wounded Knee, South Dakota, an explosive encounter that left two people dead and over a dozen wounded, and marked the beginning of the end for AIM as a significant voice in the modern Indian rights movement.

In April 1972 Richard A. "Dick" Wilson was elected tribal chairman of the fifteen-thousand-member Oglala Sioux Nation, headquartered at Pine Ridge, South Dakota. An adamant AIM opponent, Wilson had obtained support from the tribal council to ban AIM activities on the reservation during the BIA occupation crisis. He also established a tribal police force (Guardians of the Oglala Nation, or GOONs) to suppress protests by AIM as well as the activities of his political opposition. When efforts failed to impeach Wilson for mismanagement, theft, and suppressing civil liberties on the reservation, Oglala traditionalist leaders invited AIM to Pine Ridge to lead an investigation into federal violations of Native American rights under the Fort Laramie Treaty of 1868. According to historian Akim D. Reinhardt, the Wounded Knee occupation was not an AIM-inspired event but "an indictment of the entire tribal council system of government installed by the Indian Reorganization Act." The occupation may have begun as a protest against Wilson's leadership, Reinhardt argues, but was in reality an effort by Pine Ridge Lakotas to resist the colonial authority of the United States in favor of a governing structure more aligned with Oglala tradition and history.[22]

The ensuing siege at Wounded Knee pitted an estimated 200 to 250 AIM and Oglala activists against 300 FBI agents and federal marshals bolstered with armored personnel carriers, snipers, and aerial reconnaissance planes. According to Robert Burnette of the neighboring Rosebud Reservation, if federal forces tried to storm Wounded Knee, AIM would retaliate and "hit all over [the] country" including Washington, D.C., and the BIA building. After weeks of shootouts, roadblocks, negotiations, and press conferences, the occupation ended on May 8 after the activists agreed to lay down their arms and vacate Wounded Knee. Government negotiators, for their part, promised to meet with Oglala chiefs and headmen to discuss the Fort Laramie Treaty and to look into the alleged financial irregularities and civil rights abuses perpetrated by Dick Wilson and the tribal council.[23]

The NTCA's response to the Wounded Knee occupation was surprisingly and uncharacteristically subdued. Some tribal chairs were reluctant to get involved, reasoning that doing so would be interfering in the internal affairs of the Pine Ridge Sioux, which would be an attack on tribal sovereignty. Webster Two Hawk described the standoff in this way: "It's just as though someone came into a state, took over a city and demanded the state government be suspended. There is no way we can allow the takeover."[24] Robert Jim (Yakama) suggested sarcastically that federal officials should just pay the occupants sixty-six thousand dollars to leave as it had done during the BIA occupation a few months earlier. Other NTCA members declared that there was no need to get involved since the chairs' opposition to AIM was already well known. During the BIA occupation, tribal chairs had inundated federal officials with calls and letters denouncing "dissident urban Indians" and organized press conferences both to condemn the occupation and to assert their claim that the activists did not reflect the position of federally recognized tribes. Alaska Federation of Native head Donald Wright cautioned his NTCA colleagues that going to the press

William Youpee (Fort Peck Sioux) served as the NTCA's first president and as executive
director from 1972 to 1978. Courtesy of the *Billings Gazette*.

put them at a disadvantage, undermined their dignity, and would only alienate Indian youth. "We don't need to criticize or cut them up in public," Wright
warned, but instead, "stand on our record."[25]

For a variety of reasons, therefore, the NTCA adopted a low-profile approach
and was reluctant to join the media circus that accompanied the Wounded
Knee crisis. The tribal chairs grew increasingly alarmed, however, as they read
about or watched the media's coverage of government officials rushing to South
Dakota to negotiate with AIM's Russell Means, Dennis Banks, and Clyde Bellecourt. On March 7, 1973, Bill Youpee wrote to Senator Henry M. Jackson, chair
of the Committee on Interior and Insular Affairs, expressing dismay at the
media's misleading coverage, which he believed gave the appearance that federal
officials were "negotiating grievances expressed by the leadership of a reservation people." Why was it, Youpee asked, that the government only reacted to
"militant groups, whose leadership is made up of self-serving, self-styled, self-
appointed Indians" who made "unreasonable and irresponsible demands"? The
"true, elected tribal leaders" were beginning to ask whether federal authorities
had "succumbed to these threat tactics" and would "continue to listen and make
concessions out of fear." These leaders, Youpee maintained, "are also asking
whether this is deliberate, if this is not 'indirect termination'?"[26]

On March 16 interim BIA head Marvin Franklin convened an emergency consultation session with representatives from the NTCA and NCAI to discuss ways to end the Wounded Knee standoff. He informed them that he had offered to go to Wounded Knee to lend his assistance, but only after activists had laid down their arms and "nonresidents" left the reservation. He also indicated that he had no intention—nor authority—to suspend a tribal chair or council unless authorized by the tribal constitution. Tribal leaders in attendance had little to offer in the way of concrete recommendations to end the crisis. Dick Wilson was a NTCA member (albeit an inactive one), and the general consensus was that any imposed solution by the government was inconsistent with tribal sovereignty and self-determination. They also feared that if AIM was not stopped, it would "jump from reservation to reservation" and that tribal governments across the country would be in jeopardy. After further discussion, the assembled Indian leaders concluded that "this was a problem with Chairman Wilson and his people and that the group here was not really prepared to offer any opinion and not in a position to give views on what is done."[27]

While tribal leaders were unwilling to assert themselves into what they believed was an internal Pine Ridge problem best settled by the Oglala Sioux, they proved far less reluctant to criticize the media for its coverage of the standoff. The Red Lake Band of Chippewa's Roger Jourdain, for instance, charged that the American Broadcasting Company (ABC) had "joined up with outlaw and non-representative Indians in an attack on the American Reservation Indians." What Jourdain was referring to was the March 21 appearance of AIM's Vernon Bellecourt on ABC's *Dick Cavett Show*. According to Jourdain, Bellecourt had announced that, after Wounded Knee, the Red Lake Reservation along with other reservations would be next. As a result, tribal leaders had been forced to take armed precautions to prevent the announced attacks from occurring. By glamorizing and sensationalizing the acts of "a few non-representative Indians," Jourdain continued, ABC and other media outlets had "committed one of the most devastating types of exploitation by conveying to the public an image that Native Americans did not have competent leadership" and did not respect the democratic method of electing their officials. "Let me make it clear," Jourdain concluded, "that the true American Indian is sick and tired of being branded and segregated as a minority group unable to manage or take care of their own affairs."[28]

Commenting on the Wounded Knee occupation, journalist Paul R. Weick opined that "this kind of militancy is apt to get more in the way of results than the placid acquiescence of the Indians" since society operated on the principle of "ignore that which doesn't hurt."[29] The legacies of the Wounded Knee standoff, however, don't necessarily bear this out—at least not in the short term. Within two years of the occupation, many of AIM's leaders were in jail, underground, or dead, and its leadership structure had been obliterated by the overwhelming effect of state and federal prosecutions. Public approval of AIM plummeted in response to Wounded Knee, contributing to a white backlash against even mainstream Native American efforts for justice and reform. The occupation of Wounded Knee confirmed what NTCA leaders believed they already knew about the Red Power movement and further polarized the urban-reservation split. In a hard-hitting editorial published in *Akwesasne Notes* in the aftermath of the Wounded Knee episode, Vine Deloria laid blame for the rise in Native American militancy on the failures of elected tribal chairs, whom he likened to a "millstone around the Indians' necks." According to Deloria, tribal leaders in the NTCA refused to accurately report the miserable conditions on many reservations because they did not want to upset their government handlers and seemed more interested in participating in consultation sessions with government officials in posh and exotic locales. These same tribal leaders, he maintained, were silent on critical issues such as tribal sovereignty, respect for treaty rights, and self-determination. As a consequence, Deloria concluded, the NTCA brought disrespect to all tribal governments, whose leaders were increasingly regarded as "the clowns of Indian affairs."[30]

Self-Determination

Self-determination—along with cultural autonomy and land preservation—is one of the primary tributaries of sovereignty. Like "sovereignty," "self-determination" is a contested term with multiple meanings and implications. Generally speaking, "self-determination" refers to self-rule or the right to make decisions without (or with minimal) outside interference. To be truly sovereign, therefore, a nation must exercise self-determination. The Twenty Point Position Paper, interestingly, did not contain the term "self-determination," a reflection perhaps of its authors' detachment from reservation governance or their unambiguous demand for the ultimate goal of tribal sovereignty. According to Vine Deloria—who believed, incidentally, that the endless arguments over the meaning of these terms was a waste of time—self-determination simply meant "opening up a certain amount of space between tribal governments and the federal government."[31]

The NTCA's opposition to the Indian Civil Rights Act along with its refusal to intervene in the Wounded Knee crisis were couched in arguments for both sovereignty (tribal governments should have supremacy of authority over internal matters) and self-determination (tribal governments should have self-rule). As individuals with daily interactions with the Bureau of Indian Affairs, tribal chairs possessed an intimate understanding of the bureaucratic hydra that controlled or influenced virtually every aspect of reservation life, stifling self-determination and severely restricting sovereignty. Gaining greater administrative autonomy and control over tribal affairs, consequently, held understandably strong appeal. The tribal chairs had to walk a fine line, however, when pressing to "open up some space" between tribal governments and the federal government, lest they alienate the central-, area-, and agency-level bureaucrats who wielded what Thomas Biolosi termed "administrative technologies of power." Crossing these powerful individuals, as experience had shown, could have profoundly negative consequences for tribal communities made dependent upon assistance from the federal government.[32]

The NTCA's position paper *The American Indian World* did not offer a definition of self-determination but nonetheless provided recommendations for how it might be realized. Central to the chairs' approach was the process by which the federal government fulfilled its trust responsibilities to Indian nations. From the NTCA's perspective, the government's trust responsibilities were threefold: to protect tribal sovereignty, to protect tribally owned natural resources and assets, and to provide the means by which tribes could deliver community services to members of reservation communities. To advance self-determination, the tribal chairs concentrated their energies on the third point. "Self-determination will become a real and sincere effort," the chairs maintained, "when the Federal Government gets back to the business at hand of providing adequate support and resources for programs *as determined by Indian Tribes*." Instead of relying on the BIA to identify Indian needs and then administer programs and services, the NTCA was a proponent of contracting, where the federal government would channel funds to the tribes so that they could identify specific needs and then self-administer programs and services. This takeover of responsibility need not be done immediately, however, but on a gradual basis. This would give tribes the time and experience to gain mastery over the administrative details of service provision while preventing the widespread dismissal of career BIA bureaucrats—the ostensible reasons why old-liners in the BIA had obstructed contracting since its inception in the late 1960s.[33]

The promotion of self-determination via contracting gained momentum during Nixon's second term. According to Forrest Gerard, a complex array of factors explained this development. Generally speaking, they included a favorable legislative climate brought about by public and media sympathy that something be done about Indian affairs, as well as changes in congressional leadership as a consequence of the 1972 elections. As a result, a new "spirit of cooperation and compromise in Indian affairs" developed between the two major parties, between the two houses of Congress, and between the legislative and executive branches of government. The efforts of Native American leaders and organizations to give direction to and apply pressure on Congress was also critical, Gerard recalled, especially those representing the NTCA, the NCAI, and the American Indian Press Association.[34] There were undoubtedly other factors at work. The Wounded Knee occupation heightened public pressure on the federal government to take action on Indian affairs, while the Nixon administration's growing paralysis in response to the Watergate scandal shifted the legislative initiative to Congress, giving leaders there an opportunity to forge a record on Indian policy reform.[35]

While the BIA pressed ahead with contracting (negotiating or renewing over eight hundred contracts in 1971 alone), administration-backed self-determination bills (S.1573 and S. 1574) were introduced into Congress, where they sat for over a year. In May 1972 Senator Henry Jackson (D-Wash.) finally allowed the bills to come before the Senate Committee on Interior and Insular Affairs. At that time, Jackson introduced his own self-determination bill (S. 3157, the Indian Self-Determination Act of 1972), which was similar to its administration-backed counterparts with the exception that Jackson's bill allowed the secretary of the interior greater discretion in awarding or withholding contracts. On May 8, 1972, Bill Youpee appeared before the committee to share the NTCA's opinion on the proposed legislation. After expressing the association's concern for tribal sovereignty and the need for federal recognition and support of tribal governments, Youpee gave a "warm greeting" to the bill and its promise of "maximum Indian participation in the government of Indian people," or as Youpee put it, "to contract with tribes to run their own show." He requested revisions in two areas—that the bill's inclusion of technical and planning assistance for tribes be expanded and that the Interior Department be empowered to waive burdensome contracting laws or regulations that thwarted tribal participation. On August 2, 1972, the Senate passed the Indian Self-Determination Act of 1972, but the measure was not considered by the House and died at the end of the Ninety-Second Congress.[36]

On February 26, 1973, Senators Jackson and James Abourezk (D-S.Dak.) introduced a new self-determination bill (S. 1017). Like Jackson's earlier measure, the first part (Title I) of S. 1017 focused on contracting. The new bill, however, contained a second section (Title II) that stressed education reform—specifically the funding and administration of the Johnson-O'Malley Act. A New Deal–era law that provided federal aid to states and local school districts that served Indian children, the Johnson-O'Malley Act had several glaring problems. Some states, apparently, were using Johnson-O'Malley funding for general budget support rather than for meeting the needs of Indian students. Additional concerns were directed at narrow interpretations of the law. As a result, nearly two-thirds of the estimated 177,000 Indian children in public schools were left unfunded. Title II also sought to promote parental involvement in the planning and implementation of education programs, and to permit federally recognized tribes to be contractors for Indian education.[37]

In June, the Senate Subcommittee on Indian Affairs held hearings on S. 1017—the Indian Self-Determination and Education Reform Act. Testifying for the NTCA was Joseph Upicksoun (Iñupiat), president of the Arctic Slope Native Association and chair of the NTCA's education committee. After endorsing Title I and its promise of a "more realistic Indian self-determination policy," Upickson moved to the controversial aspects of Title II. While supportive of tribal contracting for education services, the NTCA preferred that the Johnson-O'Malley Act be amended to that effect rather than including contracting for education services in the proposed bill. The NTCA had "serious reservations" about the measure's complicated formula for distributing education-related funds. Uncertain about how the untried formula would affect them, some tribal leaders worried that federal assistance for education would actually decline if the bill was enacted. Other concerns focused on the reality that funding would be pegged to financial need and that cash-starved school districts would reduce their tax rates (thereby artificially inflating their need) with the expectation that "Indian funding" would make up the difference. Prospective tribal contractors, therefore, would be required to show that the taxable property in their school district was taxed at a rate equal to that of five similar school districts in the state that did not have Indian enrollment. These types of requirements, Upicksoun declared, were "too cumbersome to be useful or to be effective" and would likely discourage tribes from pursuing contracts. For that reason, the NTCA requested that the section dealing with formula funding (Part A, Section 203) be eliminated. The remainder of Title II, which called for federal funding of Indian higher education, new school construction, youth and summer programs, and adult education, had the association's strong support.[38]

On March 7, 1974, Jackson introduced amendments to S.1017 that kept the controversial formula funding provision intact but specified that at least 75 percent of Title II funding be used solely for special or supplemental programs for Indians, as opposed to general school district operations. To ensure that Native Americans had a voice in how Title II funds were spent, Jackson proposed an amendment that required school boards located in non–Indian majority districts to permit Indian parents to elect their own committees to "fully participate" in school board decisions. These changes were apparently enough for tribal chairs to support passage of the bill, which they did by formal resolution on the same day.[39]

A month later S. 1017 passed the full Senate, and on May 21 the House Subcommittee on Indian Affairs held hearings on the measure. Testifying for the tribal chairs this time around was NTCA board member Lawrence Snake (Delaware). Contrary to the association's previous Senate testimony, Snake called for revisions to Title I—specifically that the federal government provide tribes with "forward funding" so that they had adequate resources to begin implementation of contracted services. He also asked for revisions that would allow tribal governments to acquire surplus federal property as state and local governments could. Regarding Title II, Snake recommended that federal assistance for the training of Native American educators be broadened to include training in other professional areas, especially in natural resource development and preservation. After reminding committee members that the legislation would "neither surrender nor absolve the United States government of its responsibilities to the Indian people," Snake offered the NTCA's qualified endorsement.[40]

With the cautious support of national Indian organizations such as the NTCA and the NCAI, the House passed the Indian Self-Determination and Education Assistance Act on December 19, 1974, and a little over two weeks later, President Gerald Ford signed the bill into law (P.L. 93-38). In a message to NTCA leaders assembled at their Third Annual Convention in Albuquerque, Ford acknowledged the efforts of his two predecessors in laying the groundwork for the "self-determination without termination" policy and promised greater progress in the years ahead. That message resonated with the convention theme

Wendell Chino (Mescalero Apaches) served as tribal chair for over thirty years. He was one of a few Indian leaders who served as an officer in the NCAI, the NCIO, and the NTCA.
Courtesy of the Center of Southwest Studies, Fort Lewis College, Durango, Colo.

of "We Shape Our Own Future" and keynote speaker Wendell Chino's address, "The American Indian: The Final Arbiter," which stressed the need to design, plan, and implement a new national Indian policy based on the recommendations and leadership of the NTCA.[41]

Cultural Preservation

Tribal sovereignty—supreme authority within a territory—refers not only to political power but to cultural integrity as well. Just as Indian nations possess inherent rights to self-rule, so too do they possess inherent rights to embrace their values, traditions, and spirituality in a manner of their choosing. A strong and vibrant culture affirms tradition, validates Native peoples' understanding of the world around them, and helps build or rebuild community, which has always been central to Indian nations. "To the degree that a tribal nation loses its sense of cultural identity," Vine Deloria warned, "to that degree it suffers a loss of sovereignty."[42]

The Native American struggle for cultural preservation dates back to the Columbian voyages of the late fifteenth century. From the perspective of many Native peoples, the colonial period that Columbus ushered in had never ended, and Indian peoples must remain forever vigilant against the seen and unseen forces of assimilation. At the same time, cultural integrity had to be nurtured from within. As Melanie Benjamen (Ojibwe) has noted, "Our cultural existence cannot be lost, or destroyed, unless we allow it," and language, ceremonies, and traditional ways need to be practiced "all day, every day, if we are to protect the gifts of our future generations."[43]

Indian leaders of the past understood this only too well. During the eighteenth and early nineteenth centuries, cultural and religious preservation movements (sometimes referred to as nativist or revitalization movements) occurred among many eastern tribes, such as the Senecas, Munsees, Lenni Lenapes, Delawares, and Shawnees.[44] In the late nineteenth and early twentieth centuries, cultural preservation efforts provided Native Americans both a means of resisting the federal government's allotment and assimilation policies and a way to articulate individual, clan, and community identities. Among the Lakota peoples of the northern plains, for example, musical performance (drumming, singing, dancing) "served as an unexpected and highly political medium of political engagement that combined subterfuge of 'hidden' acts of resistance with blatant and effective challenges to federal Indian policy."[45]

In response to World War I, meanwhile, Indian communities across the country seized the opportunity to breathe new life into cultural practices dormant for a generation. Indian families sent off loved ones with going-away rituals and welcomed them home with new warrior society songs, victory dances, and in some cases, traditional burial rituals.[46] During the middle decades of the twentieth century, service in World War II along with ongoing efforts to assimilate Native Americans via the federal government's ill-conceived termination and relocation policies spurred renewed activism, leading to what Joanne Nagle terms an "ethnic resurgence" and cultural renascence across Indian Country.[47]

As noted earlier in this study, during the late 1960s, urban Indian activists who had embraced this cultural resurgence forged an informal coalition with reservation-based tribal traditionalists and elders, who, they hoped, would provide them a connection to their cultures and heritage. Over time, organizations such as AIM—which was originally established to combat urban Indian problems such as police harassment and racial discrimination—became unlikely yet passionate advocates of tribal sovereignty, treaty rights, and land restoration. In the Twenty Point Position Paper, cultural preservation was not strongly emphasized, save a provision calling upon Congress to "proclaim its insistence" that Indian religious freedom and cultural integrity be protected. Perhaps in response to their status as cultural neophytes, the Twenty Points' authors insisted that this protection be extended to cultural expression "even in regenerating or renaissance [sic] or developing stage" and that culturally inspired "treatment of one's own body" (such as hair length) not be interfered with.[48]

The NTCA's constitution and position statement likewise had relatively little to say about cultural preservation. The former document declared the association's intent to promote and encourage "the preservation of our cultures and traditions" while the epilogue in The American Indian World simply stated that "Indian identity is based on tribal culture, traditions, and history." That said, during the first half of the NTCA's existence, the association established a fairly substantial record on this important issue. In September 1971, just weeks after its founding, the NTCA adopted a resolution calling on Secretary Rogers Morton to direct the National Park Service, the Bureau of Outdoor Recreation, and other Interior Department agencies to assist Native Americans in preserving, protecting, and developing their cultures and traditional resources.[49]

Three years later (June 3–4, 1974), the NTCA hosted in Albuquerque a Conference on American Indian Tradition, Cultural Activities, and Critical Issues. While acknowledging the considerable complexity and diversity of Native American cultural expressions, attendees were unanimous in their understanding that traditional beliefs and styles of worship could not "be delineated from social, political, cultural, and other areas of Indian life-styles" and that modern notions about the desirability of separating church and state generally did not apply to traditional Indian communities. That said, as U.S. citizens, Native Americans were entitled to the First Amendment's guarantee of religious freedom and the Fourteenth Amendment's guarantee of equal protection under the law. Those guarantees were not being fulfilled, however, making the entire culture of the American Indian "vulnerable to regulation, suppression, and liquidation" through the imposition of "over-control measures" inimical to the principle of self-determination.[50]

The "over-control measures" in question referenced two separate but related issues. The first was the arrest in April 1974 of fourteen Native Americans in Oklahoma for alleged trafficking in the feathers of endangered birds, especially scissor-tailed fly catchers and bald eagles. According to Interior Department officials, the accused had killed thousands of endangered and migratory birds to manufacture Indian artifacts for commercial purposes. The Indians denied these allegations, claiming that they had gathered the feathers by picking them up off the road or receiving them from hunters who had voluntarily offered them. From the vantage point of the NTCA (as well as the NCAI and AIM), the feathers controversy would invariably be extended to other animals that Indians used both in their culture and in traditional acts of worship. For this reason, the NTCA passed a resolution demanding that the charges against the fourteen Native Americans be dismissed and that regulations be enacted exempting Indians from the Migratory Bird Treaty Act and the Bald Eagle Protection Act.[51]

The second issue involved the sacramental use of peyote (*Lophophora williamsii*) by members of the Native American Church. Grown exclusively in the desert regions of south Texas and northern Mexico, the small cactus (sometimes referred to as peyote buttons) contains mescaline, a psychoactive alkaloid that produces a hallucinogenic effect when consumed. For this reason, state and federal authorities regulated its sale and distribution. In addition to these restrictions, the supply of peyote was dwindling rapidly in response to changing land-use patterns on the part of farmers and ranchers more concerned with turning a profit than protecting the habitat of a seemingly innocuous little cactus plant. To protect the First Amendment rights of Native American Church members, therefore, the NTCA adopted a resolution in June 1974 calling on federal officials to work toward a solution of the problems surrounding the acquisition, possession, trafficking, and use of peyote.[52]

In the early-morning hours of January 20, 1976, six Oregon men loaded up in two pickup trucks and drove south to an Indian burial ground located near the town of Paskenta, California. Once they arrived at the sacred site, they turned off their headlights, climbed out of their vehicles, and began digging. Area residents alerted the local police, however, who quickly apprehended and arrested the men as they attempted to leave the burial ground, their trucks loaded with dirt, bones, and artifacts. According to the police, the attempted robbery and desecration of a local Indian burial site was the third that had occurred in a week.[53]

The desecration of Indian graves and other sacred sites and the associated theft of human remains and artifacts were not confined to unprincipled privateers such as those arrested at Paskenta. Museums and private collections across the nation also housed and displayed artifacts, ceremonial regalia, and skeletal remains that they too had obtained using methods hardly less unscrupulous. During the Indian Wars of the late nineteenth century, for example, federal officials had scoured battlegrounds to collect—and subsequently exhibit—the remains of Native peoples whom many in the scholarly community believed were a vanishing race.[54] In May 1976, in a prelude to what would become known as NAGPRA (the Native American Graves Protection and Repatriation Act of 1990), the NTCA passed a resolution calling on Congress to pass legislation protecting sacred, ceremonial, and religious training grounds and burial places that had been "intruded upon by persons of all races not cognizant of their significance." A second resolution that passed at the same time requested that artifacts and regalia held in public or private hands be returned for proper display or storage to the tribal groups from which they came.[55]

The NTCA also promoted cultural preservation in less direct but certainly no less significant ways. In mid-June 1976, for example, the association sponsored the first National Indian Conference on Aging. While the three-day conference's intent was to focus attention on the desperate plight of many elderly Native Americans (inadequate housing, health care, nutrition, nursing home conditions), the NTCA's Wendell Chino gave a poignant opening address that instead emphasized the role of Indian elders as "repositories" of culture, and he saluted them for preserving "all that we hold so dear and so precious in our Indianness." By seeking to address the many unmet needs of elderly American Indians, the NTCA's conference sought, albeit indirectly, to preserve this critical but vulnerable cultural resource.[56]

While protecting Indian elders as the repositories of traditional cultures, the NTCA likewise sought to protect Indian children who would one day serve as the practitioners and standard-bearers of traditional cultures. In the mid-1970s, however, the inordinately high percentage of Indian children being separated from their natural parents and placed in either adoptive or foster homes with non-Indian families cast doubt on whether this generational transition would take place. According to a 1975 study conducted of adoption statistics in nineteen states, of the 333,650 Indian residents under the age of twenty-one, 11,157 (nearly one in every thirty) were living in adoptive homes. Another 6,700 were in foster-care situations. In most states, the Indian adoption and foster-care rates were two to four times higher than that of non-Indians.[57]

In hopes of preventing the ongoing breakup of Indian families by establishing standards for the placement of Indian children in foster or adoptive homes, Senator James Abourezk introduced legislation (S.1214) in April 1977: the Indian Child Welfare Act. After the Senate passed the measure in November, it moved to the House for consideration. At hearings held in February 1978, Calvin Isaac, chair of the Mississippi Band of Choctaws, testified in support of the measure on behalf of the NTCA. "Our concern is the threat to traditional Indian culture which lies in the incredibly insensitive and oftentimes hostile removal of Indian children from their families," Isaac stated. The nontribal government authorities responsible for the removals "are at best ignorant of our cultural values, and at worst contemptful [*sic*] of the Indian way." The effects of the removals were devastating not only to the child and his family, Isaac added, but to the tribe as well. "Culturally, the chances of Indian survival are significantly reduced if our children, the only real means for the transmission of the tribal heritage, are to be raised in non-Indian homes and denied exposure to the ways of their People." Furthermore, the removal of Indian children was an affront to tribal sovereignty. "In no area is it more important that tribal sovereignty be respected," Isaac concluded, "than in an area as socially and culturally determinative as family relationships."[58] On October 14, 1978, the House passed S.1214 and President Carter signed it into law (P.L. 95-608) a few weeks later.

Land and Resource Protection

The relationship between land and Native peoples transcends the idea of land as a means of physical survival or subsistence. Ancestral lands mark the epicenter of faith and spirituality; the locus of origin stories; the provisioner of culturally significant flora, fauna, rivers, and canyons; and the final resting place of loved ones. This "indigenous spiritual rootedness to place" ensures the cultural survival of Indian people as distinct groups and nations. In the modern world, land also helps define the geographic scope of a nation's sovereignty by imposing boundaries. Richard A. Monette (Ojibwe) tells the story of a young Indian lawyer who consulted with his elders about the meaning of sovereignty. A grandfather arose, drew a line in the sand, and, pointing to one side of the line and then the other, declared, "That's the state of North Dakota, and this is Indian country. And that's sovereignty."[59]

The protection of Indian lands and the resources contained both on and beneath the surface remains a critical part of the federal government's trust responsibility: the treaty-sanctioned promises made to Indian nations in return for vast cessions of territory during the late eighteenth and nineteenth centuries. To assess how effectively the government has carried out this responsibility, one need only consider that the original Indian land base—the continental United States—encompassed 1.9 billion acres. By the early 1970s, the Indian land base stood at approximately 55.4 million acres—approximately 3 percent of their original domain.[60] Protecting that remnant was understandably a top priority for tribal leaders and Indian rights activists during the era of self-determination.

The Trail of Broken Treaties Caravan's Twenty Point Position Paper contained three articles that focused on the issue of Indian lands. The first called for a restoration of the Indian land base, but the exact size of that land base was not clearly specified. By one calculation, providing each of the estimated eight hundred thousand Native Americans with 135 acres would require approximately 110 million acres (roughly doubling the size of the existing Indian land base). A second article called for the consolidation of Indian lands that, over time, had become divided and subdivided or fractionated by multiple heirs so they could be put to more productive use. The third article called for an end to the practice of leasing tribally owned and allotted lands, often at steeply reduced rates, to non-Indians and to enable tribes to reclaim lands owned by non-Indians within reservation boundaries. In the latter case, the federal government would be responsible for compensating the non-Indian landholders since it had betrayed its trust responsibilities by allowing the lands to become alienated in the first place.[61]

The tribal chairs' *American Indian World* approached the land/resource issue quite differently. While the NTCA certainly supported the Nixon administration's limited land restoration efforts (to the Taos Pueblos, Yakamas, and Native Alaskans, for example) and had passed resolutions in favor of restoring 169,000 acres to the Havasupai Tribe of Arizona, there was no mention of a general expansion of the Indian land base like that envisioned in the Twenty Point Position Paper. Instead, the association stressed protection of the existing lands and resources based on the federal government's trust responsibility. The need for this protection, Zuni leader Robert Lewis insisted, was urgent and long overdue. "We cannot afford to be put off, bought off, or turned off any longer in questions pertaining to our last valuable resource rights." Linking the land and resource issue with tribal sovereignty and self-determination, tribal chairs declared that federal officials should not only protect tribal assets but allow tribal governments to manage them. In a jab at their Interior Department overseers, the chairs recommended, "The trustee should spend less time and energy protecting these resources from their Indian owners and more time protecting them from outside interests, including the Federal Government itself."[62]

An early victory for the NTCA in its fulfilling its "Number One priority" to protect Indian-owned lands and natural resources was, at its behest, the creation late in 1971 of a Water Rights Office within the Bureau of Indian Affairs. Bypassing the Bureau of Land Management, which many Native American leaders believed was often hostile to reservation interests, the new office reported directly to the commissioner of Indian affairs, who in turn reported to the secretary of the interior. One of the prime functions of the office was to inventory water resources and the needs of tribes in order to help them quantify their rights and develop them for future use. After identifying a specific Indian water rights problem, the office would advocate on behalf of tribes to address them. Failing that, the office would oversee the preparation of lawsuits for submission to the Justice Department.[63]

The Indian Water Rights Office operated as an independent entity within the BIA for approximately two years before bureau reorganization efforts led to its burial within the Office of Trust Responsibilities. This development was not altogether unexpected, however, since the Water Rights Office was something of a stopgap measure anyway. The tribal chairs' ultimate goal was congressional passage of the Nixon administration's proposed Indian Trust Counsel Authority. As the trustee of Indian lands and resources, the federal government (the Departments of Interior and Justice, in particular) often faced conflicts of interest when attempting to promote or protect the national interest and tribal interests simultaneously. As President Nixon stated in his July 8, 1970, special message to Congress, "There is considerable evidence that the Indians are the losers when such situations arise." The proposed Trust Counsel Authority (a three-person board appointed by the president, two of whom would be Native American) would be independent of the Departments of the Interior and Justice and would provide tribes both the authority and the means to bring suit in the name of the United States in its trustee capacity. The United States would waive its sovereign immunity from suits in connection with litigation involving the authority.[64]

Testifying in September 1973 before the House Interior Subcommittee on Indian Affairs in support of a bill (H.R. 6374) to create the Trust Counsel Authority, the NTCA's Robert Lewis offered strong support, declaring that the legislation "offers the American Indian the first real hope that his land and natural resources will be protected as they should be." That said, the NTCA recommended that the trust counsel board be expanded from three members to six or seven to give it broader representation and that the president select the board's representatives from a list of potential appointees submitted by the NTCA and other national Indian organizations. Lewis also expressed concern about whether the new Trust Counsel Authority could adequately protect them against the powerful Department of Justice with its vast resources and experience. If the department was relieved of its responsibilities as a trustee, Lewis warned, it might very well "declare full-scale attack against Indian claims." Lastly, the bill authorized federal departments to cooperate and share information with the Trust Counsel Authority. Lewis recommended that "authorized" be replaced with "required" since "cooperation might include no information and documents."[65]

The need for a mechanism such as the Trust Counsel Authority to address the glaring conflict-of-interest problem that undermined the federal government's willingness to fulfill its trust responsibilities was clear. So too was the likelihood that Indian versus non-Indian litigation would increase exponentially should the legislation pass. An editorial appearing in the *Gallup Independent* in May 1975 predicted that concerns about the potential fallout of the measure was likely to paralyze congressional action and that the odds of it gaining passage at the time were "very poor to zero." That prediction, unfortunately, turned out to be accurate. Although Congress considered several different versions of Indian Trust Counsel Authority legislation, the proposal was never enacted—the only initiative in Nixon's Special Message to Congress to meet that fate.[66]

In evaluating the NTCA's performance as an interest group seeking to advance the goals of federally recognized tribes, one must remain cognizant that the association was one of many Indian rights organizations in operation at the time. Distilling its individual impact and effectiveness in influencing a particular outcome may not be possible. As Russel Barsh and James Youngblood Henderson have observed, "Too often power is moved by combinations of subtle forces so numerous they defy accurate interpretation."[67] That said, the association was uniquely positioned by virtue of its close relationship with the BIA—and for a time the NCIO—to move power in a way that Red Power activists could not. Adopting an insider-oriented strategy to foster confidence and trust, the NTCA sought incremental change by working within the system using the traditional tools and techniques available to them at the time: letter writing, face-to-face meetings, adopting resolutions, hosting conferences, testifying at hearings, and so forth. These strategic and tactical decisions, of course, came with a steep price—the perception among some Native Americans that the reason tribal chairmen were not more forceful advocates was that they had been co-opted and manipulated by the federal government. To Indian adherents of the Twenty Point Position Paper, tribal chairs were little more than sellouts, puppets, and "the clowns of Indian Affairs." As outsiders (or, as Bruyneel suggests, occupants of a third space of sovereignty) in the battle for Indian policy reform, organizations such as AIM and Indians of All Tribes sought to move power in less conventional ways: occupations, caravans, media attention, and occasionally violence. This strategy also came with a steep price—the perception among tribal governments that urban Indian activists were publicity hounds and Native American wannabes who were primarily interested in seizing a share of the federal funding that rightfully belonged to reservation communities. By serving as the "radical flank" of the Indian rights movement, however, these organizations served a critical albeit unintended purpose—to push the federal government into the arms of moderate organizations such as the NTCA and NCAI.[68]

Even with its relatively privileged position as an insider, a position further strengthened by the federal government's recognition that working closely with tribal leaders was preferable to the Red Power alternative, the NTCA was only modestly effective in advancing its agenda in regard to the four foundational issues. The termination policy was officially repealed in 1983, but the Indian Civil Rights Act remained intact and the NTCA's requested amendment to give tribes the option of implementation was ignored. Self-determination via contracting was enacted by virtue of the 1975 Indian Self-Determination and Education Assistance Act, but the measure did little to openly transfer power to tribes to function independently of the BIA. From the point of view of critics such as AIM's Russell Means, the self-determination policy "was designed and intended to bolster rather than dismantle the whole structure of BIA colonialism."[69] Assessing the NTCA's influence on cultural preservation is a real challenge, given the difficulty in quantifying the extent that culture was or was not preserved. The association passed several preservation-oriented resolutions—to protect the traditional or ceremonial use of feathers and peyote, for example—and organized a conference on Indian culture and traditions. By placing the position of elderly Native Americans and Indian children within the context of cultural preservation, the NTCA likewise made a convincing case for important reforms that indirectly promoted that cause. The NTCA's land and resource protection efforts were partially successful. The association supported the modest land restoration efforts enacted during the Nixon administration, and was largely responsible for the creation of an Indian Water Rights Office in the BIA. The bigger prize—the formation of an Indian Trust Counsel Authority—failed to win passage despite the tribal chairs' strong support.

What were the implications of the NTCA's insider strategy, its reliance on working within the system, and its acceptance of incremental change? Had tribal chairs embraced a different strategy, could they have achieved more? On the one hand, Indian communities had to consider Foucault's warning that placing limits on goals, and the techniques employed to realize them, runs the risk of becoming entrapped in the very system one is trying to overcome. By seeking to advance their interests via court decisions, congressional legislation, or the BIA, tribal chairs representing demographically small and economically powerless Native communities had limited leverage to combat a host of powerful interests willing to use the system to limit tribal sovereignty and to exploit Indian lands and resources. The NTCA's challenge was to convince those communities that the cost of doing so (adverse public opinion, international embarrassment, legal challenges) outweighed the benefits. For tribal governments—themselves creations of the very system they were seeking to overcome—there was no real alternative. As journalist Mark Trahant (Shoshone-Bannock Tribes) noted in his study of the Native American fight for self-determination during the 1960s and 1970s, "No matter how strong the argument, no matter how right a tribal point of view might be, it meant nothing if it could not be enacted into law."[70] This was a hard truth if there ever was one, but a truth that tribal leaders accepted. As a result, the influence and authority of tribal governments gradually expanded as time passed even as the complex system of oversight (or entrapment) by the courts, Congress, and the BIA remained firmly in place.

Chapter 4

The Politics of Exclusivity

Exclusivity is an attractive albeit elusive goal of many businesses. An exclusivity strategy seeks to minimize competition, empower a business to act unilaterally, strengthen its negotiating position, and enhance its credibility and prestige. An ophthalmologist in my hometown, for example, makes much of the fact that he is the "exclusive" provider of certain vision-augmenting procedures for a popular professional football team. If star athletes use only him to correct their eyesight, so the thinking goes, he must be competent and legitimate. Exclusivity strategies are also evident outside of the business world. Labor unions, for example, claim to be the exclusive voice and representative of certain types of workers, colleges and universities create exclusive alumni organizations, and both blue-collar and white-collar professions organize associations that claim to be the "official"—if not exclusive—representative of their members.

In the spring of 1971 Bill Youpee of the National Tribal Chairmen's Association (NTCA) had argued that the association was "the only Indian organization which represents the population, tribes and reservations for which the government has a special responsibility." Tribal chairs and the NTCA bore this special responsibility, Youpee had declared, "Because they are the elected leaders and spokesmen for these particular tribes of Indians whom are federally recognized. No other Indian organization is organized in this way and cannot claim to share the responsibility with the United States government *nor can any other Indian organization claim to be the bona-fide [representative of] federally recognized Indians.*"[1] In its *American Indian World* position paper published in February 1974, the association declared, "It is time for the legally constituted reservations and other Federally recognized governments of Indian Tribes elected by democratic processes, so sacred to all segments of society, to speak out for their tribal members and exercise their legal and rightful leadership role." The chairs followed up the declaration with a query. "The National Tribal Chairmen's Association wants to know if the people in all levels and all branches of government are going to be responsive to the elected tribal leaders as the official spokesmen for Indian Tribes."[2]

As astute politicians and, in some cases, businesspeople as well, tribal leaders undoubtedly recognized that strategic advantages, credibility, and prestige would accompany recognition of their exclusive position as the voice of federally recognized tribes. That said, the NTCA appears instead to have pursued an exclusivity strategy based on principle. As "legal" and "rightful" leaders selected through "sacred" democratic processes, tribal chairs believed that they alone possessed the moral and legal authority to speak on their peoples' behalf and to interface with the federal government on matters pertaining to federally recognized tribes. As discussed earlier, some Native Americans—both on and off reservation—questioned these claims to legitimacy, criticized the process by which tribal chairs had gained office as an alien imposition, and refused to acknowledge them as legitimate leaders. The resulting fallout, as this chapter shows, contributed to the polarization evident in the national Indian community and to the NTCA's mixed legacy in the era of self-determination.

The NTCA Reorganizes

Shortly after his fall 1971 defeat for reelection as chair of the Fort Peck Tribal Council, Bill Youpee offered his resignation as president of the NTCA. Article III of the association's constitution stipulated clearly that membership was limited to "duly elected chairmen [sic], presidents, governors, or chiefs of reservation Indians or of federally recognized tribes with federal trust land," and Youpee no longer met this qualification. On November 2, 1971, however, the NTCA executive board passed a resolution authorizing Youpee to complete his full one-year term as president, which was set to expire in July 1972. At that time, a new slate of officers was elected. Webster Two Hawk was chosen as president while Wendell Chino won the vice presidency. Odric Baker and Nathan Little Soldier were reelected to their respective positions as treasurer and secretary. A year later, NTCA ended its office-sharing arrangement with the National Council on Indian Opportunity (NCIO) and moved into its own space on the fourth floor of the International Bank Building located at 1701 Pennsylvania Avenue in Washington, D.C., just west of Lafayette Square. With 146 federally recognized tribes in the organization and substantial funding from various agencies, the NTCA appeared to be in the best shape since its founding.[3]

Webster Two Hawk (Rosebud Sioux) was an NTCA founder, its second president, and a leading voice for tribal chairs during the association's early years. Courtesy of the Center of Southwest Studies, Fort Lewis College, Durango, Colo.

Webster Two Hawk brought a wealth of unique administrative experience to the NTCA. Born in 1930 on the Rosebud reservation in South Dakota, Two Hawk was a graduate of the University of South Dakota and recipient of a master's degree in theology from Kenyon College in Ohio. After serving in the Korean War, Two Hawk entered the Episcopal priesthood and received assignments on the Yankton and Standing Rock reservations before suffering a heart attack at age thirty-eight. While recuperating at home, Two Hawk was associate director of the Rosebud Community Action Program. After supporters submitted his name as a candidate for tribal leadership, he was elected president in a hotly contested match against Robert Burnette. As a man of the cloth, Two Hawk was an accomplished speaker with strong people skills, but he inherited a Rosebud tribal government in financial disarray. A month after taking office, he reported that the tribe was over one hundred thousand dollars in debt and was twenty-seven thousand dollars overdrawn at the bank. In response, Two Hawk dismissed all but two tribal staff employees and focused his attention on economic development and workforce training. In addition to the difficult task of recruiting businesses to locate on the reservation, the Two Hawk administration worked on opening a tribal college (the future Sinte Gleska College) and securing federal housing assistance. Like tribal chairs across the nation, Two Hawk contended with sporadic protests from young Indian activists. A year before the NTCA's founding, he was already voicing what would become standard association responses to Red Power–inspired activism. When protestors organized an occupation at Mount Rushmore in August 1970 to bring attention to Native American claims to the Black Hills, for example, Two Hawk responded that the protest "is not what those of us and official representatives of the people would agree with—particularly the method of doing it. We who are representative of the people have regular means by which we can be heard, and we would like to operate through those channels and legal means which are provided."[4]

Shortly after the NTCA's establishment, the association's executive board had determined that a full-time team would be required to keep up with its expanding responsibilities and activities. To that end, the board created an executive office for the association with an executive director and staff, but lacking funds to compensate any new hires, these positions were filled with interim appointments—the two staff members, James L. Sansaver and Chizu Toda, provided "on loan" by the Bureau of Indian Affairs (BIA). A month after its July 1972 election of new officers, however, the NTCA moved forward with the appointment of a full-time executive director. During an association meeting held in late August in Shawano, Wisconsin, Odric Baker asked his fellow board members to "seriously consider and accept Mr. Youpee as the Executive Director of NTCA" since he had been a prime mover in its formation. Other candidates who had expressed interest in the position included Crow Nation tribal chair Edison Real Bird and Clarence Skye (Standing Rock Sioux), director of the United Sioux Tribe Development Corp and son of Douglas Skye, the original architect of the NTCA. Since the association's constitution said nothing about requiring staff members to be duly elected chairs, Youpee was the unanimous selection. For the next six years, therefore, the individual representing the NTCA to congresspersons, senators, cabinet members, private foundations, and the press was not actually a voting member of the NTCA.[5]

In addition to representing the association, Youpee's responsibilities included organizing the NTCA's annual convention. Conventions generally lasted three or four days and included all elected chairs who were members of the association.

Attendance at these gatherings was generally strong, no doubt influenced by the fact that travel and accommodation costs were either covered or subsidized by federal agencies such as the BIA or Office of Economic Opportunity (OEO). At the NTCA's August 1972 inaugural convention in Eugene, Oregon, for example, the BIA contributed fifty thousand dollars to finance the event.[6] Conventions featured various guest speakers—area politicians, members of Congress, White House aides, BIA and Indian Health Service officials, tribal leaders— along with the obligatory panel presentations and workshops. Association members deliberated and voted on resolutions, discussed legislative priorities, and conducted elections for the ensuing year's slate of officers. As with most gatherings of this type, the NTCA convention mixed business with pleasure. Association members attending the Third Annual NTCA Convention in Albuquerque, for instance, were treated to a traditional pipe ceremony conducted by members of the Crow Tribe of Montana, toured local pueblos, and took a side trip to the Institute of American Arts at Santa Fe.[7]

The association's executive director was similarly responsible for organizing quarterly board of directors' meetings, which generally took place in Washington, D.C. Federal agencies funding the NTCA likewise bore travel and per-diem costs for these gatherings.[8] Board meetings were serious and, at times, consequential events where tribal chairs met face-to-face with the commissioner of Indian affairs, the secretary of the interior, congressional and White House staffers, and other executive department representatives. The board meetings were the venues through which tribal chairs deployed their insiders' strategy of influencing policy via consultation, relationship building, and serving as experts on reservation life. Preparations for these gatherings required a substantial investment of time in reviewing data, reading reports, and drafting position statements. As NTCA president Two Hawk observed, service on the association's board "is not all fun and games but very exhausting, time-consuming work to deliberate and discuss the vast issues that face Indians in a national sense."[9]

Funding for Urban Indians

Between 1969 and 1974 the Nixon administration doubled annual outlays for Indian programs to $1.6 billion. The BIA's budget alone grew from $249 million in 1969 to $635 million five years later. During that same time period, however, the federal government spent only $10 million to help off-reservation Indians, much of that directed to urban Indian centers that, the administration hoped, could serve as clearinghouses for domestic assistance programs and services.[10] Despite this glaring inequity in funding, the NTCA continued to claim that the BIA was shifting its resources to "illegitimate" urban Indian groups that employed "catchy things" such as "demonstrations, the sit-ins, Alcatraz, Jane Fonda, and four-letter words" to attract attention and to secure funding that came at the expense of federally recognized tribes. A consequence of the BIA's distraction, the chairs maintained, was that "the reservations continue with the same old problems."[11] In *The American Indian World*, the NTCA declared the situation "morally wrong when resources are provided by anyone to a small minority to impose its will upon the majority which the elected officials represent." Apparently oblivious to the threat this line of reasoning could pose to Indian communities that were minorities in virtually every state in the nation, the statement went on to assert, "It is wrong to expect elected officials to follow the will of anyone except the people they represent and who elected them."[12]

From the perspective of the tribal chairs, funding urban Indians was tantamount to recognizing them as the equivalent of land-based federally recognized tribes—even though urban Indian leaders were unelected and their organizations outside the pale of the federal government's trust relationship with Indian nations. If the administration recognized and funded them, the chairs reasoned, "Congress will begin to get to the level of thinking: Perhaps there ought to be an expanded relationship beyond the present scope and dilute the relationship with the federally recognized tribes." Should that occur, "Every race in the United States will clamor for the same thing."[13]

The tribal chairs believed that the efforts of urban and other nonreservation Indians to gain access to federal programs and services on the basis of their racial or ethnic claims as Indians rather than on membership in a federally recognized tribe constituted a crisis with potentially dire consequences for tribal governments and institutions. Consequently, they demanded that the federal government "honor its commitments to American Indians in *the tribal context* and not to Indians in the context of a racial minority." This approach required the federal government "to resist those of Indian blood, real or claimed, and their uninformed supporters who want to change this basic legal and moral commitment to a racial one." Members of federally recognized tribes had "nothing to gain and everything to lose in attempting a change of this nature," the chairs argued, "including their own identity which is tribal" and based on "tribal culture, traditions, and history." Urban Indian activists pushing for access to government services against the wishes of tribal government, furthermore, were violating the very principle they claimed to support: tribal sovereignty. "It would be tragic indeed if Indian people themselves destroyed their own society which has resisted these efforts on the part of everyone else throughout Indian history."[14]

In President Richard Nixon's July 8, 1970, Indian message, he was explicit that the BIA's responsibilities did not extend to Native Americans who had left the reservation. The needs of urban Indians, he insisted, should be met instead through programs designed for other disadvantaged groups, and he had charged the OEO with funding seven model Indian centers in urban areas. Perhaps in anticipation of an expansion or calls for an expansion of federal assistance to urban Indians, Frank Carlucci of the Office of Management and Budget drafted a letter on March 30, 1972, to Assistant Secretary of the Interior Harrison Loesch regarding the BIA's clientele. Citing Nixon's July message as his authority, Carlucci argued "that Indian needs on reservation are sufficiently great that resources available in the BIA should not be dissipated elsewhere," and he urged the Interior Department "to apprise OEO of reservation problems impacting on the urban Indian situation . . . which might be useful to OEO in fulfilling its lead responsibility in the urban Indian area." Upon receipt of the letter, Loesch forwarded it to Commissioner Louis Bruce and to members of the Interior Department's policy committee.[15]

Harrison Loesch needed no reminders about the BIA's spending priorities. Nearly six months before President Nixon presented his Indian message to Congress, Loesch had sent a memorandum to Commissioner Bruce with the subject line: "Adherence to our long-standing policy of not providing special Bureau of Indian Affairs services to off-reservation Indians." While he could have stopped with the subject line since it pretty much summed up his opinion about the matter, Loesch declared that the BIA "has an urgent and challenging job to meet the needs of tribal Indians of the reservations" and warned that "this is no time to be diverting our attention and limited funds from our basic responsibility." While allowing agency superintendents a degree of flexibility to assist those with "individual hardship," they were to be handled "as individual exceptions and not be allowed to compromise our basic principle as to the clientele to be served" by the BIA.[16]

Urban Indian activists, meanwhile, were working in the opposite direction. During the first week of March 1972, forty delegates supported by more than one hundred urban Indian centers met in Omaha and formed the National American Indian Council to act as "a national voice for the rural and urban

Indians no longer served by the BIA." "When you get off the reservation," stated delegate Dan Amerson (Chickasaw), "someone pushes a button and you're no longer an Indian." To rectify the problem, the new council sought to "make the transplanted urban Indians aware of the services they are entitled to" and to promote Indian involvement in federal agencies such as the Department of Health, Education, and Welfare (HEW). Conference organizer John A. Folster (Lakota) admitted that the proceedings had experienced turmoil when American Indian Movement (AIM) activists led by Russell Means tried to bring the council "under its wing rather than to set its own course." When delegates rebuffed these efforts and chose to form an independent organization, AIM refused to recognize it. "We want no part of it," Means declared. "It will eventually push the urban Indians in with the whites." In April, Grace Thorpe (Sac and Fox), the sister of Olympic star Jim Thorpe, appeared alongside Folster and Harvey Wells of the Cleveland American Indian Center before the Senate Appropriations Committee to testify in support of BIA assistance for urban Indians. A key justification offered was the ongoing transitional problems that many Native American relocatees experienced. "To move from the natural wide expanses of Arizona or the Dakotas to the concrete streets of Chicago is extremely difficult and often frustrating," Grace Thorpe stated. "The fact that an Indian has been given a six-month training program to learn welding does not qualify him to easily fit into the complex urban life in the United States."[17]

Ever the tightrope walker, Commissioner Bruce had voiced support for an expansion of government assistance to off-reservation Indians at various times during his tenure at the BIA. The degree of that support, however, often bore a direct relationship to the makeup of his audience. At a July 1971 meeting of BIA personnel in Minnesota, Bruce discussed his desire to make a "decisive break with the past," which included expanding BIA services to urban Indians. Five months earlier at a tribal chairs' conference in Billings, however, Bruce had insisted that the bureau was "reservation centered" and that the law prohibited giving urban Indians preference in federal programs.[18]

Perhaps in response to Frank Carlucci's March 1972 letter to Harrison Loesch, Bruce convened a committee cochaired by Ernie Stevens (Oneida) and John Jollie (Ojibwa) to conduct an internal BIA study that, when completed later that spring, bore the title "Indian Eligibility for Bureau Services: A Look at Tribal Recognition and Individual Rights to Services."[19] In their discussion of urban Indians, committee members argued they had not abrogated their "special" relation with the federal government because they left the reservation. To withhold government assistance from urban Indians simply because they had "exercised initiative and self-determination and made an independent transition" by leaving the reservation, therefore, was profoundly unjust. In a statement that would have irritated tribal chairs, the committee declared, "There are gross inequities in a system which discourages independent initiative by rewarding only those who use government aid to succeed."[20]

The committee also tackled the issue of cost: if urban Indians were to receive federal funding, how much money would they need and where would it come from? Estimates that serving urban Indians would require doubling the BIA's budget and that funds would be drained from reservation budgets to help cover those costs were not only "erroneous and misleading," the study noted, but also exacerbated urban-reservation tensions. Instead, the funds would come from existing executive department budgets—some of which could be funneled through the BIA. The most urgent urban Indian needs, committee members argued, were in special education, adult vocational training, and scholarships for higher education. Additional funding for those programs, they believed, would not exceed $46 million.[21]

Committee members saved "Urban Advocacy"—the subject they felt most passionate about—for their conclusion. "The BIA is a national federal agency of over 15,000 people over half of which are Indians. We assert that a few Indian desks, with no money, muzzled advocates, [and] a reactionary bureaucracy . . . does not add up to Indian advocacy." The federal government, after all, bore responsibility for the divisions between Indian people by creating and perpetuating the relocation program. It compounded the problem by ignoring the needs of urban Indians. "In the past, advocacy for off-reservation people had to be carried on quietly and informally. We have not funded them, but we think, as the agency that deals with Indians, we have the right at the very least to argue on their behalf. There are those that say we have gone too far—to them we say, it's only because they have not gone far enough."[22]

It's not clear if and when members of the NTCA gained access to the "Indian Eligibility for Bureau Services" report. If they did, the tribal chairs were not swayed by the arguments put forth on behalf of urban Indians. On April 27, 1972, Youpee wrote Commissioner Bruce concerning "an announcement which we understand was forthcoming that BIA was broadening its eligibility requirements to serve urban Indians." Youpee also alluded to a bureau "draft study" that had been completed but not released and requested that Bruce send him a copy for the NTCA's "review and comment." Not surprisingly, a month later, the NTCA board of directors passed a resolution registering "serious concern" regarding "efforts to include urban and off-reservation Indians within the scope of Bureau of Indian Affairs responsibility." The BIA was already overburdened, the resolution stated, and Nixon's July 8, 1970, message had directed the BIA "not to dissipate its resources elsewhere than to serve the reservation Indian population."[23]

While BIA funding for off-reservation Indians remained an extremely sensitive issue, Congress moved to provide them other avenues of assistance. During the mid-1970s, the federal government began to fund several pilot programs to assist urban Indian centers. The Comprehensive Employment and Training Act of 1973, meanwhile, made nonreservation Indian groups and organizations eligible for manpower programs; passage of the Native American Programs Act of 1974 provided direct support for self-determination programs aimed at improving the health, education, and welfare of Native Americans both on and off reservations; and the Indian Self-Determination and Education Assistance Act of 1975 (discussed in the previous chapter) also recognized off-reservation Indian organizations as eligible to contract for services.[24]

The issue of funding for urban Indians, along with the NTCA's insistence that elected tribal chairs were the sole representatives of federally recognized tribes, reflected poorly on the association and called into question its stated goals of unity, strength, and justice. The claims of association leaders that the BIA had been shifting its priorities and resources away from the reservations to urban and other off-reservation Indian communities were inaccurate, and the comments of some association leaders that urban and landless Native Americans were "illegitimate" and "not real Indians" only deepened the divisions within the national Indian community. The position of tribal chairs on funding for off-reservation Indians also reinforced the perception that the NTCA had been co-opted and was being manipulated by the federal government. Indian rights activist and theorist Hank Adams (Assiniboine-Sioux) went so far as to argue that the BIA had created the NTCA to buttress the federal government's efforts to "consolidate a force against commitment to urban Indians."[25] According to the "Indian Eligibility for Bureau Services" report, "Implications are made to Indian tribal leaders that the needed funds [for services to off-reservation Indians] will be taken from their reservation budgets."[26] The source of those "implications"— presumably conservatives in the BIA, budget hawks in Congress, and Interior

Department hard-liners—bear an even larger share of the blame for sowing the seeds of division, which would sprout and grow in alarming new directions on the eve of the 1972 Presidential election.

Lumbee Recognition

The 1960s were a time of considerable public sympathy for Native Americans and their ongoing struggle for self-determination, cultural preservation, and social justice. One consequence of this emerging mind-set was a growing number of individuals who began identifying themselves as Native Americans. Driven by diverse motives—the desire to express pride in their ancestry, heritage, and culture; to resurrect and reestablish tribal communities that had been long lost or forgotten, and perhaps to gain access to federal programs and services—these individuals began to mobilize in hopes of gaining federal recognition. During the late 1960s and into the 1970s, organizations of non–federally recognized Indians sprouted up across the country, especially east of the Mississippi River. In December 1972, two hundred delegates representing dozens of "ignored and sometimes forgotten Indians" formed the Coalition of Eastern Native Americans (CENA) to "remove roadblocks" to "self-determination and self-development." To those ends, the coalition demanded that each of its member tribes or confederacies receive federal recognition if they requested it, aid in rebuilding a tribal land base, seed money to reconstitute tribal offices, and access to BIA assistance.[27]

Federally recognized tribes responded predictably to the sudden and unexpected appearance of eastern groups claiming Indian ancestry and their subsequent efforts to seek federal recognition. According to Mark Edwin Miller, many reservation Indian leaders resented the "newborn Indians" and questioned their efforts to exercise Indigenous rights and their self-declared entitlement to government funding and assistance. In addition, tribal chairs distrusted "the youth-directed, intertribal and pan-Indian emphasis" of groups like CENA and AIM, although some rural-based "new tribes" shared the tribal chairs' contempt for the media-driven protests of Red Power activists.[28] As the voice of federally recognized tribes, the NTCA was quick to cast suspicion on the authenticity and legitimacy of new groups claiming Indian ancestry and was in the forefront of the counteroffensive to quash efforts to extend the groups federal recognition. Of particular concern to tribal chairs were the long-standing claims advanced by the Lumbee Indians of North Carolina, a people whose fight for federal recognition was nearly a century old. Although hardly a new group, the Lumbee

Tribe represented about 60 percent of the Indigenous people in the United States seeking federal recognition at that time. If recognized, they would constitute the second-largest tribe in the nation.[29]

The Lumbees' fight for federal recognition began in the 1880s. North Carolina legally recognized the "Indians of Robeson County" in February 1885, but several efforts in the ensuing decades to obtain federal recognition were unsuccessful. In hopes of satisfying the constantly shifting state and federal criteria to confirm their "authenticity" as Indians, the tribe agreed to four official tribal name changes between 1885 and 1956: Croatoans, Cherokee Indians of Robeson County, Siouan Indians of the Lumber River, and finally, the Lumbee Indians. The ever-changing criteria of treaty relations, anthropological measurements of culture, or blood quantum laws imposed by outsiders, historian Malinda Maynor Lowery (Lumbee) has shown, was inconsistent with Lumbee experience and tradition, which stressed kinship and place as their "foundational layer of Indian identity." Internal disagreements about the desirability of complying with these alien requirements led to increased factionalism among the Lumbees, a development that Maynor Lowery maintains was a strategic response to the government's vacillating, contradictory, and self-serving requirements for recognition.[30]

In June 1956 the Lumbees won a partial victory after Congress passed the Lumbee Act (H.R. 4656; P.L. 570), which acknowledged their claims of Indian ancestry but did not extend federal recognition. Especially problematic from the Lumbee perspective was the law's final sentence: "Nothing in this Act shall make such Indians eligible for any services performed by the United States for Indians, and none of the statutes of the United States which affect Indians because of their status as Indians shall be applicable to the Lumbee Indians." The Lumbee Act, consequently, was a double-edged sword—acknowledging them as Indians while simultaneously disclaiming any federal responsibility for their welfare.[31]

Despite these setbacks, the Lumbees persisted, and on January 22, 1974, Representative Charlie Rose (D-N.C.) introduced legislation (H.R. 12216) that sought to repeal the portions of P.L. 570 denying them federal services. While the bill would not secure federal recognition—and thus continue the Lumbees' ineligibility for BIA programs and services—Lumbee leaders hoped that removing the blanket restriction on "any services performed by the United States for Indians" might at least qualify them for public health assistance and scholarships. On October 1, 1974, the House passed the measure and sent it to the Senate Committee on Interior and Insular Affairs for consideration. Despite support from Senator Jesse Helms (R-N.C.) and a visit by Lumbee leaders to press for action, the bill never made it out of that body.[32]

The NTCA opposed the Lumbee bill for several reasons. First, many tribal chairs remained unconvinced that the Lumbees had ever constituted a tribe and were never bona fide Indians. These views were buttressed by an April 5, 1974, Interior Department report that argued that the provision in H.R. 12216 removing the language disqualifying them from receiving federal services "would appear to make the Lumbees a federally recognized tribe." That was a problem, the Interior Department's John Whitaker noted, since the Lumbees did not own common land suitable for a reservation; they were not a cohesive, identifiable ethnic group; and they had no historical relationship with the U.S. government.[33] According to the NTCA's Buffalo Tiger, chair of the Miccosukee Tribe of Florida, the Lumbees possessed "no identifiable tribal or cultural history" and, in a telegram to Bill Youpee, warned that "multi-racial groups across the country" were attempting to "identify themselves as Indians. This must not happen without proper evidence."[34]

Another influential force that helps explain the NTCA's opposition to the Lumbee legislation was the exceptionally strong and antagonistic stance of United South and Eastern Tribes (USET), an intertribal organization of federally recognized Indian nations incorporated in 1969. Like the NTCA, USET was a "fierce defender of the sovereignty and rights of federally acknowledged tribes alone," and there was a good deal of cross-pollination between the two organizations and their memberships (Buffalo Tiger, for example, held membership in both). Shortly after the House passed H.R. 12216, USET circulated a position paper that embraced the federal government's convoluted criteria for recognition and forcefully stated its opposition to the proposed changes to the Lumbee Act. "These people are multi-racial and have no evidence of history, Indian culture, Indian religion, government treaties, maintain no formal rolls of membership and [possess no] identifiable land base." In addition to these shortcomings, the Lumbees had provided "no evidence of tribalism, language or any distinct Indian cultural identity. Their principal reason, other than apparently attempting to become eligible for Indian funds, is to gain a racial and tribal identity, which we think is completely manufactured."[35]

In June 1974 the NTCA adopted a resolution opposing the Lumbee bill—a significant setback for the Lumbees, who understood the importance of securing the acceptance of federally recognized tribes. According to Mark Edwin Miller, federally recognized tribes served the function in public discourse of legitimizing "Indianness" and exercised considerable influence over the BIA's position toward unrecognized groups. In an appeal to the NTCA to reconsider its position, Janie Maynor Locklear of the Lumbee Regional Development Association Inc. requested a meeting with NTCA officials in Washington, D.C., to "informally" discuss the legislation and answer any questions the chairs might have, but there is no evidence that this meeting took place. Instead, Bill Youpee sent letters to the Labor Department, to HEW, and to President Gerald Ford making it clear that the NTCA opposed any federal funding for the Lumbees or any other group save "Federally recognized tribes, bands and groups with whom the Federal Government has historical legal responsibility for special attention."[36]

Reminiscent of its opposition to federal funding for urban Indians—even those from federally recognized tribes—the NTCA opposed federal recognition of the Lumbees for economic reasons. Convinced that the federal budget for Native American–related spending was finite and that the addition of new claimants would come at the expense of reservation communities, the NTCA resisted any action that could potentially dilute funding for existing federally recognized tribes. As noted previously, budget-conscious federal officials played on these fears, which, intentionally or not, exacerbated tensions among the various Indian groups. The potential financial impact of a tribe the size of the Lumbees was especially troubling to Native American leaders. At its thirty-first annual convention, held in October 1974, the National Congress of American Indians (NCAI) voted to oppose the Lumbees' request for support. During an at-times strident floor debate, Robert Burnette (Rosebud Sioux) warned delegates, "We may have 40,000 to 79,000 persons waiting to make an onslaught on Congress—people suddenly coming out of the woodwork. How many do we allow to 'become' Indians, while we diminish our resources every day!"[37]

A final argument NTCA leaders posed in opposition to the federal recognition of new Indian groups were the "exasperatingly vague and confusing" criteria used to determine the legitimacy of claims. Prior to the reservation period, tribes freely naturalized nonmember Indians and non-Indians based on their usefulness and willingness to abide by tribal laws and customs making race incidental to tribal citizenship. During the 1930s, however, Congress and the Office of Indian Affairs both began imposing new restrictions on such matters, presumably to limit the government's financial responsibilities. As Barsh and Henderson have noted, "The characteristic racial character of contemporary tribes is more a product of federal manipulation than tribal discrimination."[38]

Over the years, definitions of "Who is an Indian?" multiplied, often varying from agency to agency and from state to state. By one NTCA count, there were forty-seven definitions of "Indian" in use by different federal agencies by the late 1970s. Testifying before a House committee hearing held in August 1978 the NTCA's Pat Locke (Standing Rock Sioux) professed the association's support for the restoration of "bona fide" tribes—such as the Menominee, Siletz, and Klamath—that had been terminated in the 1950s, but she did not offer a specific set of preferred procedures or qualifications for determining questions of recognition. In 1980 the NTCA worked with several other intertribal organizations (including the NCAI) to formulate a resolution in response to a new Department of Education study seeking to define "Indian" and settle the matter of an individual's or group's eligibility for government services. In addition to the oft-stated complaint that tribes had not been adequately consulted about the study, the resolution declared that as sovereign entities, tribes alone have the right to make determinations about their membership and that attempts by government officials to do so undermined tribal self-determination.[39]

The NTCA's specific stand on Lumbee recognition, as well as its general position on the determination of Indian identity (especially as it pertained to eligibility for federal programs and services), were largely consistent with the government's restrictive criteria enshrined in the federal acknowledgment process (FAP). Although taking issue with specific features of this process, the chairs nonetheless employed it to limit access to Indian-related programs and services through their insistence that only members of federally recognized tribes living on or near reservations were eligible. This position gained legal standing in 1977 with the Supreme Court's ruling in *Delaware Tribal Business Committee v. Weeks* (430 U.S. 73), which held that "organized tribal Indians are something different from, and can have rights superior to those of, persons with the same degree of [Indian] blood but with no citizenship in the tribe."[40] Urban Indians, members of non–federally recognized tribes, and individuals or groups that self-identified as Native Americans, however, were entitled to the same programs and services available to non-Indian citizens. The NTCA enjoyed fairly solid support from other intertribal organizations on these stances but drew condemnation from CENA and like-minded critics who charged that the association was acting like "purity police" conducting an "ethnic purge" of Indian peoples who, for one reason or another, were not enrolled in—or recognized as—federally recognized tribes. This was politically risky since it alienated a sizeable group of potential allies who were obviously very committed to Indian issues and redefined the movement for sovereignty and self-determination (at least in the eyes of the non-Indian majority) as a struggle for racial segregation.[41]

In the Caravan's Wake

The occupation of the Bureau of Indian Affairs building in Washington, D.C., from November 2 to November 9, 1972, by Native American activists taking part in the Trail of Broken Treaties Caravan (TBTC) was a dramatic—and well chronicled—episode in contemporary Native American history. The occupation manifested the anger and frustration of Native Americans with endemic poverty, racial discrimination, economic exploitation, and their growing impatience with the slow pace of promised reforms. Ongoing factionalism and infighting within the BIA only compounded these feelings. The occupation also magnified the tensions between urban and reservation Indians, as well as the deep divisions within Indian communities and organizations over the meaning of self-determination and the appropriate strategy to bring about its realization. The focus of the national media on the occupation—especially television footage and news photos—transformed it into a momentous event witnessed by a worldwide audience. The intensity of that media spotlight produced both intended and unintended consequences for all parties involved.[42]

Having worked closely with federal officials for important, albeit incremental, changes in the direction of federal Indian policy, the tribal chairs believed that many of the activists' demands spelled out in the Twenty Point Position Paper were impractical. They took strong issue with the fact that the individuals responsible for drafting the position paper were unelected, not accountable to any constituency, and therefore illegitimate spokespersons for federally recognized tribes. Furthermore, the TBTC's tactic, planned or not, to press for their acceptance via occupation (and the subsequent damage) of the BIA building was counterproductive and threatened to stall what the tribal chairs believed was a precipitous moment in the battle for self-determination. For these reasons, the NTCA condemned the TBTC, the ensuing occupation, and the Nixon administration's decision to negotiate with the protestors and to promise consideration of the Twenty Points document.

The NTCA's participation in press conferences and other media-related events to publicize their opposition to the occupation was harshly criticized at the time and reinforced the opinion of some Indian rights groups that the tribal chairs had been co-opted and were being manipulated by federal authorities to sow inter-Indian divisions and thwart meaningful changes in federal Indian policy. The following discussion seeks to assess the validity of these criticisms since they bear directly on the NTCA's claims to be the exclusive voice of federally recognized tribes and the association's legacy in contemporary Indian history.

It perhaps goes without saying that politicians of all stripes have exploited Native Americans for political gain. During World War I, for example, Commissioner of Indian Affairs Cato Sells dragged every Indian enlistee or combat veteran he could find in front of cameras to demonstrate the remarkable "success" of the government's assimilation-oriented policies in producing such patriots. During the New Deal era, John Collier likewise used Native Americans who supported the Indian Reorganization Act to trumpet its successes or to downplay its failures. That such political gamesmanship and publicity stunts continued during the Nixon administration—especially in the days leading up to the 1972 presidential election—is indisputable but hardly exceptional. Tribal leaders were well aware of this troubling dynamic. Three months before the caravan commenced its journey to the nation's capital, Webster Two Hawk had declared that the "NTCA is concerned with fulfilling the American Indians' needs instead of being continuously used for individuals' self-gains in our political system."[43] That said, the most damning charge leveled against the tribal chairs during the BIA occupation crisis was that the Nixon administration (using the NCIO or the BIA as intermediaries) had exploited them for political purposes—to discredit the occupiers and to bolster support for the administration's handling of Indian affairs.[44] AIM's Clyde Bellecourt remembered it this way. "In response to the occupation, the BIA flew in some of the tribal leaders they had in their back pockets. These were members of the National Tribal Chairmen's Association. They put these men up in luxury, in the Hyatt Regency Hotel—wined and dined them—when we were lying on floors, had nothing to eat, and were cold."[45] According to Paul Chaat Smith and Robert Allen Warrior, the NCIO's Bob Robertson "had flown some of them in for the express purpose of criticizing the militants as well as the reformers in the BIA, and provided them with a sheet of talking points to use at the press conference."[46] Speaking for the NCAI, Chuck Trimble argued that "the Interior Department, the Bureau of Land Management, in conjunction with the Vice President's own National Council on Indian Opportunity, [was] working clandestinely to muster Tribal Leaders for the defense of the administration."[47] A related charge was that Robertson and other government officials intentionally delayed restoration efforts in the BIA building so that the media and tribal officials could conduct publicized

Federal officials review the aftermath of the November 2–8, 1972, occupation of the BIA building in Washington, D.C. Secretary of the Interior Rogers C. B. Morton is on right. The NCIO's Bob Robertson is second from left. NARA Photo Archive, College Park, Md.

tours of the wreckage. This "deliberately designed program of indoctrination and polarization," critics charged, sought to focus national attention on the destruction wrought by the occupiers rather than on the compelling points raised in the Twenty Point Position Paper.[48]

The assumption that the BIA or NCIO had summoned tribal leaders to the capital and then orchestrated the NTCA's press conferences to discredit the objectives of Indian activists and the Twenty Point document is certainly plausible and understandable given the hyperpoliticized environment at the time. For the many urban and reservation-based Native Americans who participated in the TBTC or who were sympathetic to its goals, the BIA/NCIO manipulation of tribal leaders was obvious and indisputable. While neither the BIA nor the NCIO had created the tribal chairs' association, they had unquestionably assisted its establishment by helping it secure financing, temporary office space, and even staff support. The sudden appearance of NTCA leaders during the occupation and their participation in two press conferences and a segment on NBC's *Today* show also support the scenario described above. According to an internal NTCA chronology for November 5 through November 10, tribal chairs met with Interior Department officials and White House aides Bradley Patterson and Leonard Garment on five separate occasions, and it's entirely possible that government talking points were passed along during one of these meetings. That the tribal chairs subsequently condemned the occupation and its organizers in no uncertain terms (the NTCA's Position Paper likened the occupation to "an orgy of wanton, senseless destruction"), and demanded that the federal government negotiate only with "recognized and legally elected tribal leaders" who expressed a desire to "work peacefully with the United States Government" certainly played into the hands of the Nixon administration, which sought to marginalize the protestors as extremists. The tribal chairs' subsequent request that the president accept the resignations of Interior Department and BIA officials who had failed "to take proper measures to protect the Bureau of Indian Affairs building and the records it contains" supports the accusation that tribal chairs were out to get Louis Bruce and the remnants of his reform-minded New Team—but would seem to challenge the charge that the BIA had arranged their appearance in the first place.[49]

Other circumstantial evidence, however, points to a somewhat different conclusion. The NTCA, for starters, was headquartered in Washington, D.C., and tribal chairs were most certainly already present. The chairs who arrived later denied that the government had arranged for their transportation and cited plausible reasons unconnected with the occupation crisis as an explanation for their appearance in Washington. The NCIO's Bob Robertson admitted to speaking with tribal leaders at the beginning of the occupation ("All I did was give them factual information"); he insisted that he had not summoned them to the capital but that they had called him.[50] Speaking years later, Robertson rejected charges that he had strong-armed tribal leaders into holding politically self-serving press conferences. To do so, he declared, would have been "presumptuous and manipulative."[51]

An internal NCIO memorandum dated October 30, 1972—four days before the occupation began—showed that Robertson had indeed recommended organizing a press conference on November 3 and that he had consulted with the NTCA's Webster Two Hawk, but its purpose was to announce the selection and swearing in of new Indian members of the NCIO. That event, Robertson believed, might also counter the expected "unwarranted and unkind statements" about the administration from TBTC participants.[52] While this admittedly substantiates the claim that Robertson was willing to employ Indian leaders for political purposes, it's a far cry from the charge that he flew them

Webster Two Hawk (Rosebud Sioux) shakes hands with Commissioner Louis Bruce. The BIA helped finance the NTCA throughout its fifteen-year existence. Courtesy of the Center of Southwest Studies, Fort Lewis College, Durango, Colo.

in to the capital and then strong-armed them into denouncing the occupation. During subsequent press conferences, the NTCA representatives were certainly not bashful about condemning the occupation and attendant destruction of property. They showed even less restraint in their denunciation of the occupation's leadership, whom the NTCA's position paper described as "ruthless, self-seeking, self-appointed Indian leaders." From the perspective of Webster Two Hawk, AIM leaders were little more than opportunists seeking to exploit legitimate Indian complaints for their own aggrandizement. "They may wear their hair long and they may wear beads," Two Hawk declared, "but their culture is a bastard one. It's a twisted culture." Throughout the weeklong ordeal, tribal chairs stressed the illegitimacy of the "dissident urban-oriented Indians" and demanded that federal officials negotiate solely with "recognized and legally elected tribal leaders."[53]

The point to consider here is that the tribal chairs had been saying many of these things for years. Their concerns about urban Indian activists and Commissioner Bruce's apparent willingness to accommodate them were important reasons for the NTCA's creation. No one had to pressure them into declaring what they had long believed to be true, and no BIA or NCIO official had to provide them talking points regarding topics that they had been writing and talking about well before the TBTC was ever envisioned. The BIA occupation crisis, in fact, provided the chairs an unprecedented opportunity to broadcast these beliefs before a global audience. That they chose to do so may have been uncomfortable to some Native Americans—an embarrassing admission of substantial internal Indian divisions and disagreement at a time when unity of purpose was so desperately needed. No one was more aware of this point than NCAI executive director Chuck Trimble. Rather than pointing a finger at AIM or the tribal chairs, which he feared would only serve to deepen the divisions further, Trimble argued that it was the federal government that sought to "polarize the Indian community of this nation, and sever that thread of hope that is the common cause of justice for all Indian people."[54] The federal government had absolutely proven its adeptness at such manipulations in the past, but during the BIA occupation crisis it had no need to promote divisions that already existed in abundance. Instead, during the BIA occupation crisis at least, the U.S. government simply capitalized on them.

In the years leading up to the Trail of Broken Treaties Caravan, tribal leaders had watched with anxiety—and likely a touch of envy—the growing national prominence of militant Indian groups such as AIM and the media's tendency, in Bob Robertson's words, to "go with the spectacular and the unreal."[55] Militant Indian groups, moreover, claimed that they—not tribal chairs—spoke for the broader Indian community, and the press provided the militants a national platform to recruit new members and circulate their particular vision of sovereignty and self-determination. The tribal chairs insisted that, as duly elected leaders, they should have primacy of comment—but they had to fight for that privilege with a national press that appeared more interested in drama and the spectacle of confrontation and occupation. While the timing may not have been ideal, the BIA occupation provided this opportunity. In short, the tribal chairs acted in their own best interests and what they considered was in the best interests of federally recognized tribes. One can legitimately criticize them for espousing these limited priorities, as well as the NTCA's nonconfrontational approach to reform based on establishing trust, building relationships with federal officials, and working within the system. The actions of the tribal chairs during the BIA occupation were in keeping with this strategy, but they irreparably tarnished the NTCA's reputation and strengthened existing perceptions that they had been co-opted and manipulated by the federal government.

The dissolution of the National Council on Indian Opportunity in June 1974 helped the tribal chairs to at least partially redeem the NTCA's reputation, but at a substantial cost. Like the Interior Department—if not the Nixon administration as a whole—the NCIO had sought to simplify the tribal-federal consultation process by identifying a single Native American voice or entity with whom federal authorities could negotiate. Bob Robertson, the NCIO's executive director, believed the tribal chairs' association "would become the most significant group with whom the federal government will deal in meeting the needs of reservation people." The close relationship that ensued (described by some as one of "mutual manipulation") was strongly criticized by other Indian rights organizations—especially the National Congress of American Indians—which resented the NTCA's growing access or "open door" to federal officials and its efforts (ostensibly with NCIO encouragement) to shut out the voices of other Indian organizations. The sense that the NTCA was supplanting the NCAI as "the Indian voice" on Capitol Hill was borne out in the composition of the NCIO itself. During its first four years (1968–72), the NCIO's Indian members had been selected almost exclusively from the leadership ranks of NCAI. By the end of 1972, however, not a single NCAI officer served on the council. Instead, five of the eight Indian members were affiliated with the NTCA.[56]

The NTCA proved to be a dependable ally to the NCIO and passed resolutions calling for the council to be "strengthened and expanded," and that Bob Robertson (who had announced his intention in November 1973 to step down from his post) be retained as its executive director "until such time an Indian person with comparable qualifications can be recruited." During the deliberations that surrounded the resolution, the chairs discussed how the "NCIO has been accused of dictating to the chairmen's association, which is not true." Sharing the same office space had been "a bad thing," however, which made it easy for critics to make these types of accusations. Going forward, the chairs noted, "We need to lay things on the line on how certain things happen, when we are not given a chance to give our side."[57]

Despite a last-ditch letter-writing campaign on the part of the NCIO's Indian members and the NTCA to persuade President Nixon to support an extension of the council's five-year life span, on June 30, 1974, the NCIO passed into history. The tribal chairs would miss having an advocate that fully embraced their position that the NTCA should be the exclusive voice of federally recognized tribes. They would also miss the NCIO's efforts to encourage federal agencies to expand their domestic assistance programs to tribal governments. That said, the council's dissolution liberated the NTCA from future accusations of NCIO co-optation and forced the tribal chairs to take a hard look at their insider-based advocacy strategy. That strategy, as the NTCA-NCIO relationship had demonstrated, could be interpreted negatively and produce unintended and unwelcome results.

The Impact Survey Team Debate

On November 7, 1972, after it had become clear that the interior of the BIA building was badly damaged and that irreplaceable documents had been destroyed, Louis Bruce wrote to the NCAI's Chuck Trimble requesting that he form an impact survey team to make an assessment of the occupation's financial and political costs and to formulate constructive plans for the future. Bruce asked that the team be composed of a "fair cross-section of the Indian community," including representatives from the BIA, from Indian organizations, and from tribal leaders. Three days later Trimble appeared before the National Press Club to deliver prepared remarks on the NCAI's activities during the BIA occupation. After explaining his role as a "conduit" for the transmission of OEO funds to Caravan representatives and chastising federal officials for their duplicitous behavior before and during the occupation, Trimble called on the NTCA "to reject the sinister and clandestine tactics of the conservative bureaucracy" and to participate as members of the Impact Survey Team. In keeping with the commissioner's request, Trimble also extended invitations to other Indian rights organizations, including AIM and the NIYC.[58]

The response of the tribal chairs was predictable. On November 20, Bill Youpee issued a memorandum to the NTCA executive board informing them about the creation of the NCAI-led Impact Survey Team and its intention to hold meetings later that week.[59] "NTCA is not participating in these meetings," Youpee explained, "since NTCA has plans already under way to make its own evaluation on the disruption of the BIA." The plan he had in mind was simple but not terribly imaginative—to have NTCA board members convene meetings with elected tribal leaders to solicit their views and recommendations. A second reason given for the NTCA's refusal to join the Impact Survey Team was also predictable. According to Youpee, "It was felt that since NTCA is an organization of elected tribal leaders and the legal spokesmen for the reservation Indians and Federally recognized tribes, the Federal Government should be consulting with NTCA" rather than the NCAI or the Impact Survey Team.[60]

The association's refusal to participate on the Impact Survey Team apparently did not prevent individual members from doing so. On the same day Youpee dispatched his memorandum to the NTCA executive board notifying them of the association's position, NTCA board member Peter MacDonald was named chair of the Impact Survey Team. As chair of the Navajos—the largest tribal nation in the country—MacDonald had the luxury of treading an independent path, which, on occasion, put him at odds with more conservative members of the NTCA. His advocacy for the creation of a "Truth Network" and placing the BIA under White House receivership, for example, had received rather tepid NTCA support. As a board member of the NTCA and chairman of the Impact Survey Team, MacDonald was faced with a rather profound conflict of interest and was hard-pressed to endorse the NTCA's position paper, which he refused to do. Of particular concern to the Navajo leader was the provision that the NTCA be the exclusive negotiating partner of the federal government as it pertained to Indian affairs. There were Navajos in Cleveland, Chicago, Los Angeles, and other areas, MacDonald declared, and he was ready to counsel with them "wherever they are." In a statement that likely knocked his fellow chairs out of their seats, MacDonald maintained that it was the NTCA's incessant demand that it alone represented all reservation-based Indians that had led to the BIA occupation in the first place. By trapping the BIA and Interior Department between the NTCA and other Indian groups, the tribal chairs had paralyzed the movement for meaningful reform. The association needed to be big and strong enough, and possess enough confidence, "to solicit all kinds of opinions." The NCAI also sought to contribute to the discussion, MacDonald concluded. "They do not want the chairmen's jobs. . . . They want to lend their expertise and thinking to what we are thinking, and we can discuss and talk about it."[61]

At an hourlong meeting with Secretary Morton held on the morning of December 8, 1972, NTCA executive board members learned that Commissioner Bruce, Deputy Commissioner John Crow, and Assistant Secretary Harrison Loesch had all decided to resign, retire, or accept positions elsewhere.[62] Morton touched briefly on the various reorganization plans that had been floated regarding the BIA and commented generally on the need to make "hard decisions" and to implement the "best ideas." The president's "whole philosophy," Morton added, was focused on "a new way to go; a whole new, better way to go." That "new" and "better" way included close collaboration with tribal chairs who, the secretary believed, "represented the hard-core, long-term established political base for communication with the central government by the Indian people." At that point, Morton put on a dazzling display of equivocation. Federal authorities would in no way "stiff arm" or "clip the wings" of any other organization seeking to influence Indian policy, the secretary noted, but there had to be "some well-established system of communication on policy matters with an organization that is permanent and one which has an elected, democratic structural base," and the NTCA should be the "lead agency of the Indian people." That said, making them the exclusive negotiating partner would negate his "open door policy" and "be a step backward." "We would be in tough shape," Morton argued, "if we said to AIM, NCAI, or any other organization, to stiff arm them and say we are not going to listen to you." Such an approach, he believed, would only polarize the Indian community further.[63]

There were apparently other forces at work here that explain Morton's reticence about working solely with the NTCA. According to journalist Richard LaCourse, Morton had met with representatives of the NCAI the very same day—presumably before his meeting with the tribal chairs. At the NCAI meeting, Native American leaders urged Morton to end his department's exclusive recognition of "the tribal leaders organization" and to consider forming an all-Indian task force to "redefine federal structures and Indian needs." As a result, Morton agreed to end the closed-door policy and "open his doors to other voices and groups within the total Indian community."[64] This development, a tacit admission that the government's partnership with the NTCA had indeed been polarizing to the nation's diverse Indian communities, may have been one of the most important outcomes in the wake of the Trail of Broken Treaties Caravan and BIA occupation.

The American Indian Policy Review Commission

The chaotic state of Indian affairs in the early 1970s led to calls for a "comprehensive review" of the historic relationship between tribes and the federal government. In July 1973 Senator James G. Abourezk introduced a joint resolution (S.J. 133) calling for the establishment of an American Indian Policy Review Commission (AIPRC) that would evaluate several critical aspects of federal Indian policy and make recommendations for improvement. Comprising fifteen members (five senators, five congressmen, and five Native Americans), the commission's professed purpose received the enthusiastic support of Indian leaders nationwide. That support splintered, however, over the selection of Indian participants on the commission. As envisioned, the AIPRC's Indian members would be broadly representative—three members would come from federally recognized tribes, one member would come from the urban community, and one would be from a nonrecognized tribe. Testifying at hearings held by the Senate Subcommittee on Indian Affairs, Vine Deloria Jr. recommended eliminating the three categories of Indian representation and to "leave it up to the wisdom of the congressional members chosen as to how they are going to pick the Indian members." Who represented the Indians, Deloria argued, was less important than selecting experienced people who knew what they were talking about.[65] The NCAI's Leon Cook, on the other hand, supported the idea that Native American representatives from different constituencies be included on the commission. When asked if he had any specific comments or suggestions about the selection process, Cook replied, "No, just to speed it up and get on with it."[66]

The NTCA took a decidedly different view—one that reflected its long-held insistence that the leaders of federally recognized tribes should be the exclusive voice in any discussion involving reservation-based Indian nations. Testifying before the Senate Subcommittee on July 19, 1973, Samson Miller (Mescalero) spoke on behalf of the Mescalero Apache Tribal Council and for NTCA. While commending the commission's creation as something long overdue and desperately needed, Miller asked that the Senate consider increasing the number of Indians on the commission from five to ten (or no less than seven), that five be members of federally recognized tribes, and that the NTCA be responsible for naming all Indian members. The NTCA, after all, was "the legitimate voice of the Indian people, and the only major group with clear credentials to speak for federally recognized tribes."[67]

President Ford signed S.J. 133 (P.L. 93-580) on January 2, 1975. The approved version called for a commission of eleven members—three from the House, three from the Senate, and five Indian members from the original three categories. At an NTCA Board of Directors meeting held a month later, the chairs' primary concern focused, not surprisingly, on the appointment of the commission's Indian members. After much discussion, a motion was made to recommend that the presidents of the NTCA (Wendell Chino) and NCAI (Mel Tonasket) be included as members on the commission, and the motion carried unanimously.[68] That conciliatory attitude changed abruptly following the announcement in early March of the commission's appointment of Ada Deer (Menominee), Jake White Crow (Quapah-Seneca), and John Borbridge (Tlingit) as the three members representing federally recognized tribes. None were NTCA members, none represented a large western tribe, and all three hailed from tribes lacking federal trust status.[69] Since the AIPRC would be making recommendations to Congress regulating Indian treaties, laws, courts, and natural resources, Wendell Chino maintained, "tribes with vast resources should have input and be directly involved in the commission." Without that input, he cautioned, the commission "may well close their ears" to the opinions of western tribes.[70]

When NTCA resolutions, letter-writing campaigns, and requests for a meeting with President Ford failed to secure new Indian representation on the AIPRC, the chairs filed suit on May 20, 1975, in the U.S. District Court in the District of Columbia asking for an injunction halting the commission's operation on the grounds that the Indian members appointed did not truly represent the interests of a majority of American Indian tribes. The suit charged, furthermore, that the appointments were unconstitutional since Article II, section 2 of the U.S. Constitution authorized only the president (not Congress) to appoint "officers of the United States."[71] Although the case (*NTCA v. Abourezk*) was ultimately dismissed on the grounds that Congress has plenary power in Indian affairs, the legal maneuver succeeded in delaying the AIPRC from commencing its work.[72]

The chairs' lawsuit against the AIPRC had additional consequences. Fault lines within the association were exposed after some NTCA members claimed that they had not been informed about the executive board's actions and they did not agree with the lawsuit. Navajo leader Peter MacDonald continued to demonstrate his maverick inclinations not only by criticizing the suit but by agreeing to serve on one of the AIPRC's many task forces. Senator James Abourezk, who had never been particularly supportive of the NTCA, suggested that the chairs' lawsuit had been inspired by BIA leaders who felt threatened by the commission's close scrutiny. In a news piece published in the *Albuquerque Journal,* Abourezk played on the popular perception that the NTCA was a tool of the federal government. After reminding readers that the NTCA was funded by the BIA, Abourezk claimed it was "general knowledge in the Indian community they [the BIA] are behind the court challenge."[73]

While association members (with the exception of Peter MacDonald) did not formally participate in the AIPRC, they kept a close eye on its deliberations. In mid-October 1976 the NTCA Board of Directors created a six-person committee to review the commission's work, a herculean task given the volume of materials generated by the AIPRC's various work groups. A month later, the

NTCA committee produced a three-page summary that listed various concerns with some of the AIPRC's recommendations, many centered on the charge that the recommendations lacked sufficient documentation or support. AIPRC Task Force Three, for instance, which had examined the federal administration and structure of Indian affairs, had recommended the establishment of a seat in Congress for a nonvoting delegate representing Indian tribes and the creation of an independent agency to replace the BIA. The NTCA committee disagreed with both recommendations, especially the latter. Citing "serious questions and misgivings" about the creation of a replacement for the BIA, the chairs argued that the AIPRC's study of BIA management, which had been conducted by a private consulting firm, was "misleading and incomplete." The AIPRC's recommendations for reservation economic development, meanwhile, "lacked adequate documentation or support" and "were of such a general nature to be of little or no value." The NTCA committee criticized AIPRC recommendations regarding tribal justice and jurisdictional matters as incomplete due to the commission's "failure to deal meaningfully" with the complex jurisdictional problems of Oklahoma tribes.[74]

The NTCA committee's review of the AIPRC's recommendations for reforming Indian education were particularly damning. Alarmed with the commission's apparent implication that the U.S. government had "a special and unique responsibility for the education of *all* Indians," the chairs maintained that no such responsibility existed except for federally recognized tribes. Expressing their oft-repeated criticism about the ongoing ambiguity and confusion about the definition of what exactly constitutes an Indian, the chairs maintained "There are too many American citizens who are declaring themselves to be American Indian in order to be eligible for monies intended for American Indian tribal members." In an explicit statement of their stance on this controversial issue, the chairs declared, "The National Tribal Chairmen's Association's position is that American Indians are only those persons who are members of federally recognized tribes" and that "such tribes shall determine their own membership." Going a step further down the road of exclusivity, the chairs demanded that "federal agencies, states, and other organizations such as foundations must accept the above definition and modify by amendment of rules and regulations any divergency."[75]

Although NTCA leaders were on target with their criticisms that the AIPRC did not adequately represent the interests of federally recognized tribes (particularly large tribes located west of the Mississippi River) and that there had been inadequate consultation with tribal leaders, their persistent claims to be the exclusive body and "legitimate voice" for Indian tribes was divisive and simply untenable. The association never had more than 175 to 200 tribal chairs as members, but there were twice that number of federally recognized tribes (along with tribal chairs who held membership solely in the NCAI). How could the NTCA claim to speak for them? Like the Nixon administration as a whole, the NTCA's refusal to give consideration to the legitimate needs of Native Americans who had left (or been relocated) from reservations was a serious miscalculation that unnecessarily fomented opposition from half the Indian population in the country. The tribal chairs' role during the BIA occupation (whether the government put them up to it or not) further polarized an already badly fractured Indian population and solidified the opinions of Indian rights activists like AIM's Clyde Bellecourt that the NTCA was in the government's "back pocket." The chairs' refusal to participate on the Impact Survey Team and its efforts to block the American Indian Policy Review Commission, while consistent with its claims to be the exclusive negotiator and voice for reservation-based Indian nations, evinced a distinctly puerile quality that alienated potential allies such as the NCAI. As Peter MacDonald noted at the time, the NTCA had to reach out to Native Americans from all walks of life and be "big and strong enough" to deal with its critics in an intelligent and professional manner. In reply, Robert Jim (Yakama) reminded MacDonald that the association "was formed to represent the land base, not to touch base with several Indian organizations." Webster Two Hawk agreed. "Our concern should be for all landed reservations and federally recognized tribes. NTCA does not pretend to speak for anybody else. . . . NTCA is not a Pan-Indian organization. We do not want to become diffused; we have a purpose."[76]

Chapter 5

Backlash

On November 21, 1973, President Richard Nixon sent a message of greeting to the tribal chairs assembled in Phoenix for the second annual convention of the National Tribal Chairmen's Association. Avoiding even a hint about the previous year's tense and politically charged occupations of the Bureau of Indian Affairs (BIA) building and Wounded Knee, the president instead enumerated his administration's many accomplishments since the delivery of his July 1970 Special Message to Congress.

> Important lands have been restored to the Taos Pueblo and the Yakama Nation. We have a fair and very promising Alaska Native Claims Settlement Act on the statute books. Major cases for the protection of Indian interests have been won in the Supreme Court and in lower courts. The budgets of the Federal agencies administering Indian programs have been significantly increased, the BIA's own budget going up by 224% since FY 1969. Knowledgeable and sympathetic men and women are working with Indian policy matters in many of the departments of Government, and a new Commissioner of Indian Affairs, Morris Thompson, himself an Alaska native, is taking office.

Before signing off, the president promised to continue "working to meet the needs of Indian people by measures which grow out of the closest consultation with responsible Indian leaders." Presented at the convention by Nixon aide Bradley Patterson, the letter was apparently "very well accepted" by the "responsible Indian leaders" in attendance.[1]

Nixon's expression of goodwill, however, masked a very different phenomenon that was beginning to take root across Indian Country, a phenomenon based on fear, resentment, envy, racism, and ignorance. Reid Chambers, head of the Indian Division in the Interior Department's Solicitor's Office, likened the phenomenon to "storm clouds on the horizon" and as an approaching "counterforce" that would "run through the country like a shock."[2] In part a reaction to the very types of accomplishments trumpeted by Nixon in his letter to the NTCA and in part to the confrontational tactics employed by some Native American activists, an anti-Indian backlash movement emerged in the early 1970s, expanded during the latter part of the decade, and continues (albeit in lesser form and influence) to the present day. This is not to say that any critique of Indian activism or of Indian Country was a product of the backlash, but that the various anti-Indian organizations that sprung up at the time invariably were. The backlash phenomenon constituted perhaps the greatest threat to tribal sovereignty and treaty rights since the introduction of termination legislation in the post–World War II era. The central aim of this chapter is to examine the origins, strategies, and goals of backlash adherents and to assess the NTCA's reaction. The threat posed by the backlash, as we will see, required a united response on the part of national Indian organizations, the type of collaboration that the NTCA had heretofore resisted. Did this position change? What lessons did Indian leaders take from the backlash crisis of the 1970s, and how did they apply them afterward?

Origins and Typologies of Backlash

Like any movement or event in history, the anti-Indian movement of the 1970s was a creature of complex economic, social, and political forces. Anti-Indian backlash, in other words, did not just appear out of nowhere. To many Americans in the late 1960s and early 1970s, the country seemed hopelessly divided. New Left liberals placed their faith in government to promote equality and opportunity, while New Right conservatives maintained that government was a threat both to states' rights and to individual liberties. Americans questioned the Johnson and Nixon administrations' handling of the war in Vietnam, worried about the growth of a military-industrial complex, argued over the appropriate response to the civil rights movement, and fretted about the nation's growing dependence on foreign oil. Middle- and working-class Americans felt especially pinched. The government, in their view, had one eye affixed on addressing the needs of the poor while the other focused on appeasing the rich. Their needs, consequently, appeared to be ignored or forgotten.

The modern Indian rights movement was born within this volatile milieu of protest, change, and anxiety and, like other reform efforts of the time, left its own enduring marks on the history and memory of the period. As a result of Great Society community action initiatives and the gradual shift to self-determination-oriented policies, tribes began assuming greater responsibility for programs that had formerly been administered by the federal government. Tribal governments, meanwhile, began to actively assert control over reservation lands, resources, and tribal members, as well as the activities of nonmembers and non-Indians within reservation borders. They also began to seek recognition and fulfillment of treaty rights that had long been ignored or forgotten.[3] While Indian activism had roots stretching back into the late nineteenth century, the sudden rise to prominence of Red Power–inspired protests and the much-heralded occupations of Alcatraz, the BIA building, and Wounded Knee brought their reform efforts unprecedented publicity and attention. "It is sad that the American Indian Movement [AIM] has to use these tactics," AIM's Eddie Benton (Chippewa) explained in an October 1971 interview, but they are "necessary to get the attention of a totally apathetic society."[4]

Other Indian leaders followed a different path. Bob Carr (Laguna Pueblo), director of the Upper Midwest American Indian Center in Minneapolis, argued that militant Indians were interested primarily in the publicity; they were "followers of the black movement" and weren't serious when it came to the hard work of reform. "I've never seen any of them [AIM members] involved in long-term constructive activities. If Indians hope to accomplish anything," he concluded, "there's got to be some planning."[5] National organizations such as the NTCA and the National Congress of American Indians (NCAI) provided this long-term planning along with the critical follow-through by lobbying Congress, testifying before committees, drafting and amending legislation, organizing conferences, and mobilizing their constituents to press for fundamental changes in federal Indian policy. Largely through these efforts the Nixon administration embraced self-determination without termination; land restoration for Taos Pueblo, the Yakama Nation, the Havasupi Nation, the Confederated Tribes of Warm Springs, and Native Alaskans; greater Indian control over the education of their children; expanded funding for reservation development; and stronger protections of Indian-owned lands and resources. In 1974 a federal judge issued a historic ruling (the *Boldt* decision) reaffirming the rights of Washington's Indian tribes to fish in accustomed places and allocated half of the state's annual catch to tribes. From the perspective of many, if not most, Native Americans, these developments were steps in the right direction, but the federal government still had a ways to go in fulfilling its trust responsibilities to Native nations.

Non-Indians living on or near reservations, on the other hand, grew increasingly apprehensive about the federal government's apparent willingness to concede to tribal demands for sovereignty and self-determination. From the perspective of some non-Indians, such behavior constituted preferential treatment for an undeserving minority group that invariably came at the expense of "regular" or "un-hyphenated" Americans. If left unchecked, these unwelcomed expressions of Indian self-confidence and assertiveness threatened to upend the status quo in Indian-white relations, to curtail access to tribal lands and resources, and to recalibrate the power imbalance that had historically skewed in their favor. During the early 1970s, therefore, an anti-Indian movement developed in many parts of the country marked by a combination of one or more of the following categories or typologies of backlash.

1. *Land-resource backlash.* Practitioners of this category of backlash were most concerned with tribal land restoration efforts or securing or maintaining access to Indian-owned lands and resources. In 1975, for example, a suit filed by the Passamaquoddy and Penobscot tribes of Maine brought a decision that the tribes had a potentially meritorious claim to nearly 60 percent of the state.[6] Non-Indian leaseholders of tribal grazing and other agricultural lands, meanwhile, often rented the most productive tracts on the reservation but paid rental amounts that fell far below the market average for such arrangements.[7] Any change to this process was obviously not in their financial interest. Water rights—particularly in the arid Southwest—was also a hotly contested issue frequently pitting the interests of large metropolitan areas and states against those of tribes. Land-resource backlash was especially prevalent among hunting and fishing enthusiasts, commercial and sport fishing organizations, and related businesses that resented the "special" rights accorded to tribes. The *Boldt* decision, in particular, was a cause célèbre among this group. At times, conservationist groups contributed to the backlash based on concerns that Native Americans were inefficient managers of natural resources and that cash-strapped tribes would permit logging, mining, or oil exploration activities on reservation lands. Other groups focused their attention on restricting traditional subsistence hunting practices, especially in Alaska, that they believed posed a threat to endangered species.[8]

2. *Antisovereignty backlash*. Adherents of this form of backlash adopted the position of President Andrew Jackson in the 1830s—that tribal sovereignty was a myth and that the anomalous condition of sovereign Indian nations residing within the boundaries of states was impractical and contrary to the national interest. Antisovereignty proponents argued that the legitimacy of treaties with Indian nations was suspect, that "alien tribal governments" had no authority to tax or regulate the behavior of nonmembers, and that states be empowered to extend their jurisdiction over reservations. Similar to the terminationists of the post-WWII era, antisovereignty groups employed patriotic and even civil rights rhetoric to promote their goals—for example, termination would liberate Native Americans, All Americans should be equal and no group should be treated as "super citizens," the United States is one nation under God, reservations promoted segregation akin to Red apartheid.[9]

3. *Elitist backlash*. This brand of backlash stressed the notion that Native Americans were poor stewards of their lands and were squandering precious resources. The federal government, in their view, was wasting time and money trying to sustain inept tribal governments that were tyrannical and corrupt. Elitists likened the provision of government social services to tribes as "from womb to the tomb pampering," all at taxpayer expense.[10] Native Americans would be far better served, in their view, by vacating reservations, getting jobs, and joining the mainstream. Elitists viewed tribal cultures and traditions as superstitions, barbaric, and backward. The very existence of a non-Western belief system, rooted in the middle of the most powerful Western nation, was seen as a fundamental obstacle to overcome. Reminiscent of the Carlisle Indian School's Richard H. Pratt, they espoused a philosophy of "killing the Indian to save the man."[11]

4. *Law-and-order backlash*. This particular category of backlash was inspired by the confrontational activism of Indian rights groups such as AIM and Indians of All Tribes. According to one adherent, Indian activists appeared to be "trying to reestablish the archaic term *savage* as a description of the Indian" by engaging in such activities.[12] In the aftermath of the Wounded Knee occupation, conservative activist Floyd Paxton went so far as to argue that AIM was both a terrorist organization and a "communist tool" sponsored by the government "to serve communist purposes."[13] Although this brand of backlash was ostensibly directed

only at activist groups, adherents believed that funds appropriated for Indian programs should be diverted to pay for damages caused by their activities. Proponents of law and order arguments consequently used the threat of backlash as a means of regulating Indian behavior and modes of protest.

5. *Racist-inspired backlash.* This form of backlash was the most insidious and prevalent, to some degree, in all its various manifestations. This included not only vicious slurs toward and violent harassment of Native Americans but also the widespread charge that Indians were inferior, slothful, unintelligent, drunkards, childlike, bloodthirsty, and in desperate need of guidance from the Great White Father. Anti-Indian groups sought to make an issue out of Indian people who looked white, accusing them of using their "blood quantum" to secure government benefits. The declining number of full-bloods on reservations, meanwhile, indicated that the population of "real Indians" was minute and that reservations were no longer necessary. Aware that charges of racism could undercut their appeal, most anti-Indian groups went to great lengths to deny any trace of racism and pointed to members whose great-grandmothers were Cherokee, for example, or who had "close friends who happen to be Indian" to prove their point.[14]

Although not a standalone category, a final characteristic of at least some people involved in the anti-Indian backlash movement was an incomplete or erroneous understanding of Native American history or the history of federal-Indian relations. This knowledge deficit enabled backlash organizers to advance seemingly compelling narratives based on half-truths, omissions, and falsehoods that they couched in patriotic and libertarian rhetoric for political effect.

The precise genesis of the anti-Indian backlash movement is difficult to identify with any precision. Initially, backlash was confined to local organizations combatting tribal initiatives specific to their location. Not until the mid-1970s did these widely dispersed organizations coalesce into regional and national bodies that served as umbrella organizations for local groups. This consolidation of backlash groups was at least partly in response to a surge in the number of tribal lawsuits filed during this time. During the 1960s the Department of the Interior had been involved in approximately ten to twenty cases annually on behalf of tribal nations. By 1976, however, the department was involved in nearly two hundred.[15]

An example of the nascent anti-Indian backlash movement was the response accorded to a tribal council's decision to levy a modest charge for individuals seeking to hunt, fish, or encamp on Montana's Flathead Reservation. In March 1969 the tribal council of the Confederated Salish and Kootenai Tribes passed an ordinance requiring nontribal members to purchase a five-dollar annual permit to enter designated parts of the reservation for recreational purposes. Three months later, area whites formed a backlash organization—Flathead Residents Earning Equality (FREE)—to protest the ordinance, which they claimed violated their rights. As time passed, FREE employed various arguments, most falling under the antisovereignty, elitist, and racist categories of backlash. For example, FREE spokespersons maintained that the tribal council had mismanaged and failed to invest in developing the reservation and was dependent upon federal assistance. Since public funds had been used to develop recreational areas on the reservation (to stock the rivers and lakes with fish and to build roads), "nondiscriminatory use" of the reservation was a public right. "It is the middle of the 20th century and not the days of the buffalo," remarked one FREE official. "We think this fee permit plan is no more appropriate than it would be for tribal members to pay a toll to use the facilities provided by nontribal members." Some FREE members questioned whether the Salish and Kootenai residents of the Flathead Reservation were actually Indians in the first place. According to FREE organizer Del Palmer, "If one is less than half Indian he is non-Indian," and since "there are only some 86 full bloods on the reservation . . . the reservation has outlived its intended life span and should now be terminated."[16]

Throughout the decade of the 1970s, local backlash organizations such as FREE sprouted up across the Pacific Northwest, the Northern Great Plains, the Upper Midwest, the Southwest, and along the East Coast. Most were not particularly long-lived, and after a few years of protest, they either disbanded, re-created themselves, or were absorbed by larger, better-financed backlash organizations. Like the lifecycle of the cicada bug, they started out underground and remained dormant for an extended period only to surface, briefly make a lot of noise, and then die. Unfortunately, their progeny then repeated the cycle. FREE, for example, morphed into Montanans Opposing Discrimination (MOD) in 1974.[17] MOD, in turn, provided inspiration two years later for the creation of a relatively powerful multistate backlash organization: the Interstate Congress for Equal Rights and Responsibilities (ICERR). ICERR helped refine the anti-Indian movement's message, making it more sophisticated and, in some ways, deceptively attractive. First, it portrayed tribal members as "super citizens" enjoying rights above the rest of the populace. While acknowledging the many wrongs perpetrated against Native Americans throughout history, ICERR insisted that the present generation should not feel guilty and "stumble over its tears" nor be held accountable for the sins of the past. In its "Declaration of Purpose," ICERR employed patriotic rhetoric to lend credibility to its cause. In a double whammy aimed at the rights of tribal governments to tax nonmembers and the rights of Native Americans to participate in state politics when they were exempted from most state taxes, ICERR condemned both "taxation without representation and representation without taxation" as unconstitutional. The Declaration of Purpose pronounced that the constitutional rights of all Americans superseded treaty rights, called for the application of state and local laws to all reservations, and demanded that reservation boundaries not be extended. Lastly, the ICERR Declaration of Purpose advocated a prohibition of government funding for Native Americans or "to any group of people based upon their race." Given the group's well-known stance on tribal sovereignty and treaty rights, arguments about funding based on the government's trust responsibilities would likely have fallen on deaf ears as well.[18]

If anti-Indian backlash movements such as ICERR had confined their activities to writing letters to newspaper editors, holding meetings, and passing out pamphlets, the threat they posed to Native nations would have been marginal. But this was not the case. As time passed the purported size of organizations such as ICERR and like-minded backlash organizations such as Protect Americans' Rights and Resources (PARR), Totally Equal Americans (TEA), and Citizens Equal Rights Alliance (CERA) numbered in the tens of thousands. In low-population states like Montana, North Dakota, South Dakota, Wyoming, and Nebraska, their lobbying efforts at the state and national levels were significant and consequential. "Our intentions are to make an effort at home to make our congressmen more accountable to and have more respect for the views of the voters," stated ICERR's Jack Freeman. We want "to ask our congressmen to reassess their positions and the problems." In addition, ICERR intended to challenge tribal rights in court. According to Freeman, each of the states attending a February 1976 backlash summit in Salt Lake City had a "substantial legal battery to screen and determine which cases to bring to trial."[19] No one understood this reality and the very real threat the backlash movement posed better than did tribal chairs and the leaders of national Indian organizations. How they responded to the backlash and the effectiveness of that response is the focus of the remainder of this chapter.

The Borgstrom Memorandum

Howard G. Borgstrom seemed an unlikely candidate to become a focal point in the anti-Indian backlash movement of the 1970s. A 1970 graduate of Wesleyan University's College of Social Studies, Borgstrom took a position two years later as a budget analyst for the Office of Management and Budget's (OMB) Interior Branch. At some point during the spring of 1976, Borgstrom received an assignment to draft a "think piece" on the appropriate structure for the implementation of federal Indian programs. He apparently had a collaborator or assembled a team (the subsequent report references its authors as "we") that sensibly concluded that the selection of a strategy for federal Indian policy must precede any determination of structure. To that end, Borgstrom and his collaborator(s) drafted a paper bearing the title "Organization for Indian Affairs" that actually focused on two possible strategies: long-range social problem-solving and incrementalism.[20]

Borgstrom was no politician and, not surprisingly, approached the assignment in a manner befitting a budget analyst—analytically, objectively, and dispassionately. The long-range social problem-solving strategy assumed that the government's role in policy formation was to identify a problem, prescribe a measurable end-state or goal, and then implement a strategy to bring about its realization. As applied to federal Indian programs, this involved closing the gap that existed between Indians and non-Indians in the realms of housing, education, health, and employment. Once needs-testing demonstrated that the gap was closed, federal programs would no longer be needed and the agency responsible for closing the gap (in this instance—the BIA) would become obsolete.[21]

Borgstrom's report recognized that employing the long-range social problem-solving strategy (or "social engineering strategy") faced stiff headwinds. First, Native Americans were sure to oppose any plan that called into question the "perpetual Federal-Indian relationship" and that failed to recognize federal trust obligations, tribal sovereignty, and the need for federal protections against state encroachments on Indian rights. Second, the current emphasis on Indian self-determination was not "end state"–oriented but was instead a policy geared toward strengthening tribal governments and removing the threat of termination. Third, the authors took a dim view of the capacity of the reservation-based Indian population—even if "properly pre-pared" by "social interventionist policies"—to make the transition from depen-dence on federal assistance to independence and self-reliance. Given these limitations, the long-range social problem-solving strategy would require an end to self-determination policies and the reinstatement of relocation policies, the gradual termination of federal assistance based on both reservation and individual needs testing, and the expansion of state control over the provision of health, education, and law enforcement services to reservations. Federal rec-ognition for any new tribal aspirants, Borgstrom argued, would need to end, tribal assets allotted in severalty, and school curriculums be oriented toward the assimilation of Indian children. In short, the Borgstrom report appeared to endorse the reapplication of virtually all the most controversial and devastating federal Indian policies of the late nineteenth century and post-WWII eras—policies that the authors admitted had already been tried "and are perceived to have failed." Why they had failed was not specifically discussed, but the clear implication was that it was due to faulty implementation rather than defective design. For that reason, the proposed long-range social problem-solving strat-egy would be executed not by tribal leaders or the BIA, but by "a permanent entity of 50–100 social science professionals, lawyers, and administrators" who would "impose these policies on the Indian community."[22]

The second proposed strategy—the "incrementalist strategy"—was an ambiguous one but apparently did not require "radical policy shifts" nor the abandonment of the self-determination ideal. Instead, it focused on the "per-ceptions and motives of the Indian people" as the major determinants of their futures and, significantly, that these perceptions and motives could be influ-enced to change over time. To some extent this strategy appears to utilize what Scott Lyons (Leech Lake Ojibwe) has termed "rhetorical imperialism"—the assertion of control over others by setting the terms of debate.[23] For exam-ple, the definition of self-determination could be broadened to include not only tribal choice but individual or local choice as well, and federal policies could therefore be geared toward altering socioeconomic conditions at any of these three levels. Terms such as "sovereignty" and "entitlement," meanwhile, should be viewed as "reference points" rather than as "basic" or "unconditional princi-ples." Indian perceptions and motives could likewise (somehow) be molded by avoiding dichotomies (e.g., a tribe is either recognized or not recognized; a resource is in trust or not in trust) and stressing continuums (Indians have a spiritual connection with the natural environment; Indians have a deep reverence for tribal traditions). "Actions taken under this strategy," the writers concluded, "are tentative, experimental, and correctable. Promises are modest, delivery is evaluated. The level of commitment is essentially rational and conditional, not emotional or moral."[24]

On April 19, 1976, Borgstrom submitted the confidential memorandum to James L. Mitchell, assistant OMB director for natural resources, energy, and science. Exactly who reviewed the document afterward is unknown, but someone leaked it to the press. In mid-July, the *Confederated Umatilla Journal* of Pendelton, Oregon, ran a front-page article under the title "Covert White House Plan Sees Tribal Termination," which cited the Borgstrom memorandum and its controversial contents as "the Ford policy," the "Ford proposals," and "the Ford objectives." Similar pieces ran in the *Santa Fe New Mexican* and the *Arizona Republic* a week later. In the latter publication, Borgstrom stated he had no idea how the memo was leaked and that it was not a plan of action but a "general background discussion piece." That it had caused "a bit of controversy" within Indian circles was unfortunate since "the memo is not a recommendation for anything" and was intended for internal OMB circulation only.[25]

The timing and subject matter of the controversial Borgstrom memorandum were especially embarrassing, of course, to the Ford administration. On July 14, just two days before the president was scheduled to meet with Indian leaders, word arrived at the White House that the *Confederated Umatilla Journal* had scooped the story and published the memorandum in its entirety. In hopes of containing the expected fallout, the Interior Department's R. Dennis Ickes suggested that the president emphasize that "notwithstanding the private views of a small minority of non-policymaking persons, there is no intent or policy to terminate or negatively alter the special Federal relationship with Indian tribes."[26] During President Ford's subsequent meeting with tribal leaders, he chose not to mention the Borgstrom memorandum but did acknowledge the government's trust responsibilities, voice support for self-determination, and declared that he was "strongly opposed to termination." Indians in attendance likely appreciated these sentiments, but some took issue with the fact that they were not allowed to ask questions or make statements of their own. From the perspective of the NCAI's Mel Tonasket (Colville), the meeting was little more than a photo op for the administration and that he and his colleagues were being used for political purposes. At a sidewalk press conference held outside the White House, Tonasket suggested that President Ford was "not informed on the illegal actions of his underlings"—an oblique reference, perhaps, to the Borgstrom memorandum.[27]

On October 14 the NTCA convened a board meeting in Washington, D.C., where tribal chairs took the opportunity to grill White House aide Bradley Patterson about the memorandum. Of particular concern was the troubling fact that the document was conceived at the very time the anti-Indian backlash movement appeared to be gaining momentum. Was this mere coincidence, or was federal Indian policy now reflecting the views of ICERR and its ilk? A flustered Patterson responded defensively with a wide-ranging critique of the Borgstrom memorandum. First, he described Borgstrom unflatteringly as an analyst "four levels down in the OMB" and insisted that it was incorrect to suggest that the study was a product of the White House. Second, he described the memo as "written in the most atrocious English, it is hard to read, and plow through and understand." Third, he argued that Borgstrom had not actually made any concrete recommendations but had instead discussed theoretical strategies, some of which (e.g., incrementalism) did not make any sense. "It has not got any status in OMB, it has not got any status in the White House. It is not a plan, it is not a recommendation," Patterson maintained. What did matter, he insisted, were the president's remarks of July 16, which made clear that the administration was not interested in termination nor in ceasing assistance to Indian people.[28]

Patterson's protestations that the Borgstrom memorandum "did not merit any concern among Indian people" given its lack of status within the Ford White House failed to alleviate the concerns of the NTCA board. Joe Delacruz (Quinault) was especially persistent that the White House rebut the memorandum by taking a more aggressive public stand in support of Indian rights. Specifically, he urged Patterson to ask the president to issue a statement in support of the *Boldt* decision. Patterson was wary of this sensitive topic, however, and responded evasively or pretended to be confused about what the Quinault leader was requesting. With the presidential election just a few weeks off and polls indicating a close race, Ford would not risk alienating voters in the Pacific Northwest with a politically charged pronouncement in favor of the ruling. Instead, Patterson went on the counterattack. "Don't imply that we are going to weasel," he replied. The *Boldt* decision was "the law of the land as far as the President is concerned" and he had taken an oath to uphold and defend the Constitution. That being the case, no additional statement was necessary.[29]

Bill Youpee then opened a new line of inquiry concerning a September 9 meeting of executive branch officials, including Patterson, with several representatives from ICERR. Why had the meeting taken place, and what did they want? Patterson responded that the government was "always open for the presentation of views by citizens" and that the ICERR group consisted of between fifteen and twenty individuals from several western states. What transpired was basically a roundtable discussion with a series of presentations that focused on overturning the *Boldt* decision and on various jurisdictional matters such as Indian jurisdiction over non-Indian lands on reservations. "I wouldn't characterize them as "rednecks" or as "violent or vitriolic people," Patterson declared, but as "very concerned and very articulate and very strong in their convictions." Even so, he continued, "we gave then absolutely no encouragement that we would back off on anything in Indian trust rights." Just what the organization wanted was unclear. The ICERR reps had promised to draft a list of their specific goals for the federal government to consider but had not yet done so. Patterson then made a rather absurd recommendation that the NTCA authorize one of its members to arrange a sit-down with an ICERR leader and "to try to probe him about what kinds of things he has on his mind" and to "build a little link of communication" between the two organizations.[30]

Patterson's meeting with tribal leaders at the NTCA board meeting seems to have contained the fallout from the Borgstrom memorandum, although suspicions remained that anonymous White House insiders could say "foolish things like that" and inspire others to act on them.[31] Tribal leaders, in short, would need to redouble their vigilance or the next Borgstrom memorandum could very well become the federal government's new Indian policy. The chairs were understandably noncommittal about establishing any type of relationship with a backlash group such as ICERR, given the organization's record of anti-Indian rhetoric and ongoing efforts to undermine tribal sovereignty and treaty rights. Rather than opening a "little link of communication" with backlash groups, the NTCA and other Indian organizations instead worked to counter their divisive campaign of half-truths, fear mongering, and misinformation with a wide-ranging effort to educate the broader public and their elected representatives about the meaning of tribal sovereignty and the historic basis of the government's trust responsibilities to Native peoples.

Unilateral NTCA Responses to Backlash

As the anti-Indian backlash movement expanded during the mid-1970s, the NTCA responded in diverse ways—some innovative, some proactive, and some rather self-serving. During the summer of 1976, for example, the NTCA headquarters established a legislative monitoring system to track Indian-related bills and resolutions that had been introduced in Congress. At a time when desktop computers were still in their infancy, the NTCA's "system" was basically two file cabinets with color-coded folders (green for Senate bills; blue for House bills) and a status display board that tracked where precisely a bill was in the legislative process. Although establishing the monitoring system was a tedious and timely process that took nearly four months, it was extremely organized and well thought out, with a subject matter index that provided a cross-reference to the bills filed according to their assigned number. While quaint by today's standards, the system worked reasonably well and allowed NTCA officials to keep a close eye on backlash-related legislation.[32]

The tribal chairs also sought to combat the backlash by lobbying both major parties to include an NTCA-drafted plank in their respective 1976 platforms. Each of these Indian planks—they were identical—declared the party's recognition of the government's trust responsibilities, its support for Indian cultures and traditions, its acknowledgment of the principle of quasi-sovereignty of Indian tribes, and recognition of the legislative, executive, and judicial decisions of tribal governments. True to form, the association's recommended Indian plank also called for each party to support the principles enunciated in the NTCA's *American Indian World* position paper and to declare its recognition "that it is only through the elected tribal government that an Indian tribe can endure as a viable reality in the political structure of the United States." After all, these governments "represent the national voice of Indian people by whom they are elected and to whom they are accountable."[33]

As discussed previously, a frequent backlash complaint during the 1970s was the perceived injustice of tribal governments exercising jurisdiction over both Indian- and non-Indian-owned lands within the boundaries of a reservation. A pamphlet distributed by Montanans Opposing Discrimination (MOD), for example, described tribal laws and ordinances as promoting "ever expanding inequities and infringements upon the property and individual rights of citizens."[34] In hopes of diffusing jurisdictional-related tensions between Indian and non-Indian communities, the NTCA collaborated with Dale Wing (Fort Peck Sioux) of the Law Enforcement Assistance Administration about hosting a national conference to discuss jurisdiction problems that were common to reservations (especially in western states) and to draft a "uniform model tribal civil and criminal code." The entire process would likely take two years to complete, but in the end the "model tribal code" would clarify jurisdictional issues in hopes that "if the other side knows what the law is, then they won't have the problems associated with the distrust currently that exists between them [and tribal governments]." While a completely rationale and progressive idea, the proposed conference never got off the ground. The reason may partly be attributed to the election of Jimmy Carter and the initiative being lost or forgotten amid the transition process of a new administration, but the reality was that groups like ICERR would not likely be persuaded that "Indian law isn't that bad." According to remarks by ICERR attorney Thomas Tobin, even if Indian tribal codes were perfect and the tribal governments' administration of justice unblemished, non-Indians would still not want to be subject to them. For that reason, backlash organizations increasingly sought to mount challenges to tribal authority via Congress, a particularly worrisome development. "Once the non-Indian community begins the legislative process," the chairs mused, "the simple political fact is there are more of them than there are of us."[35]

In May 1976 the NTCA board convened a meeting on the Miccosukee Reservation in southern Florida and formulated several specific objectives to be accomplished during the remainder of 1976 and 1977. One of these objectives—Objective Ten—was a response to the backlash movement and called for developing programs to acquaint state and local governments and citizens with the nature and scope of tribal sovereignty and the trust relationship.[36] According to Buffalo Tiger, chair of the Miccosukee Business Committee and the meeting's host, the underlying cause of backlash was "the general ignorance in America about Indian traditions and legitimate Indian historic and legal rights. There is no general understanding in the non-Indian community of the federal government's trust relationship to Indian tribes. There is almost total ignorance of the quasi-sovereign status of Indian tribes."[37] This assessment closely paralleled the one contained in Objective Ten, which stated that the backlash movement was based on fear, not on facts. Backlash groups, the chairs argued, "are playing on the fears of people who do not know the facts of what tribal sovereignty really means to them and how it would affect their lives." To address this problem, tribal leaders laid out a plan to "tell our story" factually and rationally as opposed to the "shrill emotional arguments" emanating from backlash organizations. One specific target was members of Congress and their staffs. Objective Ten called on tribal leaders to call on their congressional representatives when they visited the Capitol, to invite them to come to their reservation, and then to follow up with monthly correspondence. These conversations were to be conducted in a statespersonlike manner and be a "learning, positively reinforcing experience" for the congressperson.[38]

Objective Ten also contained an ambitious agenda for national outreach. This included forming a speakers' pool of tribal chairs who would make themselves available to address non-Indian groups, the preparation of radio scripts and contacting radio stations about their availability, and a plan to contact local, regional, and national newspapers and to cultivate relationships with editors. To manage and coordinate these efforts, the NTCA contacted the National Association of Counties (NACo) and the BIA. NACo agreed to assist the tribal chairs in their open dialogues with county commissioners, while the BIA promised to use its public information program to make more facts about tribal governments and treaty rights available to the public and the media.[39]

The NTCA also proposed shooting a twenty-eight-minute backlash film and three public service announcements to give Indians a medium through which "to speak to others about what it meant to be a tribal member" in contemporary America. The proposed film and announcements would "communicate an experience of pride and strength in heritage" and, if done properly, would "elicit respect and appreciation for American Indians as people." Specific issues to be discussed included tribal sovereignty, the federal trust responsibility, land claims, water rights, and tribal jurisdiction. After calculating production and distribution costs and creating special school curriculum packages to accompany the films, the estimated bill was $591,000. Just how that sum would be raised, the proposal did not specify.[40]

Finally, in an effort to get the federal government's support for the principles and strategies envisioned in Objective Ten, the tribal chairs passed a resolution in December 1976 requesting that the secretary of the interior establish a task force (under the auspices of the NTCA, of course) to plan a "comprehensive counter movement" to ICERR and its member groups. That effort would include a "counter public relations campaign" in areas experiencing backlash and would have adequate funding to carry it out. The resolution also called on the secretary to "do everything necessary to have the 95th Congress repeal H.C.R. 108 on termination."[41]

These initial NTCA efforts met with mixed results. The legislative monitoring system worked as long as there was adequate staff to keep it up to date. Neither the Democrats nor the Republicans agreed to include the NTCA Indian plank, although each party platform included a paragraph espousing recognition of the federal government's trust obligations. The model tribal code initiative was a positive and forward-thinking idea but never received the federal funding necessary to establish it. The association's plan to launch a media blitz to realize its Objective Ten was also a sound proposal but required tribal leaders already busy trying to earn a living while simultaneously running a government to invest time and energy reaching out to media outlets that appeared more interested in drama, personalities, and crises than in the complexities of tribal sovereignty and treaty rights. The backlash movement, meanwhile, metastasized across the nation. As noted in the introduction to Objective Ten, the backlash "is no longer an isolated incident, but a well-organized, well-financed and coordinated effort in many states from Washington to Maine." To contain it, the NTCA belatedly realized, would require a concerted effort on the part of all national Indian organizations.

The United Effort Trust

On September 20, 1978, the *Marshfield News-Herald* ran a story under the headline "Popularity vs. Integrity?" The piece included reflections from three retiring legislators who were concerned about "the insidious pressures that too frequently lead to individual courage being supplanted by political expediency." There were some politicians, lamented one of the retiring legislators, "who decide the job is so damned important to themselves that they're prepared to sacrifice their integrity."[42]

The retiring legislator to whom these quotes were attributed was Representative Edwin Lloyd Meeds, a seven-term congressman from Washington's Second District. First elected to the House in 1964 Meeds established a record as a staunch supporter of Native American interests. He chaired the House Subcommittee on Indian Affairs, helped champion the Alaska Native Claims Settlement Act, and was vice chair of the American Indian Policy Review Commission. During his first decade of service, Meeds was never seriously challenged for reelection in the heavily Democratic Second District. Everything changed, however, with the *Boldt* decision. Almost overnight, Meeds's record of support for Indian rights became a political albatross and in the 1976 election, Republican John Nance Garner very nearly toppled him. After absentee ballots were tallied and a recount conducted, Meeds was declared the victor by just 542 votes out of 200,000 cast (just over 0.25 percent). To an experienced political operative like Meeds, the election's lesson was abundantly clear: support for Native American sovereignty and treaty rights was a losing proposition for politicians in the Pacific Northwest. Bowing to the "insidious pressures" of the anti-Indian movement, Meeds made the politically expedient move to forsake his previous record on tribal rights and take up the mantle of backlash—a maneuver that Native

American leaders later termed "Lloyd Meeds syndrome." Even Meeds admitted that Lloyd Meeds syndrome existed. "There is a good deal of apprehension [among congresspeople] over getting caught what I got caught in," Meeds declared a year after the election. That said, he insisted that he hadn't changed his stance on Native American issues, "just the way I approach things." As the 1978 midterm elections drew near, however, Meeds apparently decided that his job wasn't "so damned important" after all and he announced his decision not to seek reelection. Native Americans looked on with mixed emotions—relief that a backlash-oriented politician was leaving the field of battle and disappointment in a former ally who had sacrificed his integrity for political gain.[43]

It didn't take long for the symptoms of Lloyd Meeds syndrome to become manifest in the halls of Congress. In the House of Representatives' Interior and Insular Affairs Committee, for example, fear of anti-Indian backlash was so intense that Chair Morris Udall could not persuade anyone on the committee, aside from nonvoting delegates from Guam and the Virgin Islands, to serve as chair of the Indian Affairs Subcommittee.[44] Legislation to help Indians, meanwhile, came under closer scrutiny than it had in the past, at times failing on the floor owing to a "small but vociferous anti-Indian faction" motivated by various backlash-inspired concerns. On January 4, 1977, Meeds had introduced H.J. Res. 1—the first piece of House legislation in the Ninety-Fifth Congress and the opening salvo in a barrage of over a dozen backlash-inspired bills. H.J. Res. 1 proposed the establishment of an eleven-member commission to study and assess the effects of the *Boldt* decision on the commercial and recreational fishing industry in the Pacific Northwest and to make "appropriate recommendations for remedial legislation." In November, Meeds introduced two additional bills. The first, H.R. 9950—the Omnibus Indian Jurisdiction Act—provided for the extension of state jurisdiction over all crimes committed on reservations by nontribal members, stripped tribes of their sovereign immunity against lawsuits, and sought to limit the *Boldt* decision's provision allowing Indians to fish in accustomed places by empowering states to regulate all hunting and fishing outside reservation boundaries. The second, H.R. 9951—the clumsily named Quantification of Federal Reserved Water Rights for Indian Reservations Act—sought to limit tribal claims to water by requiring both a "qualification of claims" and regulating the amount of water a tribe needed based on a quantification of Indian water usage over a five-year period. Since this amount was generally negligible given the long history of discriminatory water allotments, tribes would be locked in to a system guaranteeing that the discrimination would continue.[45]

Lloyd Meeds was certainly not the only backlash-oriented legislator in the "Nightmare 95th." On January 27, 1977, Representative John Dingell (D-Mich.) introduced H.J. Res. 206 that would allow states to regulate off-reservation hunting and fishing rights granted to Indians by treaty. On September 12, 1977, Representative Jack Cunningham (D-Wash.) introduced H.R. 9054—the so-called Native American Equal Opportunities Act—which, in true termination fashion, called for the abrogation of all Indian treaties, an end to the government's trust responsibilities, the allotment in severalty of tribal assets, and the dissolution of all hunting and fishing rights to Indians.[46]

While the substance of these bills was understandably troubling to Indian leaders, so too was the rhetoric employed by their sponsors in promoting passage. Meeds, in particular, appeared to be using a script drawn directly from the incendiary pages of backlash propaganda. He spoke of "Equal rights for all Americans including whites" and, echoing FREE's denunciations about paying use fees to hunt and fish on the Flathead Reservation, declared that since non-Indians were not allowed to participate in tribal government, then tribal government should not have jurisdiction over them or their activities. Similar to the cynical and disingenuous claims of backlash organizations that they were seeking justice and equality for Indian and non-Indian alike, Meeds sought to give the impression that his bills were as much for the Indians' benefit as they were about justice for non-Indians. As the NCAI's Chuck Trimble noted at the time, Meeds "is still looked to by many as a 'friend of Indians,' and he is good at making himself sound like one."[47]

In response to the ominous start of the Ninety-Fifth Congress, leaders representing a broad spectrum of national and regional Indian organizations convened on May 4–5, 1977, at the Bottle Hollow Resort on the Ute Reservation in northeastern Utah. AIM's Vernon Bellecourt attended, as did the NCAI's Mel Tonasket and Chuck Trimble. Rick Baker represented the NTCA. According to notes recorded by Lucille Echohawk (Pawnee), the group's purpose was "to preserve Indianness, tribal sovereignty and treaty and other Indian rights" and to take "positive action to combat backlash." The positive action the group had in mind was creating an alliance of Indian organizations. An alliance would promote cooperation and communication among tribal governments and Indian organizations, help avoid duplication of effort, and encourage members to coordinate their activities. After two days of meetings, participants unanimously agreed to designate the NCAI as the "ad hoc coordinating organization" of the alliance, obtain sanction for an alliance from the governing bodies of participating organizations, and develop plans for short- and long-term financing. In his report to the NTCA executive board, Rick Baker stated that he had endorsed beginning a "process of cooperative endeavor" and had stressed that the association "should be an important part of any response that may be developed."[48]

Unlike the other organizations that participated in the Bottle Hollow meeting, the NTCA did not send any of its top leaders (Baker had previously served as treasurer but was not on the NTCA executive board at the time). That the association had participated at all was something of a surprise given the chairs' history of shunning such gatherings—especially when they included urban Indians and nonrecognized groups. Strongly protective of their prerogatives as elected tribal chairs and steadfast in the belief that they alone possessed the authority and legitimacy to speak for federally recognized tribes, avoiding venues that in any way diminished their position as "the voice of the tribes" was, in their minds at least, a matter of principle. The decision to authorize Rick Baker to attend the meeting, consequently, was likely an exercise in intelligence gathering and to keep abreast of what other Indian organizations were doing regarding backlash. News that the NCAI had been designated as the lead agency for coordinating a national Indian response, meanwhile, likely stoked old resentments among NTCA hard-liners such as Bill Youpee, but the magnitude of the anti-Indian movement and very real dangers it posed prompted other association members to endorse the "process of cooperative endeavor." Should that endeavor fail, Chuck Trimble had warned, "Indian tribes will not survive the decade as governments."[49]

Over the course of the next several months, representatives from the NTCA and NCAI began holding meetings and discussing possible avenues of cooperation. In August 1977, members of both organizations met with a BIA media-relations expert and with officials from the Federal Communications Commission. A week later, they discussed Indian-state relations with members of the United Indian Planning Association and the National Governors' Conference. On the evening of November 2—the night before Meeds introduced two backlash bills (H.R. 9950 and H.R. 9951) to Congress—the NTCA's Evelyn Pickett (Cherokee) joined NCAI officials to draft a telegram to all congresspersons urging them "to exercise the greatest care and caution in examining and endorsing these proposals" and to "consider their potential impact on the inherent rights of Indian governments." They likewise put together a joint statement strongly opposing the Meeds bills that would go out to all tribes from the NTCA and NCAI presidents.[50]

On December 6–7, 1977, an Emergency Conference of Tribal Leaders convened in Phoenix to take the next step in fulfilling the promises made seven months earlier at Bottle Hollow. Participants included representatives from the NTCA and NCAI, staff members from the Senate Select Committee on Indian Affairs and House Interior Committee, and the BIA. After hearing assessments of the mood in Congress and discussing strategies to block backlash legislation, a seven-member Joint NCAI and NTCA Lobbying and Coordinating Committee was appointed to carry out a "concentrated, well-defined campaign to defeat the backlash legislation, and through a campaign of education and mass communication, to change the public attitudes that foster such legislation."[51] To some extent, this sounded very much like the NTCA's Objective Ten initiative but on a far grander scale. Wayne Ducheneaux, chair of the Cheyenne River Sioux Tribe, challenged leaders to support the effort financially and set an example by pledging ten thousand dollars from his tribe. By the end of the two-day event, over fifty thousand dollars had been pledged.[52]

Getting to this point was by no means a simple task. Tribal leaders from both associations expressed caution about creating yet another national Indian entity that would likely exacerbate existing political divisions even further. They likewise feared that the proposed joint committee would detract from the "true sanction" of the parent organizations, and that tribal leaders would shift their allegiances (and funding) to the new joint venture. There were concerns that the new committee—if successful—would invariably take on expanded responsibilities other than combatting backlash and become independent of the NTCA and NCAI executive boards. The coordinating committee's staff, meanwhile, might "unscrupulously use privy politics and favoritism to put the leadership of the parent organizations at odds with one another" for the purpose of advancing their own agendas. There were a host of financial and legal concerns expressed as well: Who would oversee and be held accountable for expenditures or mis-expenditures? Did the new committee need to file papers as an independent corporate entity?[53]

In the end, the crisis facing tribal governments along with the threats that the backlash posed to the Indian land base, water rights, hunting and fishing rights, and tribal sovereignty outweighed the strong loyalties of Indian leaders to either of the national intertribal organizations. A week following the Phoenix meeting, an account was established in the American Indian National Bank to hold tribal contributions for the joint venture, and professional staff members of the NTCA and NCAI began work on fleshing out organizational details to get the effort up and running. On January 18, 1978, NTCA president Joe Delacruz and NCAI president Veronica Murdock (Mohave) signed a "Statement of Common Concern" and thereby entered in an agreement to form the joint effort and to secure funds for "a national campaign for the survival of Indian tribal governments." Everything seemed to be advancing according to schedule up to this point . . . but then lawyers got involved.[54]

To move forward with the joint effort, each organization's corporate charter and related official documents needed to undergo a formal review. To expedite the process, Joe Delacruz gave his approval for the NCAI's outside counsel—Wilkinson, Cragun & Barker—to conduct this review for the NTCA as well. When the NTCA's outside counsel, Winston & Strawn, got wind of this and objected, the entire process came to a halt. According to one account, an attorney with Winston & Strawn stated that the joint effort was "not a good idea" and threatened legal action if the NCAI's attorneys persisted in involving themselves in NTCA business.[55] In the face of this unexpected problem, Delacruz and Murdock discussed the possibility of the NCAI "going it alone" but agreed to meet in Phoenix on March 21 to discuss other options with the principal officers of NTCA and NCAI.

On March 21, 1978, NTCA officers Joe Delacruz, Paul Tafoya (Santa Clara Pueblo), and Terald Goodwin (Shoshone-Paiute) met with the NCAI officers Veronica Murdock, Juanita Ahtone (Kiowa), and Rachel Nabahe (Shoshone-Paiute) in Phoenix. NCAI executive director Chuck Trimble also attended, as did Philip S. (Sam) Deloria (Standing Rock Sioux), director of the American Indian Law Center, and Charles Hobbs, an attorney with the NCAI law firm Wilkinson, Cragun & Barker. Conspicuously absent was Bill Youpee—a worrisome sign, perhaps, that at least some members of the NTCA were not fully onboard with the joint effort.[56]

After discussing the unexpected legal roadblock that had led to the meeting, participants decided to create a trust under the auspices of the NCAI. The trust would have a brief life span (lasting only to the next national election) and a narrow focus—to lobby against backlash legislation and to serve as a central coordinating point for tribes and Indian organizations combatting the backlash. To ensure broad support from tribes, the principal officers of the NTCA and NCAI would hold seats on the board of trustees.[57] In a somewhat aston-

As executive director from 1972 to 1978, Charles "Chuck" Trimble (Pine Ridge Sioux) helped restore the NCAI as an important voice in the modern Indian rights movement.
Courtesy of the Center of Southwest Studies, Fort Lewis College, Durango, Colo.

ishing display of collegiality and goodwill, NCAI president Veronica Murdock nominated NTCA president Joe Delacruz as board chairman while the NTCA's Paul Tafoya nominated the NCAI's Rachel Nabahe as secretary/treasurer. Under the guidance of Deloria and Hobbs, the attendees drew up and signed papers establishing a seven-member United Effort Trust (UET). According to its declaration, the trust would "resist by all lawful means the threats, such as posed by the Meeds bills, to the lands base, sovereign rights, water and mineral rights, hunting and fishing rights, and other rights of the Indian people and the very existence of tribal governments."[58]

Shortly after the creation of the UET, Chuck Trimble resigned his position as NCAI executive director to manage the new antibacklash initiative. To accomplish its stated goals, UET organized a data bank of potential allies (Indian organizations, potentially sympathetic non-Indian organizations, churches, environmental groups, etc.) as well as information about politicians and their voting records.[59] It also organized an extensive lobbying effort that targeted key congressional delegations and their staffs and compiled and published educational materials to communicate "concise information on the Indian tribes, their unique relationship with the federal government, and their unique rights." To exert pressure on politicians where it counted most—their election or reelection campaigns—the UET helped organize voter registration drives on reservations across the West. Finally, the UET worked to improve relations between tribal governments and city, county, and state governments through engagement—to get them "in a bear hug," so to speak, before backlash organizations such as ICERR could unite them in the effort to roll back recent tribal advances.[60]

A critical component of the bear-hug approach was an outreach to the National Council of State Legislatures (NCSL), a bipartisan organization established in 1975 to improve the quality and effectiveness of state government. In response to the anti-Indian backlash, the NCSL established a task force in the spring of 1977 to examine the relationship between states and tribes. During a meeting held in Albuquerque later that year, Sam Deloria proposed that the task force join with the NCAI and NTCA to study the state-tribal relationship. The resulting Commission on State-Tribal Relations consisted of twelve members (six legislators and six tribal chairs) and was, by design, not a negotiating body but instead an investigative body that sought to discern "prototype positions" in order to provide an overall framework for understanding the kinds of considerations that states and tribes might have regarding various hot-button topics.[61] Financed in part by grants from private sources such as the William H. Donner Foundation and the Ford Foundation and government funding from the BIA and the Community Services Administration, the commission held a series of national hearings on critical issues. In May 1980, for example, the commission held hearings in Helena, Montana, to explore environmental, natural resource, and wildlife conflicts between Indian and non-Indian authorities. Witnesses from five states testified that "constant communication—both formal and informal—is the key to understanding between Indian tribes and non-Indian governments."[62]

The Commission on State-Tribal Relations was instrumental in reversing the momentum of the anti-Indian backlash movement. In 1982 it published Sam Deloria's *Handbook on State-Tribal Relations* to assist Indian and non-Indian lawmakers in their efforts to work through their governments' complicated relationship. The commission also provided information via publications, conferences, and workshops on specific issues such as the Indian Child Welfare Act, tribal law enforcement, the Indian criminal justice system, and the effects of block-grant implementation on federal-tribal and state-tribal relationships. Over time, the commission's effort to promote dialog and knowledge-based decision making as an acceptable alternative to the emotional and adversarial approach *à la* the anti-Indian backlash movement prompted a change in the political atmosphere as candidates competed to see who could promise better relations with tribal governments.[63]

Although the anti-Indian movement limped on into the 1980s, not one of the backlash bills introduced during the Ninety-Fifth Congress gained passage. Instead, several pieces of important reform legislation were enacted, including the Indian Child Welfare Act, the Tribally Controlled Community College Assistance Act, the Community Reinvestment Act (which made tribes eligible for HUD community development grants), and the Food and Agricultural Act (which permitted tribes to administer food stamp programs on reservations if state agencies failed to run them properly). These victories were in large part a response to the efforts of national and regional Indian organizations that employed effective lobbying strategies, collaboration, and dialog with state and local governments, public outreach, and a tremendous amount of arduous work.[64] As the NCAI's Cal Noel confidently remarked at the close of the Ninety-Fifth Congress, Indian activists would prevail over future periods of backlash because "We have a higher profile now," and "People are starting to understand our views."[65]

Like most of its efforts to promote the rights of federally recognized tribes, the NTCA's role in combatting the anti-Indian backlash movement is difficult— if not impossible—to quantify. The decade of the 1970s has been described as an "era of cacophonous voices, all claiming to speak for Indians," but combatting the backlash movement, as we have seen, required interorganizational unity and coordination that had heretofore proven elusive. The NTCA was certainly aware of the backlash early on, recognized the threat it posed to tribal governments, and was proactive in fashioning a response. NTCA leaders challenged the Ford administration to acknowledge and explain the so-called Borgstrom memorandum, passed a resolution condemning ICERR, and devised an elaborate in-house monitoring system to track Indian-related legislation introduced during the Ninety-Fifth Congress. To address ongoing jurisdictional conflicts with state and local governments, the NTCA proposed creating a model tribal code that could clarify misunderstandings and alleviate the fears of non-Indians living (or possessing property) within tribal boundaries. The association's Objective Ten was a progressive and ambitious plan to combat the backlash through a wide-ranging lobbying and education effort—a strategy that was later adopted and implemented through the United Effort Trust.

The NTCA's degree of cooperation with the NCAI in establishing a joint effort to combat the backlash is especially difficult to assess. While it is clear that association officers were committed to the idea, there is also evidence that suggests the NTCA's board of directors, its executive director, and its outside counsel were, at the very least, cautious about committing the association to such a course of action. The same is true about the United Effort Trust. NTCA officers served on the UET's board of trustees (and Joe Delacruz as its chair) but they apparently did so without the official sanction of the NTCA board. Why some association leaders balked at the prospect of combining forces with the NCAI is unclear, but one plausible explanation is that NTCA officials feared that cooperation with a "rival" such as the NCAI would somehow damage their credibility and diminish their claim to be the voice of federally recognized tribes. The association did agree to take part in the consequential Commission on State-Tribal Relations, but its precise activities or contributions are not specified in the NTCA Papers housed in the Smithsonian, which end in 1978. In short, the NTCA played a role in resisting the backlash movement of the 1970s. By failing to fully embrace the collaboration offered by NCAI and the United Effort Trust, however, it missed an opportunity to substantially strengthen the antibacklash effort and to shore up its own position as a leader in the modern Indian rights movement.

Chapter 6

The Reagan Revolution

Native Americans had good reason to be anxious about the major-party candidates seeking the presidency in the 1980 election. Incumbent Jimmy Carter had shown little interest in federal-Indian relations, had failed to issue a presidential Indian policy statement, and seemed content to simply continue his predecessors' self-determination strategy and allow things to "go on as usual."[1] Ronald Reagan's stand on Native American issues was equally uninspiring. At a campaign stop in Missouri, Reagan's son Michael pledged that his father would "do more than President Carter for American Indians" and guaranteed there would be an "open line of communication" with a Reagan White House. As a candidate, the former California governor railed against the excesses of big government, championed tax cuts, and vowed to rein in the federal bureaucracy. During a campaign swing through Wichita in the weeks leading up to the Kansas Republican primary, Reagan singled out the Bureau of Indian Affairs (BIA) as a prime example of bureaucratic waste and inertia. The bureau had more employees than there were Indians, Reagan maintained, and joked that a BIA official was seen crying because "my Indian died."[2]

Reagan's landslide election proved to be a watershed moment in the history of the National Tribal Chairmen's Association (NTCA). Since its inception in 1971 the association had sought to advance the interests of federally recognized tribes through an insider strategy of consultation, relationship building, and working within the existing political system. That strategy became increasingly untenable, however, as the so-called Reagan Revolution brought devastating cuts to domestic spending programs and to the BIA budget. Over time, the NTCA became one of the most vociferous critics of the Reagan administration, a principled decision perhaps, but one with profound consequences for the association's economic viability. Old criticisms that the NTCA was a "rubber-stamp" organization filled with sellouts and compliant Uncle Tomahawks were no longer voiced in the 1980s, a testament to the association's new leadership and aggressive rhetoric, along with the rapid decline of militant organizations such as the American Indian Movement (AIM) that had captivated the nation's attention a decade earlier. Some tribal chairs were put out by the uncharacteristically confrontational approach adopted by some NTCA leaders, still convinced that the calm, cool deliberations advocated by the association's founders had been successful in steering federal Indian policies in a positive direction. Rumors of financial irregularities and infighting among association leadership, meanwhile, led to a decline in membership and concerns that the association's days were numbered—a situation reminiscent of the internal crises of the National Congress of American Indians (NCAI) a decade earlier. How did the NCTA respond to these challenges?

The NTCA in Crisis

According to the NTCA constitution, the activities of the association were to be governed by a twelve-member board of directors and four elected officers: president, vice president, secretary, and treasurer. To supervise the staff and to carry out the association's daily business, the position of executive director was established roughly a year after the NTCA's founding. There was always a bit of ambiguity, however, over just who was in charge and who possessed decision-making authority—not a problem if association leaders were on the same page but problematic when there were differences of opinion. The addition in May 1975 of the Winston & Strawn law firm as the NTCA's outside counsel complicated these rather fundamental questions. Over time, Winston & Strawn attorneys Joseph Fontana and John Keys became extremely influential players in association deliberations and in its various activities. They filed suits on behalf of the association and for specific tribes, attended congressional hearings and recommended changes to legislation, drafted NTCA resolutions and assisted with fund-raising efforts, and were present at all association conventions and board meetings. As advisers to the board, the officers, and to the executive director, Winston & Strawn was in a powerful position to influence virtually every aspect of association business. When NTCA president Joe Delacruz and other association officers decided to collaborate with their NCAI counterparts to form the United Effort Trust (the lobbying effort to combat the anti-Indian backlash movement), for example, Winston & Strawn attorneys questioned their authority to do so and recommended that the NTCA "monitor all UET activities to make certain that it does not misrepresent to the Indian people what it is or who it represents." Those warnings, along with the fact that the NCAI was leading the effort, help explain the board's decision not to endorse NTCA involvement but are also indicative of an apparent schism within the association's top leadership.[3]

Additional evidence of what appeared to be a growing breach between the NTCA officers on one side and its board of directors and outside counsel on the other was brought to light during a March 3, 1978, meeting held in Billings. At that meeting—with no officers and only seven board members present—the chairs discussed a recent audit of association finances conducted by the Department of the Interior that had pointed out a wide range of irregularities. Association expenditures, for example, had been inappropriately charged to contracts with the BIA and the Indian Health Service, payments to outside counsel Winston & Strawn lacked specificity, and there was no set financial policy on matters such as salaries for permanent staff, the payment of stipends, or travel-related expenses. NTCA leadership, according to the auditors' report, had to exercise more direct responsibility and control over the association's financial operations and to approve annual budgets. Board members also discussed seemingly innocuous matters such as the venue for the association's next annual convention. At the previous convention, members had voted to hold the 1978 gathering in Spokane, Washington. According to attorney Joseph Fontana, however, that vote was not binding since it had not been conducted by roll call and it was the board's responsibility to make those types of decisions for the association. At this point, Earl Old Person's (Blackfeet) motion to hold the convention in Minneapolis passed unanimously.[4]

Four months later, an article appeared in the *Southern Ute Drum*, under the headline "NTC Has Problems," that touched on some of the issues discussed at the March board meeting in Billings. The article cited NTCA president Joe Delacruz's dramatic assertion that the association was dead, "robbed and beaten by a few tribal leaders, and it died of internal injuries." According to Delacruz, NTCA officials were ignoring tribal mandates and, in collusion with their legal counsel, had mounted an intensive "stonewalling effort" to prevent disclosure of internal financial affairs and reform of the organization's administration. He went on to blast Executive Director Bill Youpee and the NTCA Board of Directors for conducting the recent Minneapolis convention "in an undemocratic and dictatorial manner" and claimed that tribal leaders from the Sioux nations, from the Northwest, from California, and from Oklahoma had walked out in protest.[5]

Delacruz's assertion about the NTCA's death was a bit premature, and the Quinault leader finished out his term as president before stepping down in August 1979, still frustrated that the association's board of directors "did not fully cooperate with its officers."[6] By this time, Bill Youpee had also left the NTCA and returned home to Fort Peck. The circumstances surrounding his departure at some point in the fall of 1978 are unclear. In August his wife, Marjorie, had been forced due to poor health to retire as tribal secretary, and Youpee may have resigned to care for her and his family.[7] Conservative, uncompromising, and at times undiplomatic, Youpee had been a founding member of the NTCA and a staunch advocate for tribal chairs as the sole legitimate representatives of federally recognized tribes. His knowledge and experience leading the association, not to mention the many contacts he had cultivated in Washington, D.C., left a considerable vacuum at the top of the NTCA hierarchy at a time when the antibacklash fight was still a work in progress and important midterm elections were looming in November.

His replacement as executive director was fifty-five-year-old Kenneth Black, a World War II veteran and long-serving member of Oklahoma's Otoe-Missouria Tribal Council. Black had served a term as NTCA treasurer and as secretary in the mid-1970s and was well versed in association operations. While he lacked the national prominence of tribal chairs like Roger Jourdain or Wendell Chino, his appointment seemed a reasonable choice. Unfortunately, like Joe Delacruz, Black quickly became embroiled in a publicized dispute with the NTCA Board of Directors. As is often the case with organizations both large and small, the central issue in the dispute revolved around power. When officials in the NTCA's Denver office applied for and received a $235,615 grant from the Office of Indian Education (OIE), Black withdrew the proposal, refused the funds, and sharply criticized the Denver office for submitting it in the first place. The resulting furor that ensued pitted Black and some members of the NTCA board against the Denver office and other members of the board, including Roger Jourdain, who argued that the executive director had "deviously misinterpreted" the board's decision to accept the grant. In this particular instance, Jourdain's opinion was at odds with association president Wendell Chino, who insisted that Black had acted appropriately. The board had rejected the grant, Chino explained, on the grounds that tribal governments seeking control over their education programs should have applied directly to the OIE and left the NTCA out of the process. To do otherwise, he added, was contrary to tribal self-determination. "We sincerely believe that the interests of all the federally recognized tribes is better served by not accepting this grant from the OIE to do a task which the tribes can do themselves." The NTCA's program officer Elmer "Sy" Savilla (Quechan) offered a different rationale for Black's rejection of the grant. "Why would grant monies be sent to a subdivision of NTCA, instead of going directly to the administrative office to be properly distributed and monitored?" After all, the NTCA central office in Washington, D.C., was "the only office that has the right to approve grants, make grant applications, and distribute grant monies."[8]

By the summer of 1981 Kenneth Black had left his position with the NTCA and was replaced by Elmer Savilla—the third executive director in the span of three years. Born at Fort Yuma in 1926 Savilla attended high school at the Sherman Institute in California, an off-reservation boarding school established in the late nineteenth century. At the age of seventeen, he enlisted in the U.S. Navy and served as a radio operator on several ships during and immediately after World War II. During the 1950s and 1960s Savilla worked as a power lineman, electrician, and contractor before returning home in 1970. A music enthusiast, Savilla played the trumpet in the Quechan Indian Band; he also served on the Fort Yuma Council on Alcohol and Drug Abuse, and in 1972 took on new responsibilities as manpower director of the Fort Yuma Community Action Agency and a member of the Quechan Tribal Council. A year later, he was elected president of the Quechan Nation and in 1974 reelected by a four-to-one margin to serve a four-year term. Under Savilla's leadership, the Quechans' long fight to recover lands erroneously taken by the federal government in the 1890s led to the recovery of twenty-five thousand acres, more than tripling the size of the tribe's land base. Savilla hoped to convert at least some of this nonirrigable land to farming and estimated that it might generate as much as $2 million a year for the tribe. He also oversaw the construction of a new office complex to house tribal offices, fought the construction of a pipeline that would carry water from the Colorado River across the Quechan Reservation to Yuma, and worked to promote business growth and job opportunities on the reservation. In his 1975 inaugural address Savilla encouraged the 1,725-member Quechan Nation to embrace change. "To refuse to go along with progress," he cautioned, "would be suicide."[9]

By the early 1980s the NTCA seems to have stabilized, but lingering problems remained. Association officers and the board of directors continued to squabble, the relationship between the NTCA and the NCAI deteriorated

once the anti-Indian backlash was defeated, and the association's long dependence on federal grants and contracts to fund its operations continued.

These problems, however, paled in comparison to the challenges posed by the
Reagan administration's domestic agenda. The NTCA's response to these challenges would have profound implications for its future as the self-proclaimed
voice of the tribes.

The Reagan Cuts

Ronald Reagan took office intent on cutting costs. Doing so, he argued, would
provide the budgetary flexibility to enact tax cuts without ballooning the deficit and, more importantly, promote the devolution of power from Washington,
D.C., to state and local governments—the so-called New Federalism. Native
American leaders were understandably cautious; any talk of limiting the federal
government's role in society and strengthening the power of states sounded ominously like termination, despite Reagan's campaign promises to respect treaties
and to promote tribal self-determination. For Reagan, there was no inconsis-
tency. "Instead of fostering and encouraging self-government," he declared in
his January 24, 1983, statement on Indian affairs, "federal policies have by and
large inhibited the political and economic development of the tribes. Excessive
regulation and self-perpetuating bureaucracy have stifled local decision making, thwarted Indian control of Indian resources, and promoted dependency
rather than self-sufficiency." To realize the concept of self-government, Reagan
argued, tribes had "to reduce their dependence on federal funds by providing a
greater percentage of the cost of their self-government."[10]

A month after Reagan's inauguration, the NTCA's Ken Black indicated that
the association was in agreement with the "general goals" of the new administration. "We accept the fact the we too will be required to make sacrifices," Black
maintained, "but in view of what the American Indian has already sacrificed
over the past two centuries, we can endure a little more."[11] This conciliatory attitude evaporated immediately, however, following the release of the administration's proposed FY 1982 budget on March 10, 1981. Presented as an effort to fight
inflation and promote economic growth, the budget called for a $136.9 million
decrease in Indian Health Service (IHS) funding, a $72.9 million cut in BIA
funding, and an end to funding for the construction of reservation water and
sanitary facilities. Funds for public service employment (e.g., jobs created under
the Comprehensive Employment and Training Act and similar programs in
the Economic Development Administration) were also cut, as were allocations

to Indian education. While administration officials justified these measures as reasonable and necessary sacrifices during difficult economic times, the impact of the cuts on reservations were especially devastating given tribal governments' dependence on federal assistance. According to the NTCA's *American Indian World* position paper, the federal government's trust responsibility included supporting tribes "in their efforts to enhance tribal sovereignty" and "providing the means by which tribes can provide community services" to their people. Federal support for Indian health care, education, and reservation economic development, therefore, were essential parts of the trust obligation, and tribal officials viewed the reductions as the ultimate breach of trust—what one scholar termed, "a callous form of termination by accountants."[12]

A week after the proposed budget's introduction, the NTCA requested a twenty-minute meeting with President Reagan "to discuss the Presidential policy relating to Indian affairs."[13] When this request, predictably, went nowhere, the NTCA agreed to cosponsor an emergency national meeting of Indian leaders and, through a "massive show of tribal support," attempt to force revisions to the proposed budget. In an invitation letter to tribal leaders, conference coordinators Elmer Savilla and Ada Deer (Menominee), of the Native American Rights Fund, declared that the conference's objective was the "survival of Indian tribes" and that they hoped to meet with President Reagan, Vice President George Bush, and Secretary of the Interior James Watt. These men had promised to consult with Native nations before implementing changes in Indian policy, Savilla declared, and that process needed to be face-to-face and not by mail.[14]

On May 6–7, 1981, over four hundred delegates representing 149 tribes and sixteen national Indian organizations attended the National Tribal Governments Conference in Washington, D.C. In a somewhat amazing display of productivity and unanimity, they drafted a new federal Indian policy, endorsed a letter to be sent to President Reagan (and gathered in front of the White House while it was delivered), and then marched to the National Press Club to hold a news conference. The proposed "American Indian Policy" stressed the sovereignty of Indian nations; the unique "government-to-government" relationship based on treaties, court decisions, and congressional laws; and the inherent right of tribal governments to control all persons and property within the external boundaries of the reservation. The proposed policy reemphasized the importance of the federal government's "self-determination without termination" policy and the challenges posed to that effort by jurisdictional disputes with state and local governments. The proposed policy also touched on the delicate issue of federal support for urban and off-reservation Indians and for members of nonrecognized tribes. There had to be ways and means of "securing better opportunities for them" without threatening, compromising, or diminishing "the treasured trust relationship of the federally recognized tribes." Finally, the proposed policy called on the Reagan administration to "address Indian affairs in a positive manner and direct that the federal government's responsibility to tribes be as mandated by treaties, statutes, and executive orders." To do otherwise, they declared, would diminish the "honor and integrity of the United States of America."[15]

The American Indian Policy was silent about the proposed budget cuts, but the letter to President Reagan that accompanied it was not. Signed by the chief executive officers of several tribal governments and national Indian organizations and hand-delivered to the White House by NTCA president Wendell Chino, the letter declared that the administration's budget would "destroy the progress we have made to date and reduce our tribal people to welfare states without resources available to help them." The nation's Indigenous peoples were not seeking "gifts or handouts," Indian leaders insisted, but only "that which our people are entitled to—bought and paid for with the bulk of our land and the blood of our people." To that end, the letter's signatories demanded that Interior Department and BIA officials meet with tribal leaders to discuss the proposed budget along with the funding priorities of Indian Nations. Second, they demanded that the president direct his staff to meet with elected and national tribal leaders and draft legislation "confirming the exclusive authority" of Indian nations within Indian Country and to provide for the resumption of tribal jurisdiction in areas that had been undermined by state infringement. Finally, Indian leaders demanded the immediate resignation of Interior Secretary James Watt for his unwillingness to consult with them as prescribed by law. (A spokesman for the Interior Department explained that because of a "mix-up," Watt had not received an invitation to address the conference until the meeting was under way).[16]

The Reagan administration's reaction to the letter and policy statement was silence, but White House aides were startled by the tribal chairs' hostile tone and "serious lack of political sensitivity."[17] An increasingly impatient Elmer Savilla, meanwhile, threatened to take their case to the World Court or the United Nations if Reagan did not agree to at least meet with tribal leaders. Noting the Japanese flags flying along Pennsylvania Avenue in honor of a visit by Prime Minister Zenko Suzuki, Savilla noted the irony of the nation's World War II

Elmer Savilla (Quechan) served as executive director of the NTCA from 1981 to 1985. His strong opposition to Reagan-era budget cuts strained NTCA relations with the federal government. Courtesy of Lorraine E. White.

foe gaining financial assistance and privileged access to the White House while "the Indian people, after 100 years of broken treaties and broken promises, [are] still trying to get up off the ground economically."[18] Over the course of the next few months, therefore, Elmer Savilla called and wrote White House officials to check on the progress of the materials drafted by the National Tribal Governments Conference. Much of that effort was directed at Morton C. Blackwell, the White House liaison to Native Americans. Not well versed in Indian affairs, Blackwell had worked for the Reagan campaign and reportedly received the liaison assignment because he was one-thirty-second Cherokee and because no one else wanted the position.[19] At any rate, his relationship with Savilla was a tenuous one. In a July 7, 1981, letter, for example, Savilla expressed concern that Blackwell had "done nothing to advance the review" of the conference's recommendations and that he had likely "trash-canned" them. In a letter sent nine days later, Savilla again pressed for an update on the recommendations and asked for a specific response about the resignation of James Watt. "Even a simple yes or no would be better than no answer," Savilla declared, before signing off with, "Waiting patiently, for now."[20]

On July 23 Blackwell finally responded. Acknowledging that the Quechan leader had "repeatedly written asking about the status of the policy papers" presented to the White House on May 8, Blackwell gave the standard boilerplate explanation that they were "under review by Administration officials." As for the resignation of James Watt, Blackwell stated that the interior secretary enjoyed "the complete confidence" of the president and would remain in his position.[21] In the face of a second round of budget cuts announced in October, the NTCA organized a march from the White House to the Capitol. Although only sixty Indian leaders "dressed in traditional clothes and business suits carrying signs and briefcases" participated, NTCA president Phillip Martin (Mississippi Choctaw) warned that if their lobbying efforts proved unsuccessful, they would have to consider legal action.[22]

The precise fate and influence of the proposed American Indian Policy document may never be known. On January 24, 1983, President Reagan did issue an Indian Policy Statement that was based, at least in part, on "suggestions from Indian leaders"; sections of it—acknowledgment of the government-to government relationship, support for self-determination without termination, the need for reservation economic development, upholding treaty rights—echoed themes enumerated by the National Tribal Governments Conference and virtually every other Indian rights effort during the preceding quarter century.[23] The day after Reagan issued his policy statement, the NTCA board passed a resolution calling (once again) for Watt's resignation, this time for controversial comments the beleaguered cabinet official had made on national television a week earlier.[24] In an interview broadcast on Satellite Program Network, Watt had described Indians as "incompetent wards" and declared that the federal government's management of Indian reservations demonstrated the "failures of socialism" that fostered the highest rates of unemployment, divorce, alcoholism, drug addiction, and social diseases in the country.[25] That statement, along with other faux pas and strong opposition by environmental groups, led to Watt's resignation on October 9, 1983.[26]

While Congress had been able to restore many of the funding cuts proposed during Reagan's first year in office, in succeeding years the administration was able to hold spending on Indian programs in check or reduce them outright. Between 1983 and 1987, federal expenditures on the BIA fell nearly 40 percent, from $1.5 billion to $923 million.[27] NTCA opposition to Reaganomics, meanwhile, continued unabated. In testimony before the Senate Committee on Indian Affairs, Elmer Savilla characterized the administration's fiscal year 1984 budget as a "flagrant violation of the legal obligation to provide for the education" of Indian children. He went on to cite insufficient funding levels for reservation economic development, contracting services, law enforcement, housing, and the Indian Health Service. Savilla concluded his remarks with a rather disturbing charge that the Reagan administration's budget proposal was part of a "hidden agenda" to sow division within the national Indian community. By shrinking the funding of various programs, the government was forcing urban and reservation-based organizations to compete for scarce resources. This was "causing disunity throughout the country," Savilla charged, "and I believe that it is planned."[28]

The Reagan-era budget cuts were not part of a "hidden agenda" to sow intra-Indian discord nor to terminate the government's trust responsibilities to Indian nations. They were part of a much larger plan to "check and reverse the growth of government" and dissolve and return power to the states. "Government is not the solution to our problem," Reagan famously intoned in his first inaugural address, "government is the problem." Like Nixon before him, Reagan viewed tribal self-determination as consistent with the New Federalism and sought (like Nixon) to promote Indian entrepreneurial activities in hopes of reducing their dependence on the federal dole. That the Reagan administration pursued such efforts without the requisite investments was, as Dean Kotlowski has observed, a serious mistake. Partly as a result, per-capita expenditures on Indians by the federal government declined from thirty-five hundred to twenty-five hundred dollars during the 1980s while the poverty rate for Native Americans rose from 23.7 percent to 27.2 percent. Despite their best efforts, national Indian organizations such as the NTCA were not able to reverse this trend, although federal spending on Indian programs witnessed a modest rebound during the administration of Reagan's successor, President George H. W. Bush.[29]

State of the American Indian Nations: 1983

A side effect of the budget-cut crisis was the BIA's announcement in February 1982 of yet another "major realignment" in its administrative structure. According to Assistant Secretary for Indian Affairs Kenneth Smith (Wasco), the proposed changes would reduce central office costs, thereby allowing for an increase in program funding at the reservation level.[30] Smith had received tepid

NTCA support during his confirmation hearings but had subsequently drawn the ire of tribal chairs with his remarks that tribal governments would be held accountable for the federal dollars they received, that transgressors had been "babied long enough," and that the BIA would no longer be "bailing out tribes when they get into trouble."[31] Smith's realignment plan also met with NTCA opposition. Allegedly a response to requests from Indian leaders to protect reservation funding by cutting BIA administrative costs—which according to some estimates absorbed nearly 70 percent of Indian service appropriations—the plan called for the consolidation of the BIA's twelve area offices into six regional "service centers" and the elimination of five hundred BIA positions, which would save $16 million annually in staffing alone. The proposed realignment, Smith argued, would "cut red tape and costs and definitely improve the Bureau's management of Indian programs." Elmer Savilla remained unconvinced. Tribal leaders had not been consulted in drafting the plan, and the NTCA's position was to stop the realignment process and start over after a task force had been created to discuss BIA reorganization.[32]

In January 1983 Secretary Watt had met separately with NTCA and NCAI leaders to discuss the realignment proposal and promised them he would create a special task force to review Indian policy reforms. He also made an important—and rather threatening—announcement: that he wanted to deal "with elected tribal leadership" and not the two associations. The preferred venues for meetings, Watt declared, was on the tribal leaders' "home turf" and not in Washington, D.C. In a parting shot aimed clearly at individuals such as Elmer Savilla who had made frequent use of press conferences to demand Watt's resignation, the interior secretary warned the Indian leaders against using the media as a platform for their complaints. "We would like your help," Watt declared, "but if we have to negotiate with the front pages of the *Washington Post* when you demand that we be fired and lose our jobs, why should we negotiate with you?" The politics in Washington, D.C., were a tough business, Watt added, and "We'll match you blow for blow."[33]

Watt apparently decided against implementing his divide-and-conquer strategy completely. On May 6, 1983, the BIA sent the proposal to realign and "streamline" its structure to a nine-member Indian Policy Review Team appointed by the NTCA and the NCAI as well as to BIA area directors with instructions to distribute the plan to every tribe within their jurisdiction.[34] Scarcely a week passed, however, before the NTCA chose to escalate its war of words with the Reagan administration. On May 11, at an association meeting held in Albuquerque, Wendell Chino charged that the policies of the current administration had turned the federal government into the "biggest enemy" facing American Indians. Recommending a very different restructuring of the BIA, Chino announced that his first recommendation would be "to burn all the Bureau of Indian Affairs manuals and regulations and start anew." He then encouraged Indian leaders "to take their complaints to Washington and use political pressure to get what [we] want." Elmer Savilla announced that Indian leaders planned to consolidate their grievances in one document—a State of the Indian Nations—and to release the document in the nation's capital.[35]

True to his word, on June 1, 1983, Elmer Savilla sent a thirty-six-page document bearing the title *State of the American Indian Nations: 1983* to President Reagan that laid out the NTCA's positions on a wide range of issues and provided the president with a report card of sorts on the effects of his policies on Indian communities at the midpoint of his first term. In hopes of adding greater weight and legitimacy to the document, Savilla's cover letter expressed the NTCA's long-held view that elected tribal chairs "be recognized as the Spokesmen for the federally recognized Indian tribes" as opposed to nonelected Indian individuals, nonelected groups, and organizations representing non–federally recognized Indian tribes.[36]

The first section of *State of the American Indian Nations* provided a damning assessment of Reagan's Indian policies, juxtaposing administration rhetoric with the reality of Indian communities that remained "largely undeveloped and without a meaningful degree of self-sufficiency." The efforts of tribal governments to alter this depressing condition, the document asserted, had been met with a "roadblock" of federal regulations, red tape, and "negative government heavy-handedness," which guaranteed failure. The president, meanwhile, had promised in his January 1983 policy statement to lessen federal control over tribal government affairs. If he was sincere in his statement, he would agree to meet with the Indian tribes "in their full assembly" and then personally order federal agencies to commence removing the roadblocks to progress. If he failed to do so, tribal leaders declared, "all of the fine rhetoric contained in the statements made by you and then delivered by remote control will deteriorate into pure hyperbole."[37]

State of the American Indian Nations also took strong issue with the BIA and other federal bureaucracies that diverted (or impounded) nearly 70 percent of Indian funding for their own perpetuation. This "deliberate impoundment" of Indian program dollars violated the intent of Congress to assist Native nations and provided an excellent example of the "trickle-down theory" of economics. As applied to Indian affairs, "trickle down" meant that "while the federal faucet appears to be turned on, the trickle regulators (the federal agencies) ensure that only a small amount is actually made available to the Indian tribes." If Reagan was serious about allowing Indian nations to have true self-determination, therefore, he would order "a transfer to tribal governments of the decision-making authority for Indian program guidelines" and shift funding away from federal agencies and instead directly fund tribal governments.[38]

Up to this point, the tone of *State of the American Indian Nations* had been decidedly negative. What came next—an interpretation of the administration's motives—was based on a conspiracy theory that, if at all true, would rightfully place Reagan alongside Andrew Jackson and William Henry Harrison as the most anti-Indian chief executives in American history. According to the chairs, tribes would no longer quietly accept the blame for the failures of presidential administrations to reduce the bureaucratic obstacles and remove the "trickle regulators" most responsible for the deplorable state of Indian nations. The Reagan administration, in fact, had aggravated the situation by a "deliberate manipulation" of these specific problem areas, and it was doing so to advance a "hidden agenda." The aim of this presumed hidden agenda was to reduce the effectiveness of tribal governments in handling their own affairs in order to terminate Indian property rights and allow corporate and state interests to acquire Indian-owned natural resources, including land and water. *State of the American Indian Nations* then offered "tangible evidence" of this impending threat, lest its authors "be accused of paranoia." Administration officials such as James Watt, for example, had adopted the language of anti-Indian backlash organizations by describing reservations as "enclaves of socialism" and calling for the "liberation" of Native Americans from a system of government oppression. Such benign rhetoric masked a sinister motive, tribal leaders charged, which was the termination of the federal trust relationship and dissolution of tribal governments to make Indians the "equal" of other Americans. Additional evidence of the government's hidden agenda was the sudden halt in social progress and opportunity that accompanied the inauguration of Ronald Reagan. Within two years' time, the gains realized by Indian communities in the late 1960s and 1970s evaporated and the delivery of services by federal agencies left in shambles. For reservations without natural resources for development, federal programs and tribal governments were the largest sources of employment. Thanks to the Reagan budget cuts, these areas were now facing mounting unemployment and skyrocketing suicide rates, alcoholism, illness, and poverty. The Reagan administration, however, had turned a deaf ear to the problems it had created and "insulated itself from the pleas and petitions of tribal governments" while simultaneously delivering huge sums to foreign countries. "Few options remain for the tribes to attract the attention of this Administration," tribal leaders warned, "before splinter groups turn to the self-help option."[39]

Additional evidence offered for a termination-oriented hidden agenda was the behavior of the BIA, an organization that *State of the American Indian Nations* described as an accomplice to the Reagan administration's intentional mismanagement of Indian affairs. In addition to absorbing federal funds intended for Native nations and squandering what little money was left, the BIA had failed in its trust responsibilities to properly manage and protect tribal resources. Rather than improving its own performance, the BIA had instead sought to redirect criticisms toward the tribal governments by claims that tribes were "unstable" and incapable of managing their own affairs. At the same time, however, tribes were being told that they must become less dependent upon the federal government—and to do so with deep cuts in their program budgets. "The logic behind these actions is completely lost to the Indian tribes."[40]

The introductory section of *State of the American Indian Nations* concluded with a litany of compelling and blistering criticisms, at times couched in questions or demands. "This Administration cannot point, with anything akin to PRIDE, to the conditions which have been re-created in Indian Country since January of 1981." Although Reagan's Indian policy team had presented some initiatives, the tribes viewed them as "only symbolic gestures," and if implemented "in the usual bureaucratic manner" and with inadequate funding would be ineffective in providing long-term and lasting solutions to the problems facing Native peoples. Tribal governments, consequently, "truly do not know, after 2½ years of patience, if this Administration is really interested in their welfare, or if the Administration really understands the unique Trust relationship which was established by the Constitution of this United States." In short, "DOES THE ADMINISTRATION REALIZE THE CONSEQUENCES OF ITS ACTIONS? DOES IT EVEN CARE?" To demonstrate his true intentions and commitment to self-determination, tribal governments demanded that

the President himself speak to them personally and in no uncertain terms enunciate what the REAL Indian Policy is, and then if he is serious in having his administration do all that can be done to alleviate the

Table 2
Summary of *State of the American Indian Nations: 1983* Position Papers

Issue	Recommendations
Operations of the Department of Interior and Bureau of Indian Affairs (BIA)	• Due to the negative connotations associated with the term "reservation," all descriptions and definitions of Indian lands should hereafter be referred to as Indian Country • The current Secretary of the Interior (James Watt) and Assistant Secretary of the Interior for Indian Affairs (Kenneth Black) have not been acting in the best interests of tribes. Both have violated the law by failing to adequately consult with the tribes. • Current efforts aimed at restructuring the BIA are inadequate and should be stopped. Elected tribal leaders should themselves name and appoint a special Tribal Commission to do this work and consider the reconstruction plan devised by the NTCA. • Indian water rights have not been adequately protected. • The Secretary of the Interior must issue a statement recognizing the authority of the NTCA, its right to exist and appoint its own representatives, and that the Secretary recognize that representative. • Reagan's Indian Policy Statement is not beneficial to Indian tribes.
Indian Country gaming	• Only tribes have the authority to regulate gaming activities on their own lands and any involvement by the federal government to interfere in such activities is an assault on tribal sovereignty and contrary to the policy of self-determination.
Health concerns	• Increased funding. • IHS Director should be elevated to Assistant Secretary of Health and Human Services. • Creation of an NTCA Indian Health Advisory Council. • Government funding for the provision of health care to off-reservation Indians should not be taken from the amount necessary to provide health care in Indian Country.
Indian education	• The federal trust responsibility includes education but only for members of federally recognized tribes. • Only tribes have the authority to determine eligibility for membership.

Table 2

(continued)

Issue	Recommendations
	• BIA-proposed minimum academic standards should be replaced by standards set by the tribe.
	• NTCA objects to the closure of federal boarding schools until adequate replacements are provided in Indian Country.
	• Increased Johnson-O'Malley funding to keep pace with expanding student enrollment.
	• Increased financial support for Early Childhood Education and Higher Education Scholarships.
Indian housing	• Support H.R. 1928 and S. 856—Indian Housing Act of 1983.

poverty and hardship which is now rampant in Indian Country, he will allow the Indian Nations to take matters in their own hands to make improvements in their own way.[41]

To prove that no hidden agenda existed to terminate Indian property rights and allow corporate and state interests to acquire Indian-owned natural resources, tribal governments also demanded

> an assurance from this Administration that their lands and resources are safe and will be diligently protected by their TRUSTEE from the grasp of the States, private utility companies, and the private corporations. Reforms must be immediately instituted in those federal agencies, such as the Interior Department, who have a responsibility to protect those resources.[42]

Finally, the authors of *State of the American Indian Nations* called upon the president to be the "prime catalyst" for new federal efforts to "remove the chains of POVERTY and NEGLECT from the shoulders of the American Indian Nations and allow them to reach their full potential and strength through their own efforts assisted by the proper levels of federal help and funding."[43]

State of the American Indian Nations also included five position papers that detailed the NTCA's specific opinions about the Department of the Interior and BIA, gaming, health issues, education, and housing (see table 2).[44]

On June 1, 1983, copies of *State of the American Indian Nations* were delivered to President Reagan (or in Winnebago tribal chair Reuben Snake's words, "the great forked-tongue liar and deceiver who sits in the White House") and to Congress. At a press conference called the next day, fifteen tribal chairs briefed reporters on the document's salient points and emphasized budget cuts, inadequate consultation, and BIA mismanagement as the primary causes of their frustration. Blackfeet tribal chair Earl Old Person commented wryly that Indians "no longer fight with bows and arrows . . . but with documents," and the position paper was then distributed to the press.[45]

If the Reagan administration had been startled by the May 1981 letter from the National Tribal Governments Conference, receipt of *State of the American Indian Nations* and the widespread negative press coverage that accompanied its release must have been truly disconcerting. While the report made a variety of substantive recommendations in its position papers, the harsh criticisms contained in its introductory assessment of the administration's Indian record were unprecedented for an organization that had long sought to position itself as an insider and to promote change through relationship building and working within the system. The association's deviation from this course deeply troubled NTCA president Phillip Martin, who resigned his position as president on June 27. As an officer in the association, Martin had sought to "work with the federal administration and the Congress" and to cooperate with the NCAI "to establish a joint mechanism to address the issues," but the NTCA board and Executive Director Elmer Savilla "changed these plans by a 180-degree turn in strategy at the [May 1983] meeting in Albuquerque." Seeking to impose its own version of BIA reorganization and establishing "extra-federal structures to prescribe decisions for federal officials are counterproductive at best," Martin declared, and the NTCA "trend toward heightening levels of rancor with the National Congress of American Indians can only be harmful to the interests of Indian peoples nationwide."[46]

Phillip Martin was certainly correct in his assessment that the NTCA had exhibited a "180-degree turn in strategy," featuring an increasingly aggressive and combative posture in its defense of federally recognized tribes. The association's relationship with the NCAI, meanwhile, had always been a tenuous one, marked by varying degrees of envy and resentment punctuated by brief periods of cooperation. In the months following the release of *State of the American Indian Nations*, the two organizations worked together to fashion a comprehensive plan to restructure and redesign the BIA that called for the bureau's eventual elimination and replacement by a new independent Indian affairs agency.[47] Although Interior Department officials ultimately rejected the plan, the fact that the two national Indian organizations cooperated in drafting it was a positive indicator that interorganizational unity—at least at times—was still possible.

The Commission on Indian Reservation Economies

President Reagan established the Presidential Commission on Indian Reservation Economies by Executive Order 12401 on January 14, 1983, to "identify obstacles to Indian reservation economic development and to promote the development of a healthy private sector on Indian reservations."[48] Nine commissioners, Indian and non-Indian, were appointed to serve on the commission.[49] The commissioners spent more than a year conducting field hearings to identify specific impediments to Indian reservation development and to devise recommendations for improvement. On November 30, 1984, the commission completed its work and submitted its report to the president.

According to the presidential executive order, the commission was to "advise the President on what actions should be taken to develop a stronger private sector on Federally recognized Indian reservations, lessen tribal dependence on Federal monies and programs and reduce the Federal presence in Indian affairs." Expanding federal funding for tribes, consequently, was not to be considered.[50] The commission's final report categorized obstacles to reservation economic development into four general areas: problems with tribes, the BIA, other federal agencies, and local governments. Of the forty specific problems identified, weak business management by tribal governments, the rapid turnover in tribal governments, and an unskilled and unreliable tribal labor force ranked among the top five (inadequate federal funding ranked number fifteen).[51]

Noteworthy recommendations offered by the commission included assuring tribes that the "penalty of success is not termination" and that a congressional repudiation of H.C.R. 108 "is an assurance that they can undertake the process of modernizing their government, privatizing business, and actually working their way free of federal dependence secure in the knowledge that support will be there when and if they fail."[52] To address the perceived problems with tribal governments, the commission recommended that they modernize their constitutions to achieve a separation of governmental powers and refrain from attempting to manage corporate business functions. To promote greater certainty for business ventures, the commission recommended that legislation be enacted to provide for appellate review of tribal court decisions to the federal court system. To protect Indian resources, the creation of an Indian Trust Services Administration was recommended that would focus exclusively on the protection of Indian resources rather than the management of them. Regarding the critical issue of water rights, however, the commission passed the buck to a future "summit conference on water resources" to be convened by the secretary of the interior. Finally, to spur the growth of tribal enterprise, the commission recommended a host of initiatives designed to encourage business planning, provide tribes with capital and technical assistance, and otherwise shift the focus of tribal enterprises from one of community-oriented job creation to one of individual profit-making.[53]

From the perspective of the NTCA's Elmer Savilla, the report compiled by the Commission on American Indian Reservation Economies was "dangerous"—the "most dangerous paper on Indian policy to be written in many a decade."[54] The commission's findings, Savilla argued, were "not factual and the study itself not scientific." To make matters worse, he added, tribes had not been adequately consulted. There had indeed been sixteen field hearings, Savilla acknowledged, "but hearings cannot in any sense be called consultation." At a hearing he attended in late October 1983, Savilla objected to the panel of "Indian experts" and raised concerns that the meeting would be used as an indication of having "consulted with tribes." He also demanded an apology for the commission's insulting identification of "incompetent management by tribal governments" as a cause for Indian economic problems. When that apology was not forthcoming, Savilla left the meeting in protest.[55] NTCA president Newton Lamar (Wichita), meanwhile, believed the commission's report was alarming in that it "could very well be the biggest single step towards the termination of the federal recognition of tribes." According to noted author and publisher Rupert Costo (Cahuilla), who attended one of the field hearings, "We've seen this kind of thing over and over for many generations. The Commission was set up to do something to help the tribes in the area of economic development on their reservations, and they go way off into left field and get into shaping Indian policy from scratch. This wouldn't be bad if they knew anything about what is happening in Indian Country, but they don't."[56]

Costo's frustration with the commission's decision to wander off "into left field" reflected that of many Native Americans who took issue with recommendations that appeared to have little to do with economic development. The recommendation to create an Indian Trust Services Administration, for example, was interpreted as an effort to abolish the BIA, while the proposal to subordinate tribal courts to the federal judiciary was seen as a direct violation of tribal sovereignty. Pyramid Lake Paiute tribal council member Joe Ely echoed the views of many tribal leaders that the effect of the commission's recommendations "would be to strip Indians of their vast holdings in energy resources, precious metals, and water rights."[57]

Approximately one week after the commission's report was released, the NTCA called an emergency meeting of federally recognized tribes to discuss the potential impact of the document and to develop a strategy in case President Reagan adopted any or all of its recommendations. On January 9, 1985, representatives from 102 tribes met at the MGM Grand in Reno and voted overwhelmingly to reject the commission report.[58] The section dealing with a repeal of termination was viewed positively, but participants felt that several other sections seriously threatened tribal sovereignty and "the dangerous parts outweighed the good." After two days of deliberations, the group voted to send a telegram to Reagan thanking him for his interest in reservation economies but asking for a summit meeting to discuss alternatives to the commission report since it did not reflect the desires of Native Americans. In a somewhat ironic move, given the commission mandate to reduce Indian reliance on government support, they also requested federal assistance for elected tribal representatives to develop their own economic initiatives and for congressional hearings to give each tribe the opportunity to express its views to Congress regarding reservation economic development. Finally, tribal representatives authorized the NTCA to establish a fifteen-member committee to devise an alternative plan to be reviewed and discussed by association members prior to its presentation to the president.[59]

Elmer Savilla was understandably pessimistic that Reagan would agree to meet with tribal leaders. "He's never acknowledged our requests before," Savilla commented, so "we don't know whether he will or not." The NTCA nonetheless pushed ahead with drafting an alternative plan for reservation economic development, and on January 28 sent a forty-page draft to tribal leaders for review and comment. After those had been considered, a final draft would again be submitted to tribal governments for approval before being sent to the president and Congress.[60]

In many respects, the NTCA draft document turned the commission's report on its head. Tribes—not individual Indian businesses—were the vanguard of reservation economic development, although tribes could, at their discretion, enter into joint ventures with privately owned Indian business endeavors. The commission recommendation to divorce tribal government from the management and operation of tribally owned businesses, the NTCA draft maintained, was foreign to the "unique traditional, cultural, political and social systems of Indian nations." Contrary to the commission report's emphasis on reducing tribal dependence on the federal government, the NTCA draft declared "what Indians want is to have the government go hand-in-hand with the tribes to improve economic development without endangering the Indian land base and trust responsibilities."[61]

There was one area of agreement between the NTCA draft and the commission report: the federal government was a serious impediment to reservation economic growth—especially in its failures to fulfill its trust obligations to protect Indian resources. The commission report had pegged "Legal Protection of Indian Natural Resources" as a problem area (albeit number thirty-four on its list of forty impediments to reservation economic development), stating, "There is competition between enforcing Indian trust responsibility and the public interest within the Interior Department, competition between Interior and Justice on case theory, and competition within Justice on case management where it simultaneously sues and defends the United States. This competition contains the potential for legal conflicts of interest to arise."[62] The NTCA draft focused its attention on water rights and the Interior and Justice Departments' conflict of interest when called upon to protect this resource, which was "central to economic growth on many reservations." The two departments, the NTCA draft charged, provided inaccurate surveys and incomplete information to tribes whose water rights were being threatened, and sought to push Indian water cases into state courts without providing tribes with adequate funding for litigation.[63]

News of President Reagan's decision on September 26, 1985, to nominate commission cochair Ross Swimmer (Cherokee) to be the new assistant secretary of the interior on Indian affairs was another discouraging development for the NTCA. The association's persistent criticism of the commission report—and, on occasion, the "loyalty" of its Indian members—poisoned its relationship with the BIA's top administrator and prompted the Cherokee leader to respond in kind. Shortly after the report's release, Swimmer had argued that tribes should endorse the commission's recommendation for block-grant funding from the federal government so that they could quit acting like a "puppet to the BIA" and warned that if "tribal governments don't start acting like tribal governments, and start issuing their own taxes and running their own schools, then Congress is going to find very little reason why the tribes should be around."[64]

In October, NTCA president Richard LaFromboise (Turtle Mountain Chippewa) informed a group of Indian leaders that the association had formulated its reply to the commission report and was attempting to convince Reagan and Swimmer that none of its recommendations be implemented without first consulting with tribes. What the commission was really after, LaFromboise surmised, was to model tribal governments after the U.S. government. "We don't think their system is working so hot," he concluded. "They are $3 trillion in debt. Maybe they are the ones who need a new Constitution."[65]

As is often the case with efforts to reform the structures, processes, and cultures of huge bureaucracies, the end result rarely justifies the time and effort expended to create it. During the early 1980s the competing BIA realignment ideas proposed by the Interior Department and the joint NTCA-NCAI task force went nowhere, and the bureau's structure remained largely in place. The Commission on American Indian Reservation Economies, meanwhile, spent nearly two years and approximately $865,000 conducting its study and preparing recommendations. The NTCA, as we have seen, responded by drafting a counter-proposal and spent months refining it with input from the tribes. In the end, few if any of the recommendations made by either body were enacted. This is not to say, of course, that working to reform and improve bureaucracies or bureaucratic processes is not a meaningful or worthwhile endeavor. Without such efforts there would have been no tribal contracting and no empowerment of tribal governments, and the specter of termination might again reign supreme.

While failing to produce significant changes in federal Indian policy, the bureaucratic warfare of the 1980s over the structure of the BIA and the plight of reservation economies were instructive in what they revealed about their participants—the NTCA in particular. During the 1980s, for instance, the rhetoric that association leaders used in their communications with policymakers and their publicized assessments and descriptions of the Reagan administration's domestic policies (and the motives behind them) demonstrate what can only be described as a radical departure from the strategies that association leaders employed a decade earlier. As noted in this study, NTCA leaders of the 1970s pursued a conventional insider's strategy based on establishing trust and confidence with their federal counterparts, making themselves indispensable to Interior Department officials by serving as "experts" on tribal governance and about problems on reservations, and promoting the interests of federally recognized tribes via close and frequent consultation with legislative and executive branch policymakers. After Robert Lewis's election as association president at the end of 1973, the press had praised the Zuni leader as a voice for "steady, deliberate progress amidst cries for revolution, calm where there is confusion, and cool debate where there is a heated argument."[66]

Lewis's associates in the NTCA, meanwhile, routinely condemned the often harsh and impolitic language (four-letter words in particular) used by Red Power groups as dangerous, counterproductive, and irresponsible. During the 1980s, however, it was NTCA leaders who were publicly denouncing the federal government as an "enemy" and President Reagan as a "liar," indifferent to Indian welfare, and dedicated to a sinister "hidden agenda" that sought the termination of federal obligations to Native Americans and the expropriation of their lands and resources. The NTCA of the 1980s organized protest marches, held press conferences outside the White House and Capitol, and threatened to take their concerns to the federal judiciary, the World Court, or the United Nations if their demands were not addressed. At a press conference held in April 1982 Elmer Savilla sought to embarrass the BIA into relaxing its purse strings by announcing that the NTCA was working with unnamed Indian groups to obtain low-interest loans from Japanese business interests to provide desperately needed economic aid for reservations.[67]

How do we account for this rather remarkable change? For starters, NTCA leadership was—by design—constantly changing. In accordance with the NTCA constitution, association officers and board members changed every one or two years. During the 1980s, new leaders (e.g., Elmer Savilla and Newton Lamar) joined with older ones (e.g., Wendell Chino and Roger Jourdain) who were not afraid to take their gloves off when engaging the federal government. The departure of more conservative Indian leaders such as Bill Youpee, Webster Two Hawk, and Robert Lewis from NTCA leadership positions made this transition possible.

Explaining the possible motives for the change is a bit more complex. The decade of the 1970s was, to some extent, a golden age in federal Indian policy. Tribal contracting became the norm under the Indian Self-Determination and Education Assistance Act, federal expenditures for Indian programs substantially expanded, several tribes received land restoration awards, and federal courts issued important decisions in support of Indian rights. Expectations for continued progress along these lines gave many Native Americans cause for cautious optimism. The Reagan budget cuts shattered these hopes, however, and rising expectations among Indian peoples were replaced by anger and a sense of betrayal. The administration's unwillingness to meaningfully consult with elected Indian leaders or to adequately explain its intentions compounded such feelings, and nurtured suspicions that Reaganomics housed a hidden agenda to weaken tribal governments and to promote termination. No longer possessing a privileged insider position within the Department of the Interior or the BIA, NTCA leaders apparently sought to capture the attention of decision makers in another way—by adopting inflammatory rhetoric that was reminiscent to an extent to that used by Red Power organizations such as AIM. Tribal chairs had historically resented the media's fascination with activists such as Russell Means and Dennis Banks and were especially frustrated when federal officials appeared willing to accommodate them. The NTCA, consequently, may have simply been applying to the changing circumstances of the 1980s the squeaky-wheel lesson derived from their Red Power counterparts.

During the 1970s the Nixon and Ford administrations had sought to nurture a close relationship with national Indian organizations such as the NTCA and the NCAI by consulting with them regularly about matters that concerned Indian Country. Critics charged that this was little more than a government ploy to manage or co-opt Indian opposition, but the relationship provided tangible benefits to all parties. Consultation allowed federal officials to obtain important information and feedback from Indian leaders, which in turn empowered them to move forward with policies—whether Indians approved of them or not—that had at least been "vetted" by representatives of the national Indian population. Indian leaders, for their part, gained status and legitimacy by having a seat at the table with their federal counterparts. Consultation with policymakers, furthermore, was not always just window dressing but a genuine opportunity to influence government priorities and to secure commitments of assistance. During the 1980s, however, the Reagan administration was on an ideological crusade to reduce the size and scope of government. Disinterested in or disinclined to pursue a co-optation strategy, the president allowed the relatively close consultation process that had figured so prominently in federal-Indian relations during the previous decade to lapse. Since there were no longer rewards for continuing its accommodationist-oriented position, the NTCA leadership became increasingly radicalized in response to Reagan-era budget cuts and the controversial proposals recommended by the Commission on American Indian Reservation Economies. Weak internal controls within the NTCA and the development of schisms between association leaders, meanwhile, gave license to individuals such as Elmer Savilla and Wendell Chino to promote the interests of federally recognized tribes in a manner quite different from those employed in the past. Reflecting on this period years later, Savilla maintained that federal officials responded to the NTCA's new confrontational approach by employing a "secret weapon to divide the tribes." When tribal chairs "pushed too hard, from 1980 to 1985, in opposition to policies or regulations," Savilla recalled, "Interior could turn to the National Congress of American Indians (NCAI) for approval."[68]

Regardless of its specific motives for doing so, the NTCA's movement from insider to outsider status during Reagan's first term was consequential to say the least. As an interest group that relied exclusively on federal assistance, the association's apparent disregard for the idiom "biting the hand that feeds you," as we will see, would figure prominently in its future as the voice of the tribes.

Conclusion
Lessons and Legacies

The drum is a powerful instrument. Native Americans have used drums for centuries in spiritual and sacred ceremonial practices. Some say the beat of the drum has the power to change natural elements, including the weather, and can be used to send messages to the spirit world. The earliest drums were used for religious rituals, social dances, sporting events, feasts, and special ceremonies; in preparation for hunting; and as a prelude to war. The drum's original purpose, however, was to communicate, many times over long distances, as a warning or signal.[1]

The power of the drum—both as a sacred instrument and as a warning or signaling device—may explain why the tribal chairs positioned a ceremonial drum near the speaker's podium when National Tribal Chairmen's Association (NTCA) members gathered for their conventions. The individual standing next to the drum to address the convention would have been mindful of its spiritual and sacred significance. To be permitted to share its space conveyed dignity and honor. In late June 1986 the tribal chairs hosted a conference on treaty rights in Washington, D.C. As Assistant Secretary of the Interior Ross Swimmer approached the podium to give his talk, however, NTCA executive director Ray Field (Pawnee) raced ahead of him and removed the drum. After Swimmer concluded his remarks, Field returned the drum to its former location, explaining that "he didn't feel it was appropriate for the drum to be up there" while Swimmer was speaking.

From the perspective of the tribal chairs present at the conference, the Cherokee leader had betrayed them. In addition to serving on the much-maligned Commission on American Indian Reservation Economies, Swimmer headed a Bureau of Indian Affairs (BIA) reeling from budget cuts and had the unpleasant duty of rallying reservation communities to do more with less. Tribal leaders responded to such overtures with charges that he was a "dangerous apple" and "the token Indian of this administration," a "very capable leader who can pick fights when we are weak." Swimmer claimed that he hadn't noticed the drum insult, and that his "feelings don't get hurt that easily." He understood that Indian leaders nationwide were angry but attributed much of their resentment to a "knee-jerk reaction to the BIA not providing them with whatever they think they need." The tribes, in Swimmer's opinion, were basically saying, "Give us a blank check and leave us alone. Give us money. We don't want to be held accountable."[2]

The End of the NTCA

The NTCA's "hostile reception" of Ross Swimmer during its June 1986 conference was undoubtedly based on an additional factor. On January 27 Swimmer had sent letters informing National Congress of American Indians (NCAI) president Reuben Snake and NTCA president Richard LaFromboise that the BIA would no longer continue funding the two organizations. The bureau's practice of tapping tribal program funds to assist the NCAI and NTCA could not continue, Swimmer explained, since BIA funding had been cut and then cut further by the requirements of recently passed deficit reduction legislation—the Gramm-Rudman Act. Continuing funding for the NTCA, Swimmer bluntly stated, would take funds away from the tribes. In the future, therefore, "the organizations should be supported by the tribes and the people they represent."[3]

While certainly unwelcome news to both national Indian organizations—as was the BIA's subsequent request for an Office of Inspector General audit of the two—the NCAI's reliance on federal funding was minimal compared to that of the NTCA, whose operations had been largely dependent upon such assistance since its founding.[4] Board members from both organizations believed that their funds were cut because they had been too vocal in their criticisms of Swimmer's Indian policies, particularly his habit of making important decisions without first consulting with the national tribal leadership. NTCA leaders, in fact, had long suspected that their decision to "push hard" against the Reagan administration could trigger this eventuality and had attempted to protect the association should it occur. During the BIA reorganization fight two years earlier, for example, the tribal chairs drafted a proposal for "An Independently Funded National Tribal Chairmen's Association" that called for an annual guaranteed line-item appropriation for the NTCA to serve as a "national Indian consultative body." This would obviate the threat of "terminated funding," the proposal stated, "in cases where the BIA takes unpopular stands." Like the rest of the NTCA's plan to restructure the Indian bureau, however, the funding proposal was never adopted.[5] In the spring of 1984, meanwhile, the association implemented a different strategy and began running newspaper solicitations under the headline "The National Tribal Chairmen's [*sic*] needs your help!" Donations of five to twenty-five dollars were requested to help the association "carry on the fight for Indian survival and Tribal sovereignty" and to "occasionally take strong issue with Administration positions."[6] How effective this approach was in raising funds is not clear. The fact that the ads stopped appearing a few months later suggests that the appeal fell on deaf ears or on empty pockets.

The impact of the funding cut was felt almost immediately. Anecdotal evidence suggests that the NTCA responded by attempting to levy annual dues of $250 on members, but this Band-Aid approach did little to stop the bleeding. According to an article in the *Seminole Tribune,* during its June 1986 conference in Washington, D.C., "the NTCA was going broke because only 65 tribes (out of more than 400) had paid yearly dues."[7] Turmoil among the association's leadership compounded the financial pressures. In August 1985 Elmer Savilla had left his position as executive director and was replaced by Raymond Field, a Pawnee from Oklahoma who had served in the army during the Vietnam War. A graduate of Georgetown University Law School and a member of the Native American Church, Field took up his duties just weeks before Ross Swimmer announced that the BIA was cutting the association's funding.[8] NTCA president Richard LaFromboise, meanwhile, came under fire from the association's board of directors. According to Roger Jourdain, the board had asked for LaFromboise's resignation in the fall of 1986 because "we felt that his lack of credibility in Indian Country was damaging our chances of raising badly needed funds to keep the organization going." LaFromboise denied the charges and refused to step down.[9]

By February 1987 the internal squabble among NTCA leaders no longer mattered. Unable to pay its twenty-two-hundred-dollar monthly rent nor the salaries of staff, the NTCA closed its office (according to media accounts, it was "forcibly evicted") in Washington, D.C., and moved remaining office equipment and supplies to the home of a former secretary who attempted to set up a temporary headquarters in her basement.[10] There was talk—or at least wishful thinking—that the move was "temporary" and that the association would soon be back on its feet. This was not the case, however, and the NTCA's fifteen-year reign as the self-proclaimed "voice of the tribes" came to an igno-minious close.

Postmortem

The National Tribal Chairmen's Association passed into history with barely a whimper. Native Americans, who had always viewed the organization with a certain degree of ambivalence, greeted the news with apparent indifference (the *Indian Country Today* piece announcing the closure ran under the rather insensitive headline "Going Belly Up"). As an exclusive organization of elected tribal leaders, the NTCA had never inspired the same widespread loyalty as the membership-driven NCAI, and thanks to the Reagan budget cuts, the NTCA did not appear to be delivering discernible results in approving life on reservations. The talents and loyalties of the elected tribal chairs, moreover, remained suspect. Writing in January 1986 Dean Chavers (Lumbee) had declared them "the most vilified people" in the country. "If tribal leaders stand on principle, they are condemned as being unrealistic. If they are diplomats and try to bargain and negotiate, they are labeled as Uncle Tomahawks."[11] As time passed, the association and its efforts on behalf of federally recognized tribes were largely forgotten. Studies of contemporary federal-Indian relations contributed to this memory deficit by either ignoring the NTCA or casting it simplistically as a creation of the Nixon administration, an organization financed by the federal government (and therefore suspect), or a tool of policymakers to manipulate, stall, or otherwise sow discord within the Indian rights movement. While an element of truth undoubtedly resides in all these assertions, this study has challenged them based, whenever possible, on the words and actions of association leadership. The NTCA, to be fair, should not be assessed or remembered exclusively for its harsh criticisms of the American Indian Movement (AIM) and urban Indian activism during the early 1970s. Like an insect ensconced in amber, the one vivid memory of the NTCA that appears in studies of contemporary federal-Indian relations tends to fixate on the controversial behavior of the tribal chairs during the BIA occupation crisis of November 1972. The one-dimensional image that emerges from this singular event, however, does not reflect the totality of the association's fifteen-year history—especially the last third.

As an interest group promoting the goals of federally recognized tribes, the NTCA was moderately successful. Convinced that elected tribal chairs alone possessed the legitimacy and authority to speak on behalf of Indian nations, they adopted a conventional or accommodationist advocacy strategy of working within the system, building relationships with decision makers, and serving as brokers between federal and Indian governments. From the perspective of Indian rights activists and organizations who believed that a more confrontational approach might have brought quicker and more profound results, the NTCA's strategy played into the hands of federal officials who sought to manipulate tribal leaders and to co-opt the Indian rights movement. This friction over the appropriate strategy to bring about reform was never fully resolved and remains a divisive issue to the present day.

According to its stated mission, the association sought close and frequent consultation with decision makers in the federal government, and the documentary evidence is voluminous that this consultation occurred. At its board meetings and annual conventions, association officials met face-to-face with leaders in the BIA, from various executive branch departments, with members of Congress, and with White House staffers. These meetings were occasionally contentious and not always productive, but during its first decade of existence, the NTCA's access to federal officials surpassed that of any other Indian rights organization. During the 1980s, as we have seen, this consultation process broke down amid the NTCA's profound disagreements over Reagan administration budget cuts and the recommendations contained in the report issued by the Commission on American Indian Reservation Economies.

As discussed in chapter 3, the NTCA was also moderately successful in its efforts to promote tribal sovereignty, self-determination, cultural preservation, and the protection of Indian lands and resources. While Indian activism helped bring these issues into public view for the first time in a century, it was unclear how high-visibility demonstrations and takeovers would translate into substantive results.[12] Organizations such as the NTCA, employing conventional strategies, made this happen. Consulting with policymakers, testifying before congressional committees, studying and amending proposed legislation, and personally lobbying key legislators and their staffs were not activities that commanded the attention of the media nor did they stir the imaginations of reservation-based Indian families trying to make ends meet, but they were critical in translating desires into actions. As NTCA president Webster Two Hawk observed, service in the association "is not all fun and games but very exhausting, time-consuming work to deliberate and discuss the vast issues that face Indians in a national sense."[13]

The NTCA was likewise moderately successful in helping defeat, or at least diminish, the burgeoning anti-Indian backlash movement. Like its other work on behalf of federally recognized tribes, this was no lone accomplishment but part of a national Indian response to the threat to Indian rights posed by backlash organizations such as ICERR and the Citizens Equal Rights Alliance. The association's participation in the United Effort Trust and as a member of the Commission on State-Tribal Relations helped defeat proposed backlash legislation in Congress and initiated an important dialogue with state officials over sensitive issues and long-standing conflicts over state-tribal jurisdiction.

A recurring challenge in its efforts to promote the interests of federally recognized tribes was the NTCA's consistent and persistent claim to be their exclusive voice. While understandable from a strategic sense, the assertion was problematic for several reasons. First, the NTCA never had more than 175 to 200 tribal chairs as members at a given time, but there were approximately twice that number of recognized tribes in the country. That reason alone disqualified their claim to speak for the tribes. There are even problems with the association claiming to be the voice of its members. Navajo tribal chair Peter MacDonald, for example, was frequently at odds with the NTCA and proved perfectly willing to plot a different course when the NTCA failed to speak for the Navajos. Both Joe Delacruz and Phillip Martin left the association over bitter disagreements with its leadership or the association's strategies and goals, or both.

A second problem was that many tribal chairs held membership only in the NCAI while others held membership in both the NTCA and the NCAI. How could the NTCA claim to be the voice of tribes affiliated only with the NCAI? The NTCA compounded this problem by behaving in a manner that was divisive, at times unprofessional, and in the end, self-destructive. As the self-proclaimed voice of the tribes, the NTCA insisted on taking the lead on any Indian-related government task force or commission. After the BIA occupation crisis, for example, Commissioner Bruce had requested that NCAI executive director Chuck Trimble lead a task force to consider ways to reconcile the fractured relationship between Native Americans and the federal government. The NTCA chose not to participate, however, because of its claim to be the sole legitimate voice of federally recognized tribes. If it wasn't leading the effort, then it wasn't going to participate. The association had initially applauded the creation of the American Indian Policy Review Commission, but abruptly pulled its support, and filed a lawsuit, when the chairs learned that they would not be able to dictate which Indians were to be included on that body. In the face of the anti-Indian backlash movement, a broad-based effort took place to create a unified Indian resistance under the direction of the United Effort Trust. The backlash was a serious threat, warned the NCAI's Veronica Murdock, but "our greatest challenge is whether we as Indian leaders can put aside suspicion, vanity and our quarrels over who will lead in order to work together."[14] Joe Delacruz and other NTCA officers agreed to accept this challenge, but NTCA board members proved unwilling to do so, a failure that reflects poorly on the association's legacy in the modern Indian rights movements—and rightfully so.

As discussed in chapter 4 the NTCA's claim to be the voice of federally recognized tribes dovetailed with its engagement in the politics of exclusivity. Unwilling to meet with or seriously discuss the needs of urban Indians and non-recognized tribes—people whom Bill Youpee noted were not "real" Indians to begin with—the NTCA deepened the divisions within the national Indian community and alienated half the Indian population in the country. Understandably concerned about the potential financial impact on finite Indian-related appropriations if the BIA decided that its responsibilities extended beyond the borders of reservations, the NTCA could or should have used its access to federal officials to promote a solution along the lines recommended by Ernie Stevens and John Jollie to assist off-reservation Indian peoples by funneling monies from other federal agencies through the BIA. At the very least, such an approach would have cost the NTCA nothing but time to show that it was genuinely interested in their welfare and was not an implacable foe.

The election of Ronald Reagan was a watershed moment in the NTCA's history. Although initially optimistic that Reagan would promote self-determination by freeing tribal governments from the BIA's incessant paternalism, the budget cuts introduced shortly after his inauguration triggered alarm bells across Indian Country. As the self-proclaimed voice of federally recognized tribes, the NTCA expected to hold meetings with administration officials to consult about the proposed budget, but these requests were denied. As the budget-cutting process moved forward, the tribal chairs grew increasingly frustrated that their conventional advocacy strategies appeared to be hitting a brick wall and that accommodation to government processes no longer carried with it the requisite rewards. That being the case, they adopted a far more confrontational approach, employing heated rhetoric that at least some administrative officials characterized as "militant" and "irresponsible."[15] While the NTCA stopped short of staging occupations, its leadership held press conferences, demanded the resignations of government officials, threatened to take Indian complaints to the United Nations, organized at least one protest march, and held a vigil outside the White House. This "new" NTCA succeeded in capturing the Reagan administration's attention, but not in the way that the tribal chiefs had hoped. In January 1986 the BIA announced it would no longer provide funding for the association, a decision that NTCA officials attributed to their criticisms of the administration. A year later, the NTCA was finished and closed its office in Washington, D.C.

Two obvious lessons can be gleaned from the NTCA's rather rapid dissolution. The first is the tenuous position that organizations can find themselves in should they become too reliant on a particular form or source of financial assistance. The tribal chairs were aware of the potential hazards posed by their near complete dependence on government funding but were never able to secure adequate financing from private sources. The association received a ten-thousand-dollar grant from tobacco conglomerate Philip Morris in mid-1986 to establish a new computer database system, but this was a case of "too little too late."[16] Association leaders may have believed that their position as the voice of federally recognized tribes rendered them irreplaceable and that the administration had little choice but to maintain their current level of funding. This, in hindsight, was a serious miscalculation. The NCAI was still very much alive and had been consulting with the federal government for over four decades. There was no reason for that relationship not to continue. Another plausible explanation for the NTCA's behavior is that association leaders were taking a principled stand by strongly criticizing their government benefactors, adopting an attitude of "let the chips fall where they may." Their uncharacteristically muted response to the BIA's decision to cut the association's funding suggests they understood this dynamic and accepted its implications.

The second lesson concerns the NTCA's decision to alter its traditional advocacy strategy and embark on a new course that involved biting the hand that fed them. This decision, they must have known, would have consequences. In the previous decade, the federal government had pulled out all the stops to repress AIM, not only cutting its funding but unleashing a concerted effort of infiltration, surveillance, and indictment by the BIA, the Federal Bureau of Investigation, and other agencies. By the end of the 1970s, consequently, AIM had ceased to be a significant player in federal-Indian relations.[17] The NTCA and AIM were, of course, very different organizations that employed decidedly different strategies in their pursuit of Indian rights. The point here is that interest groups must carefully weigh the risks and benefits of ratcheting up criticisms of the entity they are seeking to influence and that holds the purse strings. Limiting that criticism, as Foucault had warned, can lead to entrapment in the very system of power that reformers or revolutionaries are trying to overcome. Disregarding those limits, however liberating, can bring about the extinguishment of the movement altogether.[18]

In the 1974 edition of *Behind the Trail of Broken Treaties,* Vine Deloria described elected tribal chairs as occupying a tenuous "middle ground of progressive ideology." On one side stood "traditional Indians" who sought cultural preservation and the restoration of tribal governance based on custom and treaty rights. On the other side stood urban Indian activists who looked to the traditional Indians for guidance and in turn provided them the enthusiasm and energy necessary to bring about change. The "middle ground" occupied by elected tribal chairs, Deloria believed, was "fast eroding" and a "desperate confrontation was in the air" over the nature of the modern Native American community.[19]

Eleven years later, a new edition of *Behind the Trail of Broken Treaties* was published that included an afterword in which Deloria addressed the significant changes in federal-Indian relations that had occurred during the preceding decade. At least some of these changes must have surprised him. The position of elected tribal chairs, for example, was no longer "fast eroding" but instead strengthening in response to what Deloria described as the federal government's "zealous" support and a series of legislative and judicial victories. The positive movement in legislation, he stated, was "the culmination of various strands of thought which had been advocated by the tribes and national organizations for over a decade." Notable legislative achievements included the State and Local Fiscal Assistance Act of 1972, which made tribes eligible for revenue-sharing funds in the same way as state and municipal governments; the Indian Self-Determination and Education Assistance Act of 1974, which allowed tribes to contract for and self-administer certain programs and services; the Tribally Controlled Community College Act, which provided funds for the establishment of these institutions on reservations; and the Indian Child Welfare Act of 1978, which provided for the participation of tribal governments in the disposition of Indian children who were tribal members.[20]

Although Deloria suggested that the underlying cause for these legislative victories was that "many Indians saw them as advances and believed they were meeting some of the objections raised by traditional people," he offered no evidence to support this conclusion. He likewise attributed decreasing animosity between traditionals and tribal governments to "traditional people having strong impact on the way that tribal officials look at themselves and their programs."[21] There is likely some truth in these assertions, but a more compelling case, I have argued, can be made that the efforts of elected tribal chairs—alongside national organizations such as the NTCA and NCAI—were ultimately responsible. In August 1972 the NTCA adopted a resolution endorsing revenue-sharing legislation, citing it as a "test of Congressional willingness to grant Reservation Indians the right to shape their own future," and like the NCAI, lobbied extensively for its passage.[22] As discussed in chapter 3, the NTCA likewise drafted resolutions, testified before Congress, and lobbied on behalf of other legislation cited by Deloria. These types of exhausting, time-consuming, and unglamorous efforts account for the significant changes in federal Indian policy enacted during the so-called era of self-determination. Federal officials confirmed this dynamic during a meeting with Indian participants taking part in the Trail of Self-Determination march of 1976. "It is the elected leadership of Tribal government," they declared, "that will have the greatest influence upon the policies of this Administration."[23]

As the oldest continuing political institutions in the United States, tribal governments have demonstrated remarkable tenacity, adaptability, and resourcefulness to preserve tribal sovereignty in the face of overwhelming obstacles. "Today," writes legal scholar Charles Wilkinson, "the tribes, not the BIA, govern Indian Country," and the tribes "are full-service governments" responsible not just for carrying out the usual government functions but for preserving a way of life and a homeland for their people.[24] Regarding Deloria's prediction of a "desperate confrontation" over the nature of the modern Indian community, therefore, it is clear that the leaders of federally recognized tribes—buttressed by the NTCA's service as their voice—were the ultimate victors.

Epilogue

The dust had hardly settled in the vacant offices of the defunct National Tribal Chairmen's Association (NTCA) before two former members cobbled together a replacement. In April 1987 Wendell Chino and Roger Jourdain formed the Alliance of American Indian Leaders, an organization comprising chairs from several western tribes based in Minnesota, South Dakota, New Mexico, Washington, Montana, Colorado, and Oklahoma. At a two-day meeting held in Minneapolis during the last week in April, Chino and Jourdain announced they were working with the Native American Rights Fund and the Indian Rights Association to conduct a study of five clauses in the U.S. Constitution that related to Indian tribes. "We want members of Congress to acknowledge that they must give due respect to members of tribal governments," Chino stated, "and ensure that this country continues to honor those obligations that they accepted when they entered into many, many treaties with the Indian tribes."[1]

From October 10 to 13, 1987—as part of the bicentennial celebration of the signing of the U.S. Constitution—alliance members joined with Indian leaders and scholars from across the nation at a symposium titled "In Search of a More Perfect Union: American Indian Tribes and the United States Constitution," held in Philadelphia. Chino and Jourdain gave speeches that stressed the nation's obligation to "honor its constitutional relationship with American Indian tribes" and called for a restoration of the "nation-to-nation" status that had eroded over time.[2]

The second occasion that brought the Alliance of American Indian Leaders into the media spotlight was its response to a Senate Special Committee on Investigations report that recommended the dissolution of the Bureau of Internal Affairs (BIA) and the Indian Health Service and the transfer of their programs and funds to tribal governments. At a January 19, 1990, meeting held at the Inn of the Mountain Gods in Mescalero, New Mexico, alliance members representing around twenty western tribes rejected the proposal, which they interpreted as yet another example of the federal government trying to avoid its trust responsibilities to Indians. "The tribes have no desire to accept the transfer of underfunded and mismanaged agencies," Wendell Chino declared, and "the waste and corruption of these two agencies must be solved by Congress before any transfer is offered or made to tribes." Employing an analogy to underscore this point, Chino stated "It's like a state offering the county something that's run down and old. I'm sure the county would accept something if it were restored and improved."[3] As with previous attempts to dissolve the BIA or transfer oversight to a different entity, this effort went nowhere, and the bureau remained under the watchful eye of the Department of the Interior.

The Alliance of American Indian Leaders appeared in the media for a third (and final) time in late September 1990 in response to an invitation from Secretary of the Interior Manuel Lujan to attend a one-day "National Tribal Leaders Conference to Strengthen Self-Determination Policy" in Albuquerque. Billed as an opportunity for Indian leaders to meet "key people" in the Interior Department and BIA and as "the first such conference in modern times," the proposed summit met with criticism from two very different sources. Speaking for the Alliance of American Indian Leaders, Wendell Chino complained that a one-day conference would provide insufficient time for tribal leaders to express their views and that it was "ridiculous" to expect individuals from as far away as Alaska or Florida to travel all the way to New Mexico for a one-day meeting.[4]

The second critic of the Albuquerque conference was James L. Mitchell, vice president of the Citizens Equal Rights Alliance (CERA), an anti-Indian backlash organization based in South Dakota. Mitchell's criticism was that the conference would be closed to the general public. CERA members wanted to observe the proceedings, he maintained, because they were "concerned about the expansion of tribal powers" and possible federal "concessions to tribal governments." CERA members did not plan to carry signs of protest or attempt to force their way into the meeting, Mitchell promised. "We're not anti-Indian. We just think the meeting should be open to members of the public who want to know what's going on."[5]

In the end, the conference went on as planned. CERA members were not granted access to the conference, and Secretary Lujan made his presentation on restructuring the BIA to promote greater Indian autonomy and self-determination. Many Native American leaders were furious that the plan appeared to be a "done deal" and that they had not been consulted in its formulation. In his remarks to reporters after the conference, BIA head Eddie Brown commented wearily, "You will never at any time have all the 500 tribes happy. You will never have maybe 50 percent of the tribes happy." The lack of details offered on how the restructuring would affect tribal budgets and funds compounded the problem. "This is like giving the Indian tribes a Christmas tree," Wendell Chino declared. "It looks nice but there are no presents under the tree for the Indian[s]."[6]

———

The Alliance of American Indian Leaders apparently never gained traction and the organization vanished from sight at some point in the early 1990s. The positions it embraced during its brief existence clearly resonated with those of its NTCA predecessor, not surprising given the pedigree of its cochairs. Indian leaders like Wendell Chino and Roger Jourdain remained in the fight for Indian rights, however, advocating the same fundamental issues that had consumed their energies for over four decades. Just months before his death from a heart attack in November 1998, seventy-four-year-old Wendell Chino responded to plans announced by forty-seven-year-old Navajo Nation resident Albert Hale to stage a daylong shutdown of interstate highways and county roads that crossed the reservation as a demonstration of Navajo power and authority. "Closing a road is a poor way to defend tribal sovereignty," Chino counseled. "Our fellow Indian nations should not resort to radicalism about sovereignty" but instead address it through the legislative process and through the courts.[7] If his former protégés in the NTCA were listening, they would have undoubtedly been nodding their heads in agreement.

Appendix
NTCA Constitution and Bylaws
(All amendments are underlined.)

Formative Constitution and Bylaws

Preamble

We, the elected or appointed chairmen of all Indian reservations and federally recognized Indian tribes, of the United States of America, in order to establish unity among our succeeding generations, <u>and to serve as official voice of Indian leaders</u>; to reaffirm our faith in fundamental Indian rights, as specified in all Indian Treaties <u>and Indian reservations or rancherias as established by executive order</u>; and the United States Constitution; to establish conditions under which justice and respect for Treaty rights, and other laws can be maintained and to promote, encourage the preservation of our cultures and traditions and finally; to promote[] social, educational, economic and political progress among our Indian people, with the belief in the Great Spirit, do hereby establish this Constitution of the National Tribal Chairmen's Association.

Article I

Name of Association

The name of this association shall be the National Tribal Chairmen's Association. It shall be a non-profit organization.

Article II

Purpose of the Association

The purpose of this Association shall be:

1. To provide, improve and direct meaningful consultation between the U.S. Government and reservation Indian, including federally recognized Indian tribes and their elected officials.

2. To help and assist in directing and administering federal programs, funds, in order to aid reservation Indians, including federally recognized Indian tribes.

3. To approve the local and national Indian policies before they are implemented by the federal, state and local governments and keep all Indians, including federally recognized Indian tribes and elected officials apprised on policies and programs that the Association acts upon or becomes aware of. This information shall be by telephone followed with a letter of confirmation.

4. To demand that Indian people receive their full share of all federally funded programs.

5. To insure [sic] that the historic trust relationship between the U.S. Government and the reservation Indians, including federally recognized Indian tribes[,] is not modified and not terminated.

6. To demand that every federal agency recognize the Indian population for whom the U.S. Government has trust responsibility as enacted by the laws of the Congress of the United States, by executive orders, judicial decisions and treaties unique to Indian tribes.

7. To employ treaty rights and privileges for the promotion and protection of the human and natural resources of Indian reservations or groups and federally recognized tribes.

8. To cultivate relationships among Indian reservations, as well as with their duly elected leadership based on respect for the principle of equal rights and self-determination.

9. To represent the reservation and federally recognized tribes and demand that prior consultation by the U.S. Government, as expressed by President Nixon in his July 8, 1970, Message to the Congress, becomes a fact.

10. And for other purposes that may be deemed proper and necessary by this Association.

11. To continue to support, promote and complement the National Congress of American Indians.

Article III

Membership

The membership of this organization shall be composed of duly elected or appointed chairmen, presidents, governors or chiefs of reservation Indians or of federally recognized tribes with federal trust land or whose members live on or nearby federal reservations <u>having a local governing entity, and by the 12 Alaska Regional Corporations as created by the Alaskan Native Claims Bill</u>. The members must have approved credentials from their tribes before they can be admitted to the membership of the organization. <u>The member may designate an alternate who shall qualify pursuant to Article VIII hereof.</u>

Article IV
Officers
The Association shall have a President, a Vice-President, a Secretary and a Treasurer.

Term of Office: The President and Vice-President shall be elected for one year by the Association. The Secretary and Treasurer shall be elected for two years by the Association. All officers shall be members and directors of this Association. <u>All officers shall be a current tribal chairman of a tribe to be eligible to hold an office. The Board of Directors shall in any event fill the vacancy in any office of the Association until the next general meeting of the Association.</u>

Article V
Board of Directors

1. The activities of the Association shall be administered by a Board of Directors and the Officers of the Association.
2. The Board of Directors shall consist of a member elected at each annual meeting by each of the respective Bureau of Indian Affairs areas.
3. The Board of Directors, except as specified in Article IV, shall hold office for one year and until their successors are elected and qualified.
4. The Board of Directors shall have general charge of the affairs, funds and property of the Association. It shall have the duty to carry out the purposes of the National Tribal Chairmen's Association.

Article VI
Meetings
The Association shall meet twice a year. Time and place of the meetings shall be decided by the Association. Special meetings of the Association may be convened by the President or at the request of five members of the Board of

Directors. Fifty (50) percent of the membership shall constitute a quorum for a regular meeting.

Article VII
Committees
Standing and permanent committees may be established as the need of the Association demands. The committee members shall be appointed by the President and at least five board members.

Article VIII
Voting
All Association members shall be entitled to one vote on all issues by roll call vote. No proxy vote shall be allowed; provided however, any member may designate a person to vote in his behalf if that person (a) presents written authority signed by the member and (b) is an elected official of the same tribe.

Article IX
Amendments
This Constitution may be amended at any duly called meeting of the National Tribal Chairmen's Association provided that fifty-one (51) percent or more of the membership present cast their votes for the amendments.

Article X
Prohibited Activities
No action shall be taken by the Association to infringe upon or interfere with the expressed or inherent residual sovereign powers of the individual Indian tribes.

Article XI
Parliamentary Authority
All meetings of the Association shall be governed by Roberts' Rules of Order Revised.

> Constitutional Convention
> Albuquerque, New Mexico
> July 12, 1971
> Further amended at the NTCA annual convention held August 7–11, 1972, Eugene, Oregon.

Source: Amended Formative Constitution and Bylaws, General Correspondence, Folder 1, Box 5, Series 1, National Tribal Chairmen's Association Records, 1971–1978, National Museum of the American Indian, Smithsonian Institution Archive Center, Suitland, Md.

Amended Formative Constitution and Bylaws, Record of the Office of the Assistant for Public Liaison, Jane Wales, Indians, December 1976, Box 85, Jimmy Carter Presidential Library and Museum, Atlanta, Ga.

Notes

Introduction

1. "Indian Protest Planned during Election Week," *Navajo Times* (Window Rock, Ariz.), October 26, 1972, B-13.

2. Paul Chaat Smith and Robert Allen Warrior, *Like a Hurricane: The Indian Movement from Alcatraz to Wounded Knee* (New York: New Press, 1996), 149–54; Woody Kipp, *Viet Cong at Wounded Knee: The Trail of a Blackfeet Activist* (Lincoln: University of Nebraska Press, 2004), 99.

3. Smith and Warrior, *Like a Hurricane*, 153–55; George Pierre Castile, *To Show Heart: Native American Self-Determination and Federal Indian Policy, 1960–1975* (Tucson: University of Arizona Press, 1998), 118–22.

4. House Subcommittee on Indian Affairs, *Seizure of Bureau of Indian Affairs Headquarters* (Ninety-Second Congress, second session, December 4–5, 1972, Serial No. 92–54); Kipp, *Viet Cong at Wounded Knee*, 99–105; Smith and Warrior, *Like a Hurricane*, 159–65; Jon Katz, "Damage to BIA Third Heaviest Ever in U.S.," *Washington Post*, November 11, 1972, 4; Robert Burnette and John Koster, *The Road to Wounded Knee* (New York: Bantam Books, 1974), 212.

5. Messages Received from Tribal Leaders RE: "Trail of Broken Treaties" Activities, November 3–8, 1972, Series 12, Box 65, National Tribal Chairmen's Association Records, 1971–1978, National Museum of the American Indian, Smithsonian Institution Archive Center, Suitland, Md. (hereafter cited as NTCA Papers).

6. Paul R. Wieck, "Zuni Leader Ends Tension with Speech," *Albuquerque Journal*, November 7, 1972, 1; statement of Mrs. Genevieve Hooper at NTCA press conference at the Roger Smith Hotel, November 6, 1972, Series 12, Box 65, NTCA Papers.

7. Donald P. Baker, "Amnesty Denied to Indians," *Washington Post*, November 10, 1972, A1; NTCA Position Paper on Occupation of BIA, November 11, 1972, Series 12, Box 65, NTCA Papers.

8. "Led Building Takeover: Criminal Record of 3 Indian Leaders Told," *Chicago Tribune*, November 13, 1972, 3.

9. At the November 6 press conference, AIM participants accused NTCA members of coming to Washington, D.C., at the behest of Assistant Secretary of the Interior Harrison Loesch. See Wieck, "Zuni Leader Ends Tension with Speech," 1.

10. Donald P. Baker, "News Conference Confrontation," *Washington Post*, November 11, 1972, A1.

11. Tassie Hanna, Sam Deloria, and Charles E. Trimble, "The Commission on State-Tribal Relations: Enduring Lessons in the Modern State-Tribal Relationship," *Tulsa Law Review* 47 (Spring 2002): 578.

12. Carole Goldberg-Ambrose, "Of Native Americans and Tribal Members: The Impact of Law on Indian Group Life," *Law and Society Review* 28 (December 1994): 1125–32.

13. R. David Edmunds, *American Indian Leaders: Studies in Diversity* (Lincoln: University of Nebraska Press, 1980), viii–ix; Martha McLeod, "Keeping the Circle Strong: Learning about Native American Leadership," *Tribal College Journal of American Indian Higher Education* 13 (Summer 2002): 10–12; Linda Sue Warner and Keith Grint, "American Indian Ways of Leading and Knowing, *Leadership* 2 (May 2006): 226–27.

14. Robert F. Berkhofer, *The White Man's Indian: Images of the American Indian from Columbus to the Present* (New York: Vintage, 1979), 183–85; Graham D. Taylor, *The New Deal and American Indian Tribalism* (Lincoln: University of Nebraska Press, 1980), 82; Thomas Biolosi, *Organizing the Lakota: The Political Economy of the New Deal on the Pine Ridge and Rosebud Reservations* (Tucson: University of Arizona Press, 1988), 3–4.

15. Wilcomb Washburn, "A Fifty-Year Perspective on the Indian Reorganization Act," *American Anthropologist* 16 (June 1984): 280.

16. Ibid., 280–81; Akim D. Reinhardt, *Ruling Pine Ridge: Oglala Lakota Politics from the IRA to Wounded Knee* (Lubbock: Texas Tech University Press, 2007), 23.

17. Lawrence C. Kelly, "The Indian Reorganization Act: The Dream and the Reality," *Pacific Historical Review* 44 (August 1975): 296–312; David E. Wilkins and Sheryl Lightfoot, "Oaths of Office in Tribal Constitutions: Swearing Allegiance, but to Whom?" *American Indian Quarterly* 32 (Fall 2008): 390–92; S. Lyman Tyler, *A History of Indian Policy* (Washington, D.C.: Department of the Interior, 1973), 132; Richmond L. Clow, "The Indian Reorganization Act and the Loss of Tribal Sovereignty: Constitutions on the Rosebud and Pine Ridge Reservations," *Great Plains Quarterly* 7 (Spring 1987): 131–33; Thomas Biolosi, "The IRA and the Politics of Acculturation: The Sioux Case," *American Anthropologist* 87 (September 1985): 657–58; Tom Holm, "Indian Concepts of Authority and the Crisis in Tribal Government," *Social Science Journal* 19 (July 1982): 59–60; Laurence M. Hauptman, *The Iroquois and the New Deal* (Syracuse, N.Y.: Syracuse University Press, 1981), 63–64; Felix S. Cohen, *On the Drafting of Tribal Constitutions* (Norman: University of Oklahoma Press, 2006), xxii–xxix; Taylor, *New Deal and American Indian Tribalism*, 65, 68, 82, 96–98, 102.

18. Robert Burnette, *The Tortured Americans* (Englewood Cliffs, N.J.: Prentice Hall, 1971), 14.

19. Brian Calliou, "The Culture of Leadership: North American Indigenous Leadership in a Changing Economy," in *Indigenous Peoples and the Modern State*, ed. Duane Champagne, Karen Jo Torjesen, and Susan Steiner (New York: Alta Mira Press, 2005), 51.

20. Goldberg-Ambrose, "Of Native Americans and Tribal Members," 1135; Biolosi, *Organizing the Lakota*, xxi; Holm, "Indian Concepts of Authority and the Crisis in Tribal Government," 59.

21. Biolosi, *Organizing the Lakota*, 180.

22. Laura E. Evans, "Expertise and Scale of Conflict: Governments as Advocates in American Indian Politics," *American Political Science Review* 105 (November 2011): 664.

23. "Sioux Leader Prays with President for Guidance," *The Indian*, February 27, 1970, 1. *The Indian* was a South Dakota–based publication of the American Indian Leadership Council.

24. Guy B. Senese, *Self-Determination and the Social Education of Native Americans* (New York: Praeger, 1991), 146.

25. Political scientist Andrew Rehfeld refers to this as the "standard account" of political representation. See Andrew Rehfeld, "Towards a General Theory of Political Representation," *Journal of Politics* 68 (February 2006): 3.

26. Tom Brown, "Who Speaks for the Indians?" *Billings (Mont.) Gazette*, January 5, 1971, 4; Mary E. Fleming Mathur, "The Duke Had a Word for It: Local-Level Competition between Tribals and Non-Tribals," in *Political Anthropology: The State of the Art*, ed. S. Lee Seaton and Henri M. Claessen (New York: Mouton, 1979), 123.

27. David E. Wilkins, *American Indian Politics and the American Political System* (New York: Rowman and Littlefield, 2002), 210–11; Jerry D. Stubben, *Native Americans and Political Participation* (Santa Barbara, Calif.: ABC-CLIO, 2006), 68–69; Bradley G. Shreve, *Red Power Rising: The National Indian Youth Council and the Origins of Native Activism* (Norman: University of Oklahoma Press, 2011), 192.

28. Shreve, *Red Power Rising*, 94–143; Daniel M. Cobb, *Native American Activism in Cold War America: The Struggle for Sovereignty* (Lawrence: University of Kansas Press, 2008), 58–60; Charles T. Powers, "Bitter Look at Uses of Red Power," *Kansas City (Mo.) Times*, March 16, 1968, 16.

29. "Manifesto," Indians of All Tribes *Newsletter* 1 (1970) in Box 6, Temporary Committees, Commissions, and Boards, Records of the National Council on Indian Opportunity, 1968–1974, Record Group 220, National Archives Building at College Park, Md. (hereafter cited as NCIO Records); Shreve, *Red Power Rising*, 184–85; Stubben, *Native Americans and Political Participation*, 105.

30. Laura Montanaro, "The Democratic Legitimacy of Self-Appointed Representatives," *Journal of Politics* 74 (October 2012): 1094–106.

31. Vine Deloria Jr., *Behind the Trail of Broken Treaties: An Indian Declaration of Independence* (New York: Dell, 1974), 40–41; Deloria, "This Country Was a Lot Better Off When the Indians Were Running It," *New York Times*, March 8, 1970, 17; Burnette and Koster, *Road to Wounded Knee*, 209.

32. Kevin Bruyneel, *The Third Space of Sovereignty: The Postcolonial Period of U.S. Indigenous Relations* (Minneapolis: University of Minnesota Press, 2007), xvi, 93.

33. See Castile, *To Show Heart*, and *Taking Charge: Native American Self-Determination and Federal Indian Policy, 1975–1993* (Tucson: University of Arizona Press, 2006); Charles Wilkinson, *Blood Struggle: The Rise of Modern Indian Nations* (New York: W. W. Norton & Co., 2005). Paul C. Rosier provides an excellent discussion of Indian politics and "hybrid patriotism" in *Serving Their Country: American Indian Politics and Patriotism in the Twentieth Century* (Cambridge, Mass.: Harvard University Press, 2009). Daniel M. Cobb's *Native Activism in Cold War America: A Struggle for Sovereignty* (Lawrence: University of Kansas Press, 2008) places Native American activism within the international context of the Cold War; David E. Wilkins, *American Indian Politics and the American Political System* (New York: Rowman and Littlefield, 2002), examines the structures and functions of Indigenous governments from a political science perspective.

34. See, for example, Vine Deloria Jr., *Custer Died for Your Sins: An Indian Manifesto* (Norman: University of Oklahoma Press, 1969); Dennis Banks with Richard Erdoes, *Ojibwa Warrior: Dennis Banks and the Rise of the American Indian Movement* (Norman: University of Oklahoma Press, 2005); Shreve, *Red Power* Rising; Bradley G. Shreve, "'From Time Immemorial': The Fish-In Movement and the Rise of Intertribal Activism," *Pacific Historical Review* 78 (August 2009): 403–34; American Friends Service Committee, *Uncommon Controversy: Fishing Rights of the Muckleshoot, Puyallup, and Nisqually Indians* (Seattle: University of Washington Press, 1970); Stephen Cornell, "The New Indian Politics," *Wilson Quarterly* 10 (New Year's 1986): 113–31.

35. Daniel M. Cobb and Loretta Fowler, eds., *Beyond Red Power: American Indian Politics and Activism since 1900* (Santa Fe, N.M.: School for Advanced Research Press, 2007), x.

36. Cobb, *Native Activism in Cold War America*, 2.

37. Thomas W. Cowger, *The National Congress of American Indians: The Founding Years* (Lincoln: University of Nebraska Press, 2001).

38. Wilcomb W. Washburn, "Legitimate Indian Leaders," *Wilson Quarterly* 10 (Autumn 1986): 173–74; Cornell, "New Indian Politics," 123–24.

Chapter 1. Genesis

1. Anthony J. Nownes, *Interest Groups in American Politics: Pressure and Power* (New York: Routledge, 2013), 25–26, 30–32. The PIGS reference came from the author's correspondence with Philip S. Deloria. This self-deprecating label was apparently what some public-interest groups called themselves in the 1960s–70s (Deloria, email message to author, March 16, 2018).

2. Norman J. Ornstein and Shirley Elder, *Interest Groups, Lobbying, and Policymaking* (Washington, D.C.: Congressional Quarterly Press, 1978), 65, 226–27; Nownes, *Interest Groups in American Politics*, 30–34; Mark Chaves, Laura Stephens, and Joseph Galaskiewicz, "Does Government Funding Suppress Nonprofits' Political Activity?" *Sociological Review* 69 (April 2004): 293; Lester M. Salamon, ed., *The State of Non-Profit America* (Washington, D.C.: Brookings Institution Press, 2002), 12.

3. Vine Deloria Jr., *Behind the Trail of Broken Treaties: An Indian Declaration of Independence* (New York: Dell, 1974), 40–41; Deloria, "This Country Was a Lot Better Off When the Indians Were Running It," *New York Times*, March 8, 1970, 17.

4. "Community Action: Main Features of the Program," *Congressional Digest* 47, February 1, 1968, 36–40, 64.

5. Daniel M. Cobb, "Philosophy of an Indian War: Indian Community Action in the Johnson Administration's War on Indian Poverty, 1964–1968," *American Indian Culture and Research Journal* 22 (1998): 73–74; E. Fletcher McClellan, "The Politics of American Indian Self-Determination, 1958–1975: The Indian Self-Determination and Education Assistance Act of 1975" (Ph.D. diss., University of Tennessee, 1988), 102; "Community Action: Main Features of the Program," 36–40.

6. American Indian Policy Review Commission, *American Indian Policy Review Commission Final Report*, May 17, 1977 (Washington, D.C.: Government Printing Office, 1977), 431, 434; Lewis Meriam et al., *The Problem of Indian Administration* (Washington, D.C.: Brookings Institution, 1928), 669; Lee J. Sclar, "Participation of Off-Reservation

Indians in Programs of the Bureau of Indian Affairs and the Indian Health Service,"
Montana Law Review 33 (Summer 1972): 207.

7. Tom Brown, "Who Speaks for the Indians?" *Billings (Mont.) Gazette*, January 5,
1971, 4.

8. Nancy Oestrech Lurie, "The Voice of the American Indian: Report on the American Indian Chicago Conference," *Current Anthropology* 2 (December 1961): 481.

9. BIA estimates of the Indian population in 1970 differ from that of the decennial census. The BIA census counted 792,730 Indians, with 478,000 living on or near reservations—just over 60 percent. See Sar A. Levitan and Barbara Hetrick, *Big Brother's Indian Programs—With Reservations* (New York: McGraw Hill, 1971), 7–9.

10. U.S. Census Bureau Decennial Census, 1970, Subject Report: American Indians, Table 11: Social Characteristics of the Indian Population, 138–47; S. Lyman Tyler, *A History of Indian Policy* (Washington, D.C.: Department of the Interior, 1973), 207; Levitan and Hetrick, *Big Brother's Indian Programs*, 108; James E. Officer, "The American Indian and Federal Policy," in *The American Indian in Urban Society*, ed. Jack O. Waddell and O. Michael Watson (New York: University Press of America, 1984), 55–56.

11. Cobb, "Philosophy of an Indian War," 74–75, 82–83; Thomas Clarkin, *Federal Indian Policy in the Kennedy and Johnson Administrations, 1961–1969* (Albuquerque: University of New Mexico Press, 2001), 126–27.

12. Tassie Hanna, Sam Deloria, and Charles E. Trimble, "The Commission on State-Tribal Relations: Enduring Lessons in the Modern State-Tribal Relationship," *Tulsa Law Review* 47 (Spring 2002): 556–57.

13. Steve Nickeson, "The Structure of the Bureau of Indian Affairs," *Law and Contemporary Problems* 40 (Winter 1976): 61; *The Public Papers of the Presidents of the United States, Richard Nixon: 1971: Containing the Public Messages, Speeches, and Statements of the President* (Washington, D.C.: U.S. Government Printing Office, 1972), 990.

14. Joseph H. Cash, "Louis Rooks Bruce, 1969–73," in *The Commissioners of Indian Affairs, 1824–1977*, ed. Robert M. Kvasnicka and Herman J. Viola (Lincoln: University of Nebraska Press, 1979), 333–40; "Commissioner Bruce Calls for More Indian Involvement," *Northwest Indian Times* (Spokane, Wash.), October–November 1969, 6.

15. Cash, "Louis Rook Bruce," 336–40; Alvin M. Josephy, *The American Indian and the Bureau of Indian Affairs—1969: A Study with Recommendations* (February 11, 1969)—copy obtained from Arizona State University College of Law Library; Homer Bigart, "American Indian Activists Winning Bureau Reform," *New York Times*, January 9, 1972, 1, 56; Charles Trimble, "Uncle Louie and the Katzenjammer Kids," *Indian Country Today*, March 7, 2008; Richard Halloran, "Reform in Indian Bureau," *New York Times*, December 3, 1970, 1; Cleve Mathews, "Indian to Head Indian Bureau," *New York Times*, August 8, 1969, 16; Nickeson, "Structure of the Bureau of Indian Affairs," 66–67.

16. Transcript of NTCA Consultation session with Marvin Franklin, July 23, 1973, Series 4, Box 5, Folder 4, National Tribal Chairmen's Association Records, 1971–1978, National Museum of the American Indian, Smithsonian Institution Archive Center, Suitland, Md. (hereafter cited as NTCA Papers).

17. Testimony of Gerald Wilkinson before Senate Subcommittee on Indian Affairs, August 20, 1973, Series 10, Box 49, Folder 1, NTCA Papers.

18. Russel L. Barsh and James Youngblood Henderson, *The Road: Indian Tribes and Political Liberty* (Berkeley: University of California Press, 1980), 226–27.

19. Ibid., 227–28.

20. "Nixon's BIA Policies in Doubt," *Nishnawbe News* (Ishpeming, Mich.), November 1971, 6; "BIA Disputes Divide Tribes," *Northwest Indian Times* (Spokane, Wash.), November 1971, 4; Cash, "Louis Rooks Bruce," 337; William M. Blair, "Indians Say Trust in Nixon is Shaken," *New York Times*, August 29, 1971, 35; Bradley G. Shreve, *Red Power Rising: The National Indian Youth Council and the Origins of Native Activism* (Norman: University of Oklahoma Press, 2011), 193–94; AIM to Richard Nixon, September 22, 1972, Series 4, Box 5, Folder 1, NTCA Papers.

21. Seth Mydans, "Indians Say U.S. Has Ignored Their Views in New Program," *Santa Fe New Mexican*, September 30, 1990, 3.

22. "Indians Bristle at New Order," *Havre (Mont.) Daily News*, December 4, 1970, 1; "Metcalf Makes Effort to Block BIA Shakeup," *Independent Record* (Helena, Mont.), December 4, 1970, 6.

23. "BIA Policies Worry Tribes," *Northwest Indian Times* (Spokane, Wash.), December 1970, 4; Brown, "Who Speaks for the Indians?," 4; McClellan, "Politics of American Indian Self-Determination," 179–84.

24. David T. Early, "Stories of Ruckus Irk Tribal Leaders," *Billings (Mont.) Gazette*, October 7, 1971, 1; "Crow Says BIA Head Is Unfairly Criticized," *Billings (Mont.) Gazette*, December 22, 1970, 19.

25. "Changes in Policy," *Jicarilla Chieftain* (Dulce, N.Mex.), July 13, 1970, 4.

26. "BIA Policies Worry Tribes," 4; Jerry Cohen, "Leadership of U.S. Indians in Open Schism," *Los Angeles Times*, May 2, 1971, F-4–7; Brown, "Who Speaks for the Indians?," 4.

27. For a discussion of the ongoing dissension and factionalism in the NCAI during the 1960s, see Thomas W. Cowger, *The National Congress of American Indians: The Founding Years* (Lincoln: University of Nebraska Press, 1999), 128–49.

28. According to Hank Adams, the NCAI was a creation of the Interior Department and for a time took the lead in planning for termination. See "Activism and Red Power," in *Indian Self-Rule: First-Hand Accounts of Indian White Relations from Roosevelt to Reagan*, ed. Kenneth R. Philip (Logan: Utah State University Press, 1995), 239.

29. Charles Trimble, *Iyeska* (Indianapolis: Dog Ear Publishing, 2012), 59–65; Stephen Cornell, *The Return of the Native: American Indian Political Resurgence* (New York: Oxford University Press, 1990), 194.

30. Charles Trimble, "NCAI Made It through Rocky Era," Keynote Address to the NCAI, October 14, 2009, see http://64.38.12.138/News/2009/017098.asp; "Alcatraz," *Akwesasne Notes* (N.Y.) 3 (Summer 1971): 2; Hazel W. Hertzberg, "Indian Rights Movement, 1887–1973," in *Handbook of North American Indians*, vol. 4, ed. Wilcomb E. Washburn (Washington, D.C.: Smithsonian Institution, 1988), 320–21; Trimble, *Iyeska*, 61–62.

31. "Activist Elected Chief by Indians," *Dallas Morning News*, November 12, 1971, 15; "Indian Leader Hopes to Establish Rapport," *Reno Evening Gazette*, November 22, 1971, 8; "Tribes Will Form a Chairmen's Association," *Northwest Indian Times* (Spokane, Wash.), March 1, 1971, 5.

32. "Indian Leader Hopes to Establish Rapport," 8; Homer Bigart, "Indians Open Reno Conference; Urban-Reservation Rift at Issue," *New York Times*, November 16, 1971, 34; Trimble, *Iyeska*, 154–55.

33. Richard Nixon, "Special Message to the Congress on Indian Affairs," July 8, 1970, *The American Presidency Project*, http://www.presidency.ucsb.edu/ws/?pid=2573;

Dean J. Kotlowski, *Nixon's Civil Rights: Politics, Principle, and Policy* (Cambridge, Mass.: Harvard University Press, 2002), 200–201.

34. Kotlowski, *Nixon's Civil Rights*, 207.

35. Ibid., 207–8; Daniel P. Moynihan, *The Politics of a Guaranteed Income: The Nixon Administration and the Family Assistance Plan* (New York: Random House, 1973), 66; McClellan, "Politics of American Indian Self-Determination," 151–55.

36. "Self-Determination Conference Raised Questions—Not Answers," *Northwest Indian Times* (Spokane, Wash.), March–April 1971, 4.

37. The definitive treatment of this period is Donald Fixico's *Termination and Relocation: Federal Indian Policy, 1945–1960* (Albuquerque: University of New Mexico Press, 1986).

38. The White Paper, 1969, The Canadian Encyclopedia Online, https://www.thecanadianencyclopedia.ca/en/article/the-white-paper-1969; J. Anthony Long, Leroy Little Bear, and Menno Boldt, "Federal Indian Policy and Indian Self-Government in Canada: An Analysis of a Current Proposal," *Canadian Public Policy* 8 (Spring 1982): 190.

39. Long, Little Bear, and Boldt, "Federal Indian Policy and Indian Self-Government in Canada," 190; "Indians Plan Red Paper in Response to Government Proposals," *Lethbridge (Alberta) Herald*, January 9, 1970, 2; "Harold Cardinal Plans Second Book," *Brandon (Manitoba) Sun*, September 22, 1970, 8; "Trudeau Informs Jews to Insist on Rights," *Lethbridge (Alberta) Herald*, February 9, 1970, 2.

40. "Lucille Hendrickson, "Indians Pin Hopes on Tribal Chairman," *Bismarck Tribune*, November 28, 1969, 1; "If You Help a Man . . . ," *Bismarck Tribune*, June 21, 1971, 12; "Funeral Service Set for Tribal Chairman," *Bismarck Tribune*, October 12, 1970, 19; Clarence Skye, phone interview with author, August 14, 2018.

41. Pat Locke, "Unlocking Education: NTCA Alive and Fighting Despite Financial Difficulties," *Indian Country Today*, April 1, 1987, 5; Kelly was a founding member of the National Indian Brotherhood and the Assembly of First Nations and in 1973 was selected as president of the Grand Council Treaty Number Three association. See obituary in *Winnipeg Free Press*, December 23, 2012, https://passages.winnipegfreepress.com/passage-details/id-198009/Tobasonakwut_Kinew; "Indians Vote for One Voice," *Colorado Springs Gazette Telegraph*, May 23, 1970, 1–2. Clarence W. Skye confirmed that his father (Douglas Skye) had met with "Chairman Kelly" in 1969 (Clarence Skye, phone interview with author, August 14, 2018).

42. "Tribes Will Form a Chairman's Assn.," *Northwest Indian Times* (Spokane, Wash.) (March 1, 1971), 5.

43. Locke, "Unlocking Education," states that Edison Real Bird was responsible for organizing the conference. Other published accounts of the meeting state that William Youpee chaired the conference. See Dave Earley, "Second Little Bighorn: This Time Indians Talk," *Billings Gazette*, February 18, 1971, 8. There is no mention about how—or by whom—the conference was funded.

44. The National Council on Indian Opportunity (NCIO) was established by executive order during the closing months of the Lyndon B. Johnson administration. Chaired by the vice president and including cabinet members and six presidentially appointed Native American leaders (later raised to eight), the NCIO was intended to promote intergovernmental coordination and cooperation in regard to programs and services for

Native Americans and to encourage Native Americans to take advantage of those programs. See Thomas Britten, *The National Council on Indian Opportunity: Quiet Champion of Self-Determination* (Albuquerque: University of New Mexico Press, 2014).

45. Dave Earley, "Pow-Wow Beckons Indians," *Billings (Mont.) Gazette*, February 10, 1971, 40; Georganne Louis, "Indians Say They Are Not Heard," *Billings (Mont.) Gazette*, February 18, 1971, 7; Earley, "Second Little Bighorn," 8; Georganne Louis, "Indians Seek Funds Control," *Billings (Mont.) Gazette*, February 21, 1971, 28; Dave Earley, "Feds Too Concerned over Urban Indians," *Billings (Mont.) Gazette*, February 21, 1971, 16; Dave Earley, "Indians Swap Jokes about Custer and BIA," *Billings (Mont.) Gazette*, February 21, 1971, 19.

46. "Tribes Will Form a Chairman's Assn.," 5.

47. Jack Anderson, "Washington Merry Go-Round," *Camden (Ark.) News*, December 19, 1972, 4.

48. Robert Bennett, Comments at Tribal Chairmen's Conference, February 19, 1971, NTCA Working Papers, Series 1, Box 1, Folder 1, NTCA Papers.

49. Ibid.

50. Ibid.; Bennett was likely referring to the NCIO-sponsored Urban Indian Leaders meeting at the Airlie House conference center in Washington, D.C., that took place on December 14–15, 1970. Some of the urban Indian attendees vandalized the property, causing over thirty thousand dollars in damages. See Britten, *National Council on Indian Opportunity*, 209–12. According to Sam Deloria, Bennett confided in him that he had suggested to several tribal chairs the desirability of creating an organization along the lines of the National Association of Mayors (Deloria, email correspondence with author, March 17, 2018).

51. Rob Burnes, "Director Says Bureau Reservation Oriented," *Billings (Mont.) Gazette*, February 19, 1971, 1, 5.

52. Wendell Chino had served as president in 1967–68, Benny Atencio had served as recording secretary, and Roger Jourdain had served as a regional vice president.

53. "Tribes Will Form a Chairman's Assn.," 5; "Two Important Indian Meetings Held," *NCIO News*, March–April 1971, 1–2; Chuck Trimble, interview with author, Omaha, Neb., March 2, 2018.

54. Britten, *National Council on Indian Opportunity*, 168–69; "National Conference on Indian Self-Determination," *Indian Center News*, April 1971, 1–2; "MacDonald-Bennett Comment on Current Indian Policy," *Navajo Times* (Window Rock, Ariz.), March 18, 1971, 18–19.

55. "Conference of Indian Leaders and Government Officials Held Recently in Kansas City," *Southern Ute Drum* (Ignacio, Colo.), March 26, 1971, 4–5; Cohen, "Leadership of U.S. Indians in Open Schism"; "Aim Official Blasts Conference," *Albuquerque Journal*, March 11, 1971, 36.

56. Cohen, "Leadership of U.S. Indians in Open Schism"; "Conference of Indian Leaders and Government Officials Held Recently in Kansas City," 4–5.

57. "Tribal Group Opens Meet in Pierre," *Daily Plainsman* (Huron, S. Dak.), April 22, 1971, 14. According to an article in the *Los Angeles Times*, at an AIM conference held in Cleveland a week before the tribal chairs met in Pierre, Russell Means suggested sabotaging the meeting by stealing the dais. See Cohen, "Leadership of U.S. Indians in Open Schism." Elmer Hunt's comments can be found in NTCA Pierre Constitutional Con-

vention Transcript, MS 654–57, p. 01064, American Indian Research Project, University of South Dakota, Vermillion, S. Dak. (hereafter cited as NTCA Pierre Constitutional Convention transcript).

58. NTCA Pierre Constitutional Convention Transcript, pp. 01043, 01052, 01117–18.

59. Ibid., pp. 01047–51.

60. Ibid., pp. 01087–91.

61. Ibid., pp. 01094.

62. Ibid., pp. 01096.

63. "Constitution Adopted for National Indian Chairmen's Conference," *Mitchell (S. Dak.) Daily Republic*, April 24, 1971, 1; "Commissioner Looks Forward to Working with Group," *Mitchell (S. Dak.) Daily Republic*, April 24, 1971, 1; "Tribal Chairmen's Conference Formed," *Daily Plainsmen* (Huron, S. Dak.), April 25, 1971, 11, 19; Resolution to Create NTCA, April 24, 1971, Series 3, Box 4, Folder 4, NTCA Papers; Resolution Calling on Louis Bruce to Create a 15-Member All Indian Commission on BIA Reorganization, April 23, 1971, Series 3, Box 4, Folder 4, NTCA Papers.

64. NTCA Pierre Constitutional Convention Transcript, pp. 01047–51 (emphasis added).

65. Robert Burnette portrays Commissioner Bruce as "feverishly organizing" the National Tribal Chairmen's Association (Burnette and Koster, *Road to Wounded Knee*, 173–74). Vine Deloria states that the Nixon administration, "fearful of the quickened pace of Indian discontent, created its own organization called the National Tribal Chairmen's Association" (*Behind the Trail of Broken Treaties*, 43). Glenn T. Morris argues that the Nixon administration pursued a policy to "chill" forces for social change by channeling federal support to the NTCA, whose primary purpose was "to provide a native voice endorsing the status quo in Indian affairs" ("International Law and Politics: Toward a Right to Self-Determination for Indigenous Peoples," in *Native American Sovereignty*, ed. John Wunder [New York: Routledge, 1999], 302).

Chapter 2. Genesis

1. "Chippewas End 40-Year Rule of Graves Family," *Minneapolis Star*, January 8, 1959, 6B.

2. Charles Wilkinson, *Blood Struggle: The Rise of Modern Indian Nations* (New York: W. W. Norton & Co., 2005), 125; Chuck Haga, "A Champion of His People," *Minneapolis Star Tribune*, March 12, 2002, 1, 18–19; "Chippewas Take Exception to Ad Paleface Now Redface Bites Dust," *Albuquerque Journal*, January 16, 1967, A-11; Robert Franklin, "At 84, Jourdain Proud of His Role in History," *Minneapolis Star Tribune*, September 24, 1996, B1, B19.

3. Matt Mygatt, "Chino Honored as Faithful Fighter for Tribe's Progress," *Santa Fe New Mexican*, November 6, 1998, 12; Kate McGraw, "A Great Leader," *Santa Fe Reporter*, November 11, 1998, 59; Sharon Simonson, "Mescaleros Quietly Pick Successor to Chino," *El Paso Times*, November 6, 1998, 1.

4. Norman J. Ornstein and Shirley Elder, *Interest Groups, Lobbying, and Policymaking* (Washington, D.C.: Congressional Quarterly Press, 1978), 28–33, 54; Anthony J. Nownes, *Interest Groups in American Politics: Pressure and Power* (New York: Routledge, 2013), 65, 76, 82.

5. Letter to tribal leaders from Benny Atencio, Wendell Chino, and Peter Mac-Donald, June 8, 1971, NTCA Working Papers, Series 1, Box 1, Folder 1, National Tribal Chairmen's Association Records, 1971–1978, National Museum of the American Indian, Smithsonian Institution Archive Center, Suitland, Md. (hereafter cited as NTCA Papers); Tentative Agenda of the Constitutional Convention of the NTCA, July 12–14, 1971, NTCA Working Papers, Series 1, Box 1, Folder 1, NCTA Papers; Memorandum on NTCA Constitution Convention, Bylaws of the NTCA, Series 1, Box 4, Folder 3, NTCA Papers; Transcript of NTCA Introductions, July 12, 1971, NTCA Constitutional Convention, Series 1, Box 1, Folder 2, NTCA Papers; Keynote Address of Alonzo Spang at NTCA Constitutional Convention, July 12, 1971; Bylaws of the NTCA, Series 2, Box 4, Folder 3, NTCA Papers.

6. Amended Formative Constitution and Bylaws of the NTCA, General Correspondence, Series 4, Box 5, Folder 1, NTCA Papers.

7. Ibid.

8. David Miller et al., *The History of the Assiniboine and Sioux Tribes of the Fort Peck Indian Reservation: 1600–2012* (Poplar, Mont.: Fort Peck Community College, 2012), 491–93.

9. "William Youpee," *Billings (Mont.) Gazette*, October 22, 1990, 10; Addison Bragg, "No Baby Kissing for This Politician," *Billings (Mont.) Gazette*, February 28, 1971, 50; "Tribal Leader Blasts Ban on Elk Delivery," *Billings (Mont.) Gazette*, December 8, 1961, 33; "Tribal Industries Plant," *Great Falls (Mont.) Tribune*, August 8, 1969, 6; "$1.5 Million Contract Goes to Indians," *Independent Record* (Helena, Mont.), August 28, 1969, 2.

10. Bill Hume, "Tribal Chairman Unit Adopts Constitution," *Albuquerque Journal*, July 13, 1971, 1. Santo Domingo Pueblo voted against ratification pending consultation with its tribal council.

11. Comments of Commissioner Louis R. Bruce at NTCA Constitutional Convention, July 13, 1971, Bylaws of the NTCA, Series 2, Box 4, Folder 3, NTCA Papers; Bill Hume, "Sioux from Montana Elected President of Indian Group," *Albuquerque Journal*, July 14, 1971, A-5.

12. First Executive Session of the NTCA, 8 A.M., July 14, 1971, Bylaws of the NTCA, Series 2, Box 4, Folder 3, NTCA Papers.

13. Section 501(c)(3) is the portion of the U.S. Internal Revenue Code that allows for federal tax exemption of nonprofit organizations, specifically those that are considered public charities, private foundations, or private operating foundations. It is regulated and administered by the U.S. Department of Treasury through the Internal Revenue Service.

14. Charles Trimble, interview with author, March 2, 2018; "Indian Education," *Syracuse Herald American*, August 8, 1975, 15; Biographical/Historical Note on Arrow Inc., National Museum of the American Indian Cultural Center, http://nmai.si.edu/sites/1/files/archivecenter/AC013_arrow.html.

15. John Lundquist, "ALC Bypasses Issues on Education, Pornography," *Winona (Minn.) Daily News*, October 8, 1971, 14; "Naval Air Station Commander Questions Group Helping AIM," *Austin Daily Herald*, August 3, 1971, 5; "Project Seeks Aid to Indians," *Abilene Reporter News*, July 14, 1974, 15; "Books by Indians about Indians," *Newark (Ohio) Advocate*, May 2, 1975, 2; "Freeze on Indian Funds Challenged," *Austin*

Daily Herald, April 5, 1973, 11; James A. Carlson, "Indians Have Mixed Emotions over Takeover in Milwaukee," *Hattiesburg (Miss.) American*, August 30, 1974, 6.

16. Message from Webster Two Hawk to NTCA members, September 30, 1972, Box 54, Richard M. Nixon Presidential Papers, Bradley M. Patterson Files, Richard M. Nixon Presidential Library, Yorba Linda, Calif. (hereafter cited as Nixon Papers).

17. Fundraising idea for the NTCA, Series 10, Box 39, NTCA Papers.

18. Proposal by the National Tribal Chairmen's Association to Make Consultation and Indian Self-Determination a Reality, Series 10, Box 59, NTCA Papers.

19. Notes on September 29 Session, NTCA Board & BIA Representatives in Chicago, NTCA Board Meeting Minutes, Series 1, Box 1, Folder 5, NTCA Papers; Funding Proposal, December 26, 1971, General Correspondence, Series 4, Box 5, Folder 1, NTCA Papers; "Small Group of Detractors at Indian Chairmen's Convocation," *Daily Republic* (Mitchell, S. Dak.), April 26, 1971, 1; Miller et al., *History of the Assiniboine and Sioux Tribes of the Fort Peck Indian Reservation*, 455–56.

20. First Executive Session of the NTCA, 8 A.M., July 14, 1971, Bylaws of the NTCA, Series 2, Box 4, Folder 3, NTCA Papers.

21. Bylaws of National Tribal Chairmen's Fund Inc., Bylaws of the NTCA, Series 2, Box 4, Folder 3, NTCA Papers; Certificate of Incorporation for the National Tribal Chairmen's Fund, Inc., By-laws of the NTCA, Series 2, Box 4, Folder 3, NTCA Papers; Minutes of the First Meeting of the Board of Directors of the National Tribal Chairmen's Fund Inc., Bylaws of the NTCA, Series 2, Box 4, Folder 3, NTCA Papers; BIA meeting with board of directors of National Tribal Chairmen's Association, July 27–28, 1971, NTCA Board Meeting Minutes, Series 1, Box 1, Folder 4, NTCA Papers.

22. Lyndon B. Johnson, "Executive Order 11399—Establishing the National Council on Indian Opportunity," March 6, 1968, *The American Presidency Project*, http://www.presidency.ucsb.edu/ws/?pid=76359. For a history of the NCIO, see Thomas A. Britten, *The National Council on Indian Opportunity: Quiet Champion of Self-Determination* (Albuquerque: University of New Mexico Press, 2014).

23. David E. Wilkins, *American Indian Politics and the American Political System* (New York: Rowman and Littlefield, 2002), 193–94; Letter to William Youpee, NTCA, from Bob Robertson, March 17, 1972, Series 3.5, Box 19, General Documents, NCIO Folder, Spiro T. Agnew Papers, Special Collections, University of Maryland Libraries, College Park, Md.; Robert Robertson Speech before the NTCA Annual Convention, Phoenix, Ariz., December 6, 1973, Box 54, Bradley Patterson Papers, Nixon Papers. The Alaskan Federation of Natives also offered the NTCA office equipment. See Memo for Files, October 14, 1971, General Correspondence, Series 4, Box 5, Folder 1, NTCA Papers.

24. Memorandum from Louis Bruce, October 14, 1971, General Correspondence, Series 4, Box 5, Folder 1, NTCA Papers; James Sansaver to Leo Vocu, October 8, 1971, Series 4, Box 5, Folder 1, NTCA Papers; Robert F. Keller, deputy comptroller of the United States, to Representative James Abourezk, chairman of the House Subcommittee on Indian Affairs, January 18, 1974, http://www.gao.gov/assets/200/193719.pdf.

25. The Position of the National Tribal Chairmen's Association, December 5, 1973, Box 54, Bradley Patterson Papers, Nixon Papers.

26. Jennifer E. Mosley, "Keeping the Lights on: How Government Funding Concerns Drive the Advocacy Agendas of Nonprofit Homeless Service Providers," *Journal of Public Administration Research and Theory* 22 (2012): 841–44. Statement of William

Youpee, October 4, 1971, Briefing Book and Master Copies, Series 10, Box 55, Folder 6, NTCA Papers.

27. Mark Chaves, Laura Stephens, and Joseph Galaskiewicz, "Does Government Funding Suppress Nonprofits' Political Activity?" *Sociological Review* 69 (April 2004): 293–96; Steven R. Smith and Michael Lipsky, *Nonprofits for Hire: The Welfare State in the Age of Contracting* (Cambridge, Mass.: Harvard University Press, 1995).

28. Chaves, Stephens and Galaskiewicz, "Does Government Funding Suppress Nonprofits' Political Activity?," 296–98; Smith and Lipsky, *Nonprofits for Hire.*

29. Dean J. Kotlowski, *Nixon's Civil Rights: Politics, Principle, and Policy* (Cambridge, Mass.: Harvard University Press, 2002), 211.

30. Meeting between Commissioner of Indian Affairs and 15-Man Interim Committee, the All Indian Commission on BIA Reorganization, May 13–14, 1971, NTCA Working Papers, Series 1, Box 1, Folder 1, NTCA Papers.

31. William M. Blair, "Indians Say Trust in Nixon Is Shaken," *New York Times*, August 29, 1971, 35.

32. The members were Webster Two Hawk, Ed Cline, Benny Atencio, Wendell Chino, Lee Motah, William Youpee, Edison Real Bird, Don Wright, Roger Jourdain, Overton James, Peter MacDonald, Adrian Fisher Sr., Robert Jim, Peter N. Jackson, and Buffalo Tiger. See Roster of 15-Member Interim Committee on BIA Reorganization, NTCA Working Papers, Series 1, Box 1, Folder 1, NTCA Papers.

33. Minutes of Meeting between 15-Member Interim Committee on BIA Reorganization and Department of the Interior, May 14, 1971, NTCA Working Papers, Series 1, Box 1, Folder 1, NTCA Papers; "Conferred with Morton," *Southern Ute Drum* (Ignacio, Colo.), June 4, 1971, 4.

34. Transcript of NTCA meeting with Bradley Patterson, July 28, 1971, NTCA Board Meeting Minutes, Series 1, Box 1, Folder 4, NTCA Papers.

35. Summary notes of NTCA meeting with BIA in Albuquerque, August 19, 1971, NTCA Board Meeting Minutes, Box 1, Series 1, Folder 4, NTCA Papers; NTCA Resolution opposing transfer of William Veeder, August 19, 1971, NTCA Board Meeting Minutes, Series 1, Box 1, Folder 4, NTCA Papers.

36. Transcript of NTCA Window Rock, Ariz., conference, September 10, 1971, NTCA Board Meeting Minutes, Series 1, Box 1, Folder 4, NTCA Papers.

37. Ibid.

38. Peter Iverson, "Peter MacDonald," in *American Indian Tribal Leaders: Studies in Diversity*, ed. R. David Edmondson (Lincoln: University of Nebraska Press, 1980), 222–38.

39. Chuck Trimble, email to author, May 22, 2018.

40. Transcript of NTCA Window Rock, Ariz., conference, September 10, 1971.

41. While serving as president of the NCAI, Wendell Chino had made a similar recommendation. See Bill Hume, "Indians vs. Bureaucracy," *Albuquerque Journal*, September 17, 1971, 4.

42. Notes on Chicago Session of NTCA Executive Board meeting, September 29, 1971, NTCA Board Meeting Minutes, Series 1, Box 1, Folder 4, NTCA Papers.

43. Jack D. Forbes, *Native Americans and Nixon: Presidential Politics and Minority Self-Determination, 1969–1972* (Los Angeles: UCLA American Indian Studies Center, 1981), 56.

44. Transcript of meeting between NTCA, BIA, and Secretary Morton, September 21, 1971, NTCA Board Meeting Minutes, Series 1, Box 1, Folder 5, NTCA Papers. On the same day, Representative Steiger called a press conference on behalf of Peter MacDonald where the Navajo leader reiterated his charges that John Crow and Wilma Victor were thwarting the president's self-determination policies. See "BIA Forces Indians to Fight, Navajo's Leader Declares," *Arizona Republic* (Phoenix), September 22, 1971, 1.

45. The "Jammer" era refers to the derisive nickname "Katzenjammer Kids" affixed to Bruce's team of administrative assistants. See Statement of William Youpee, October 4, 1971, Briefing Book Master Copies, Series 10, Box 55, Folder 6, NTCA Papers.

46. Notes on Chicago Session of NTCA Executive Board meeting, September 29, 1971.

47. "Bruce: Liberals in Command of the BIA," *Northwest Indian Times* (Spokane, Wash.), March 1972, 9.

48. "Activist Indian groups interrupt Reno Convention," *Reno Evening Gazette*, November 16, 1971, 6; Homer Bigart, "Indians Open Reno Conference; Urban-Reservation Rift at Issue," *New York Times*, November 16, 1971, 34; "Reservation, Urban Indians Split over Organization," *Silver City (N.Mex.) Daily Press*, November 17, 1971, 2; "Indian Leader Hopes to Establish Rapport," *Reno Evening Gazette*, November 22, 1971, 8; "Activist Indian Council Formed," *Navajo Times* (Window Rock, Ariz.), April 6, 1972, A-6.

49. Jack Anderson, "Sensitive Diplomatic Balance," *Eureka (Calif.) Times Standard*, November 20, 1973, 4.

50. David E. Earley, "Veteran Youpee Retired at Peck," *Billings (Mont.) Gazette*, November 1, 1971, 6.

51. According to sociologist Peter Selznick, co-optation is "the process of absorbing new elements into the leadership or policy determining structure of an organization as a means of averting threats to its stability or existence" (Selznick, *TVA and the Grass Roots: A Study in the Sociology of Formal Organization* [Berkeley: University of California Press, 1949], 13).

52. Fundraising Idea for the NTCA.

53. Patrick G. Coy and Tim Hedeen, "A Stage Model of Social Movement Co-Optation: Community Mediation in the United States," *Sociological Quarterly* 46 (Summer 2005): 409, 428.

54. Selznick, *TVA and the Grass Roots*, 217.

55. As quoted in Daniel M. Cobb, *Native Activism in Cold War America: A Struggle for Sovereignty* (Lawrence: University of Kansas Press, 2008), 119.

Chapter 3. Foundational Issues

1. Eunice Larrabee, "Health Education," in *Indian Education Confronts the Seventies*, ed. Vine Deloria Jr. (Washington, D.C.: Office of Education, Department of Health, Education, and Welfare, 1974), 153–68 (see https://files.eric.ed.gov/fulltext/ED113074 .pdf).

2. Speech by Eunice Larrabee to NTCA Convention, January 8, 1975, Series 10, Box 57, Folder 6, National Tribal Chairmen's Association Records, 1971–1978, National Museum of the American Indian, Smithsonian Institution Archive Center, Suitland,

Md. (hereafter cited as NTCA Papers); Larrabee, "Health Education," 153–68; Ann Grauvogl, "Spirit Catcher," *Sioux Falls Argus-Leader*, August 28, 1994, 53.

3. Amanda J. Cobb, "Understanding Tribal Sovereignty: Definitions, Conceptualizations, and Interpretations," *American Studies* 46 (Fall/Winter 2005): 115–18; Daniel Philpott, "Sovereignty," The Stanford Encyclopedia of Philosophy (Summer 2016 ed.), ed. Edward N. Zalta, https://plato.stanford.edu/archives/sum2016/entries/sovereignty/.

4. Joseph P. Kalt and Joseph W. Singer, "Myths and Realities of Tribal Sovereignty: The Law and Economics of Indian Self-Rule," *Harvard University Native Issues Research Symposium* (March 2004): 4.

5. Michael A. Dorris, "The Grass Still Grows, the Rivers Still Flow: Contemporary Native Americans," *Daedalus* 110 (Spring 1981): 49.

6. Cobb, "Understanding Tribal Sovereignty," 115–18.

7. The Twenty Point Position Paper, November 1, 1972, Series 10, Box 58, Folder 10, NTCA Papers.

8. Charles Wilkinson, *Blood Struggle: The Rise of Modern Indian Nations* (New York: W. W. Norton & Co., 2005), 139–41.

9. Twenty Point Position Paper.

10. Kevin Bruyneel, *The Third Space of Sovereignty: The Postcolonial Period of U.S. Indigenous Relations* (Minneapolis: University of Minnesota Press, 2007), 167; Wilkinson, *Blood Struggle*, 139–41.

11. George Pierre Castile, *To Show Heart: Native American Self-Determination and Federal Indian Policy, 1960–1975* (Tucson: University of Arizona Press, 1998), 128–29.

12. *The American Indian World*, February 9, 1974, Records of the Office of the Assistant for Public Liaison; Jane Wales, Indians: NTCA, 12/76 [O/A 4471], Jimmy Carter Presidential Papers, Jimmy Carter Presidential Library and Museum, Atlanta, Ga. (hereafter cited as Carter Papers).

13. Ibid.

14. Ibid.

15. Carole Goldberg-Ambrose, "Of Native Americans and Tribal Members: The Impact of Law on Indian Group Life," *Law and Society Review* 28 (December 1994): 1134–35; W. Roger Buffalohead, "Self-Rule in the Past and the Future: An Overview," in *Indian Self-Rule: First-Hand Accounts of Indian-White Relations from Roosevelt to Reagan*, ed. Kenneth R. Philip (Logan: Utah State University, 1986), 270–71.

16. "R. Lewis Dies," *Albuquerque Journal*, January 10, 1996, 23; "A Wise Choice," *Gallup (N.Mex.) Independent*, December 11, 1973, 2.

17. Brent L. Pickett, "Foucault and the Politics of Resistance," *Polity* 28 (Summer 1996): 447.

18. Youpee statement before the Senate Committee on Interior and Insular Affairs, October 1, 1971, Series 10, Box 55, Folder 6, NTCA Papers; Mark Trahant, *The Last Great Battle of the Indian Wars* (Fort Hall, Idaho: Cedars Group, 2010), 50–51. SRC 26 passed on December 11, 1971.

19. Testimony of Wendell Chino on S. 2010 and repeal of PL 83–280, December 4, 1975, Series 10, Box 44, Folder 3, NTCA Papers; Robert V. Beier, "Call for Indian Sovereignty Issued at Leaders' Meeting," *Albuquerque Journal*, January 10, 1975, 11.

20. Carol Chiago Lujan and Gordon Adams, "U.S. Colonization of Indian Justice Systems: A Brief History," *Wicazo Sa Review* 19 (Autumn 2004): 18–19; Castile, *To Show*

Heart, 65–66; Michael M. Pacheco, "Finality in Indian Tribunal Decisions: Respecting Our Brothers' Vision," *American Indian Law Review* 16 (1991): 138–39.

21. NTCA Resolution vs. the Indian Civil Rights Act of 1968, December 7, 1973, Series 2, Box 2, Folder 5, NTCA Papers; NTCA Resolution to amend the Indian Civil Rights Act of 1968, May 13, 1976, Series 10, Box 33, Folder 3, NTCA Papers. In *Santa Clara Pueblo v. Martinez* (1978), the U.S. Supreme Court established that tribal governments retained a large degree of sovereign immunity from suits in federal courts. See Castile, *To Show Heart*, 66.

22. Akim D. Reinhardt, *Ruling Pine Ridge: Oglala Lakota Politics from the IRA to Wounded Knee* (Lubbock: Texas Tech University Press, 2007), 202, 209.

23. Jeffrey Stotik, Thomas E. Shriver, and Sherry Cable, "Social Control and Movement Outcome: The Case of AIM," *Sociological Forces* 27 (February 1994): 59–60; "U.S. Negotiators Rebuff Indians on New Talks," *Washington Post*, April 10, 1973, A2; Robert Burnette's notes on Wounded Knee, March 20, 1973, Series 12, Box 66, Folder 2, NTCA Papers; Joane Nagel, *American Indian Ethnic Renewal: Red Power and the Resurgence of Identity and Culture* (New York: Oxford University Press, 1997), 171–72; Agreement between Feds and AIM at Wounded Knee, April 6, 1973, Series 12, Box 66, Folder 2, NTCA Papers.

24. Paul R. Wieck, "Indians Stir Up Dust," *Albuquerque Journal*, March 18, 1973, 5.

25. Notes on Chicago NTCA executive session, September 29, 1971, Series 1, Box 1, Folder 5, NTCA Papers; speech by Robert Jim before the Affiliated Tribes of Northwest Indians, April 12, 1973, Northwest Tribal Oral History Interviews, 1963–1973, 1/45, Western Washington University, Center for Pacific Northwest Studies, Bellingham, Wash.

26. William Youpee to Henry Jackson, March 7, 1973, Series 10, Box 49, Folder 3, NTCA Papers.

27. William Youpee to NTCA members, March 23, 1973, Series 10, Box 2, Folder 5, NTCA Papers.

28. Roger Jourdain to ABC News, March 28, 1973, Series 10, Box 49, Folder 3, NTCA Papers.

29. Wieck, "Indians Stir Up Dust," 5.

30. Vine Deloria Jr., "On Wounded Knee," *Akwesasne Notes* (N.Y.), early Spring 1973, 38.

31. Cobb, "Understanding Tribal Sovereignty," 115; Vine Deloria Jr., "Intellectual Self-Determination and Sovereignty: Looking at the Windmills in Our Minds," *Wicazo Sa Review* 13 (Spring 1998): 25–26.

32. Thomas Biolosi, *Organizing the Lakota: The Political Economy of the New Deal on the Pine Ridge and Rosebud Reservations* (Tucson: University of Arizona Press, 1988), 3–4.

33. *American Indian World*.

34. Speech by Forrest Gerard to NTCA convention, January 8, 1975, Series 10, Box 57, Folder 6, NTCA Papers.

35. E. Fletcher McClellan, "The Politics of American Indian Self-Determination, 1958–1975: The Indian Self-Determination and Education Assistance Act of 1975" (Ph.D. diss., University of Tennessee, 1988), 210–11, 216.

36. "Statement on Indian Affairs by Secretary of the Interior Rogers C. B. Morton," Department of the Interior News Release, October 4, 1971; Geoffrey D. Strommer and

Stephen D. Osborne, "The History, Status, and Future of Tribal Self-Governance Under the Indian Self-Determination and Education Assistance Act," *American Indian Law Review* 39 (2015): 19–20; Castile, *To Show Heart*, 105–6; testimony of William Youpee on Indian Self-Determination Act (S. 3157), May 8, 1972, Series 4, Box 5, Folder 2, NTCA Papers.

37. McClellan, "Politics of American Indian Self-Determination," 221–22.

38. Indian Self-Determination and Education Program, Hearings on S.1017; analysis of S. 1017; Karen Ducheneaux, American Indian Press Association Report MR032 (March 1974), Series 1, Box 59, NTCA Papers.

39. Committee Print No. 1 on S. 1017, Series 10, Box 59, NTCA Papers.

40. Lawrence Snake testimony before House Subcommittee on Indian Affairs, May 21, 1974, Series 10, Box 59, NTCA Papers.

41. Castile, *To Show Heart*, 168–69; NTCA Convention Highlights, January 7, 1975, Series 10, Box 57, Folder 6, NTCA Papers.

42. Donna Ennis, "It's Time to Take Back Our Cultural Sovereignty," *Indian Country Today*, July 22, 2015; Wallace Coffey and Rebecca Tsosie, "Rethinking Tribal Sovereignty Doctrine: Cultural Sovereignty and the Collective Future of Indian Nations," *Stanford Law and Policy Review* 12 (Spring 2001): 197–99.

43. Ennis, "It's Time to Take Back Our Cultural Sovereignty."

44. See, for example, Alfred A. Cave, *Prophets of the Great Spirit: Native American Revitalization Movements in Eastern North America* (Lincoln: University of Nebraska Press, 2006); Gregory Dowd, *A Spirited Resistance: The North American Struggle for Unity, 1745–1815* (Baltimore: Johns Hopkins University Press, 1993); Adam Jortner, *The Gods of Prophetstown: The Battle of Tippecanoe and the Holy War for the American Frontier* (Oxford: Oxford University Press, 2012), 5.

45. John Troutman, "The Citizenship of Dance: Politics of Music among the Lakota, 1900–1924," in *Beyond Red Power: American Indian Politics and Activism since 1900*, ed. Daniel M. Cobb and Loretta Fowler (Santa Fe: School for Advanced Research Press, 2007), 91–93.

46. Thomas A. Britten, *American Indians in World War I: At Home and at War* (Albuquerque: University of New Mexico Press, 1997), 149–52.

47. Nagle, *American Indian Ethnic Renewal*, 114–19.

48. Twenty Point Position Paper.

49. NTCA Resolution calling on the Department of the Interior and National Park Service to protect and develop culture and resources, September 9, 1971, Series 1, Box 1, Folder 4, NTCA Papers.

50. Position paper of the Association of American Indian Traditional and Cultural Activities, June 4, 1974, Series 10, Box 58, Folder 1, NTCA Papers.

51. "Indian Feathers Ruffled across Nation by State Arrests," *Daily Oklahoman* (Oklahoma City), April 13, 1974, 13; AAITCA resolution calling for NTCA assistance, June 3, 1974, Series 10, Box 58, Folder 1, NTCA Papers. The case was not dropped and at least five of the accused Indians were convicted. See Mike Hammer, "Three Convicted of Feather Sales," *Daily Oklahoman* (Oklahoma City), June 25, 1974, 63. In response to the controversy, the BIA recommended establishing a nationwide feather registry whereby Native Americans would register them and obtain a permit to possess them. See Vivian

Vahlberg, "Registration Proposed for Indian Ceremonial Feathers," *Daily Oklahoman* (Oklahoma City), May 30, 1974, 49.

52. Position paper of the Association of American Indian Traditional and Cultural Activities; AAITCA resolution calling for NTCA assistance.

53. "Six Suspected of Desecrating Indian Graves," *Arizona Daily Star* (Tucson), January 21, 1976, 35.

54. Michael Kilian, "Indian Bones in the Nation's Cupboard," *Chicago Tribune*, April 16, 1997, sec. 5, p. 1.

55. NTCA Resolution calling for protection of Indian artifacts, May 13, 1976, Series 10, Box 33, Folder 3, NTCA Papers. On May 24, 1974, President Nixon had signed S.514 into law (P.L. 93-291), which sought to protect historical and archaeological data (relics and specimens) uncovered or likely to be uncovered in federal construction projects. See Bradley H. Patterson Jr. to William Youpee, July 1, 1974, Box 54, Central Files: Staff Member and Office Files, Richard M. Nixon Presidential Papers, Bradley M. Patterson Files, Richard M. Nixon Presidential Library, Yorba Linda, Calif. (hereafter cited as Nixon Papers).

56. Juana Lyon, "The Indian Elder, a Forgotten American. Final Report on the First National Indian Conference on Aging," Phoenix, Ariz., June 15–17, 1976.

57. Hearings before the Subcommittee on Indian Affairs and Public Lands on Indian Child Welfare Act of 1978, S. 1214, Ninety-Fifth Congress, second session, February 9, 1978, 190–98.

58. Ibid. The bill was passed and signed into law (P.L. 95-608) on November 8, 1978.

59. Coffey and Tsosie, "Rethinking Tribal Sovereignty," 204–5; Henrietta Mann, "Earth Mother and Prayerful Children: Sacred Sites and Religious Freedom," in *Native Voices: American Indian Identity and Resistance*, ed. Richard Grounds, George E. Tinker, and David E. Wilkins (Lawrence: University of Kansas Press, 2003), 194; Richard A. Monette, "Sovereignty and Survival: The Status of Indian Tribes under American Law Is a Key to Their Cultural Existence," *ABA Journal* 86 (March 2000): 64.

60. Sar A. Levitan and Barbara Hetrick, *Big Brother's Indian Programs—With Reservations* (New York: McGraw Hill, 1971), 125.

61. Twenty Point Position Paper.

62. *American Indian World;* Robert Lewis to Rogers Morton, March 5, 1974, Accession Number 1501, Box 100, Indian Opportunity-1974, Julia B. Hansen Papers, Special Collections, University of Washington; notes on NCTA Phoenix executive board meeting, December 7, 1973, Series 2, Box 2, Folder 5, NTCA Papers.

63. Hearings before the Subcommittee on Administrative Practice and Procedure on Federal Protection of Indian Resources, Ninety-Second Congress, first session, January 3, 1972, 1708–9, 1712; Lewis to Morton, March 5, 1974.

64. Richard Nixon, Special Message to the Congress on Indian Affairs, July 8, 1970. The American Presidency Project, https://www.presidency.ucsb.edu/node/240040.

65. NTCA Comments on Trust Counsel Authority, H.R. 6374, September 28, 1973, Series 4, Box 5, Folder 4, NTCA Papers; Karen Ducheneaux, "Indian Spokesmen Oppose Specifics of Proposed Trust Counsel," *Navajo Times* (Window Rock, Ariz.), June 7, 1973, A-21.

66. "Indian Bills Stand Strong before Congress," *Gallup (N.Mex.) Independent*, May 19, 1975, 6; Daniel I. S. J. Rey-Bear and Matthew L. M. J. Fletcher, "We Need Protection from Our Protectors: The Nature, Issues, and Future of the Federal Trust Responsibility to Indians," *Michigan Journal of Environmental and Administrative Law* 6 (2017): 426–27.

67. Russel L. Barsh and James Youngblood Henderson, *The Road: Indian Tribes and Political Liberty* (Berkeley: University of California Press, 1980), 222.

68. Nagle, *American Indian Ethnic Renewal*, 224–28. Clarence Skye and Chuck Trimble noted this dynamic in separate interviews.

69. Barsh and Henderson, *The Road*, 228; Kotlowski, *Nixon's Civil Rights*, 188. Michael P. Gross argues that while the Self Determination and Education Assistance Act "changed formerly passive recipients of government handouts into active initiators of social reform," the education provisions "did nothing to give Indians a greater voice in the policies of the schools attended by their children. See Gross, "Indian Self-Determination and Tribal Sovereignty: An Analysis of Recent Federal Indian Policy," *Texas Law Review* 56 (1978), 1197, 1206.

70. Wilkinson, *Blood Struggle*, 139–41; Trahant, *The Last Great Battle of the Indian Wars*, 120.

Chapter 4. The Politics of Exclusivity

1. NTCA Pierre Constitutional Convention Transcript, MS 654–57, American Indian Research Project, University of South Dakota, Vermillion, S. Dak. (hereafter cited as NTCA Pierre Constitutional Convention transcript), pp. 01047–51 (emphasis added).

2. *The American Indian World*, February 9, 1974, Records of the Office of the Assistant for Public Liaison; Jane Wales, Indians: NTCA, 12/76 [O/A 4471], Jimmy Carter Presidential Papers, Jimmy Carter Presidential Library and Museum, Atlanta, Ga. (hereafter cited as Carter Papers).

3. Resolution #5, November 2, 1971, NTCA Board Meeting Minutes, Series 2, Box 1, Folder 5, National Tribal Chairmen's Association Records, 1971–1978, National Museum of the American Indian, Smithsonian Institution Archive Center, Suitland, Md. (hereafter cited as NTCA Papers); "NTCA Will Open D.C. Office," *Southern Ute Drum* (Ignacio, Colo.), February 25, 1972, 7.

4. "Webster Two Hawk Is USD Alumnus of Year," *Daily Republic* (Mitchell, S. Dak.), April 18, 1972, 14; "Rosebud Tribal President Says Tribe Broke, in Debt," *Argus-Leader* (Sioux Falls, S. Dak.), January 7, 1970, 28; "Two Hawk's Past Riddled with Variety," *Argus-Leader* (Sioux Falls, S. Dak.), December 18, 1983, 29; "Indian Leader Disagrees with Rushmore Vigil," *Argus-Leader* (Sioux Falls, S. Dak.) August 19, 1970, 5.

5. Transcripts of Executive Session, Keshena and Shawano, Wisc., August 29–31, 1972, NTCA Correspondence, Series 4, Box 5, Folder 2, NTCA Papers.

6. Louis R. Bruce to William Youpee, July 28, 1972, Bradley Patterson Papers, Richard M. Nixon Presidential Papers, Bradley M. Patterson Files, Richard M. Nixon Presidential Library, Yorba Linda, Calif. (hereafter cited as Nixon Papers).

7. NTCA Convention highlights and agenda, January 7, 1975. Series 1, Box 57, Folder 6, NTCA Papers.

8. Webster Two Hawk to NTCA Membership, September 30, 1972, Bradley Patterson Papers, Series 3, Box 54, Nixon Papers.

9. Ibid.

10. Dean J. Kotlowski, *Nixon's Civil Rights: Politics, Principle, and Policy* (Cambridge, Mass.: Harvard University Press, 2002), 208–9. For an examination of the role and activities of urban Indian centers, see Thomas Britten, "Urban American Indian Centers in the Late 1960s–1970s: An Examination of Their Function and Purpose," *Indigenous Policy Journal* 27 (Winter 2017): 1–18.

11. Dave Early, "Second Little Bighorn: This Time Indians Talk," *Billings (Mont.) Gazette*, February 18, 1971, 8.

12. *American Indian World.*

13. Minutes of NTCA executive session meeting with Bradley Patterson, May 9, 1974, Series 2, Box 2, Folder 6, NTCA Papers.

14. *American Indian World* (emphasis added).

15. Frank Carlucci to Harrison Loesch, March 30, 1972, and Harrison Loesch to Interior Department Policy Committee, April 4, 1972, Series 2, Box 2, Folder 3, NTCA Papers.

16. Lee J. Sclar, "Participation of Off-Reservation Indians in Programs of the Bureau of Indian Affairs and the Indian Health Service," *Montana Law Review* 33 (Summer 1972): 229 (see appendix C).

17. "Urban Indians Form Council," *Arizona Republic*, March 6, 1972, 7; Connie Koenenn, "City Indians' Problems Discussed Here," *Arizona Republic*, April 15, 1972, 1; "More BIA Aid South for Indians in Cities," *Arizona Daily Star*, April 12, 1972, 11.

18. "Signs of Change in the BIA," *Minneapolis Star Tribune*, July 5, 1971, 6; Rob Burnes, "Director Says Bureau Reservation Oriented," *Billings (Mont.) Gazette*, February 19, 1971, 1, 5.

19. Other committee members included Sandy McNabb, Jim Egar, David Etheridge, Lou Conger, Peter Three Stars, and Velma Garcia.

20. Draft BIA Study on Indian Eligibility for Bureau Services, April 27, 1972, Series 2, Box 2, Folder 3, NTCA Papers.

21. Ibid.

22. Ibid.

23. William Youpee to Louis Bruce, April 27, 1972, and NTCA Resolution on federal services for federally recognized tribes, May 22, 1972, Series 2, Box 2, Folder 3, NTCA Papers.

24. American Indian Policy Review Commission, *American Indian Policy Review Commission Final Report*, May 17, 1977 (Washington, D.C.: Government Printing Office, 1977), 434n15; Donald F. Fixico, *The Urban Indian Experience in America* (Albuquerque: University of New Mexico Press, 2000), 131.

25. "Activism and Red Power," in *Indian Self-Rule: First-Hand Accounts of Indian White Relations from Roosevelt to Reagan*, ed. Kenneth R. Philip (Logan: Utah State University Press, 1995), 241.

26. Draft BIA Study on Indian Eligibility for Bureau Services.

27. Mark Edwin Miller, *Forgotten Tribes: Unrecognized Indians and the Federal Acknowledgment Process* (Lincoln: University of Nebraska Press, 2004), 32–33;

Richard LaCourse, "Forgotten Eastern Indians Organize," *Gallup (N.Mex.) Independent*, December 27, 1972, 6.

28. Mark Edwin Miller, *Claiming Tribal Identity: The Five Tribes and the Politics of Federal Acknowledgment* (Norman: University of Oklahoma Press, 2013), 112–13.

29. David E. Wilkins, "Breaking into the Intergovernmental Matrix: The Lumbee Tribe's Efforts to Secure Federal Acknowledgment," *Publius* 23 (Autumn 1993): 138.

30. Malinda Laynor Lowery, *Lumbee Indians in the Jim Crow South: Race, Identity, and the Making of a Nation* (Chapel Hill: University of North Carolina Press, 2010), xiv–xv.

31. Copy of H.R. 4656 (PL-570), Lumbees of North Carolina, Series 10, Box 45, Folder 4, NTCA Papers.

32. Karen Vela, "House Okay of Lumbee Bill Is Hailed," *Robesonian* (Lumberton, N.C.), October 10, 1974, 1; "Lumbee Bill Reborn in U.S. Senate," *Robesonian* (Lumberton, N.C.), January 23, 1975, 5; Toni Goodyear and Karen Vela, "Robeson Kept Moving in '74 . . . And Usually It Was Forward," *Robesonian* (Lumberton, N.C.), January 3, 1975, 9.

33. Assistant Secretary of the Interior John Whitaker to Representative James Haley, April 5, 1974, Series 10, Box 45, Folder 4, NTCA Papers.

34. Telegram from Buffalo Tiger to William Youpee, April 9, 1974, Series 10, Box 45, Folder 4, NTCA Papers.

35. Miller, *Claiming Tribal Identity*, 112–13; USET position paper on Lumbee status as Indians, October 7, 1974, Series 10, Box 45, Folder 4, NTCA Papers.

36. William Youpee to Alexander McNabb, October 1, 1974; William Youpee to Stan Thomas, October 1, 1974; William Youpee to Gerald Ford, October 1, 1974, Series 10, Box 45, Folder 4, NTCA Papers.

37. "Indian Congress Opposes Lumbee Efforts," *Navajo Times* (Window Rock, Ariz.), November 17, 1974, B-4.

38. Russel L. Barsh and James Youngblood Henderson, *The Road: Indian Tribes and Political Liberty* (Berkeley: University of California Press, 1980), 243–46; Lowery, *Lumbee Indians in the Jim Crow South*, 126–27.

39. Hearings before the House Subcommittee on Indian Affairs and Public Lands, Federal Recognition of Indian Tribes, Ninety-Fifth Congress, second session, August 10, 1978, Serial No. 95–39; Jeanette Henry and Rupert Casto, "Who Is An Indian?" *Wassaja* 13 (June 1980): 15–18.

40. Keith Werhan, "The Sovereignty of Indian Tribes." *Notre Dame Lawyer* 54 (October 1978): 24.

41. Ward Churchill, *Perversions of Justice: Indigenous Peoples and Angloamerican Law* (San Francisco: City Lights, 2003), 218–20; Barsh and Henderson, *The Road*, 245–46.

42. William A. Gamson, "Reflections on 'The Strategy of Social Protest,'" *Sociological Forum* 4 (September 1989): 459.

43. NTCA Proposal for Consultation and Self-Determination, Series 4, Box 5, Folder 1, NTCA Papers.

44. "Damage to Capital Building by Indians Put at $1.98 Million," *Washington Post*, November 10, 1972, 2.

45. Clyde Bellecourt, *The Thunder before the Storm: The Autobiography of Clyde Bellecourt as Told to Jon Lurie* (St. Paul: Minnesota Historical Society Press, 2016), 121.

46. Paul Chaat Smith and Robert Allen Warrior, *Like a Hurricane: The Indian Movement from Alcatraz to Wounded Knee* (New York: New Press, 1996), 160. George Pierre Castile maintains that Bob Robertson solicited and received statements of support from the National Tribal Chairmen's Association, the NCAI, and the NCIO during the occupation. See Castile, *To Show Heart: Native American Self-Determination and Federal Indian Policy, 1960–1975* (Tucson: University of Arizona Press, 1998), 125.

47. "For the Record," *ILIDS Legislative Review* 2 (November 1972): 29.

48. Donald P. Baker, "U.S. Accused of Exhibiting BIA Damage," *Washington Post*, November 23, 1972, A1.

49. Trail of Broken Treaties Caravan, November 6, 1972, Series 10, Box 49, NTCA Papers.

50. "Government Finds Support in N.T.C.A.," *Akwesasne Notes* (N.Y.), early Winter 1973, 19.

51. Bob Robertson, interview with author, Smithfield, Va., August 18, 2007.

52. Bob Robertson to C. D. Ward, October 30, 1972, Box 16, National Council on Indian Opportunity Records, 1968–1974, Record Group 220, National Archives Building at College Park, Md. (hereafter cited as NCIO Papers).

53. NTCA Position Paper on BIA Occupation, November 10, 1972, Box 16, NCIO Papers; Finlay Lewis, "BIA Protests Endanger Indian Progress, Unity," *Minneapolis Star Tribune*, November 26, 1972, 1.

54. "Government Finds Support in N.T.C.A.," *Akwesasne Notes* (N.Y.), early Winter 1973, 19.

55. Robertson interview.

56. Bob Robertson to William Youpee, March 17, 1972, Box 19, Spiro T. Agnew Papers, Special Collections, University of Maryland Libraries, Hornbake Library, College Park, Md.; Aldren Cross, "Indians' Resolution May Mark Turning Point," *Spokesman Review* (Spokane, Wash.), April 15, 1973, 7; Charles Trimble, "The Betrayal of Crazy Horse," Manataka American Indian Council, October 2011, https://www.manataka.org/page2547.html; Thomas Britten, *The National Council on Indian Opportunity: Quiet Champion of Self-Determination* (Albuquerque: University of New Mexico Press, 2014), 232.

57. NTCA press release calling for NCIO funding, June 29, 1973, Series 4, Box 5, Folder 4, NTCA Papers; NTCA resolution endorsing Bob Robertson as executive director of NCIO, December 5, 1973, Series 2, Box 2, Folder 5, NTCA Papers; notes of NTCA meeting in Phoenix, December 7, 1973, Series 1, Box 2, Folder 5, NTCA Papers.

58. "For the Record," 27–29.

59. Trimble notes that he "backed away from the Impact Survey Team soon after it organized itself, in part to make it clear that it was not a 'tool' of NCAI and to make it safe for NTCA to take part in the process" (email to author, May 22, 2018).

60. William Youpee to NTCA membership, November 20, 1972, Series 4, Box 5, Folder 2, NTCA Papers. According to Richard LaCourse, the NTCA leadership decided to formulate their own recommendations at the urging of Bob Robertson. See LaCourse, "In the Caravan's Wake: An Unstable Status Quo," *ILIDS Legislative Review* 2 (November 1972): 18.

61. NTCA Position Paper, December 7, 1972, and Notes on Meeting with Rogers Morton, December 8, 1972, Series 2, Box 2, Folder 4, NTCA Papers.

62. According to Morton, Loesch "was asked to step aside as he had many things to do in the other public land management areas." Crow's resignation was "in the form of retirement." Louis Bruce's resignation was accepted after "some discussion by the Secretary with the President and his immediate staff." See Notes on Meeting with Rogers Morton, December 8, 1972.

63. Ibid.

64. LaCourse, "In the Caravan's Wake," 20.

65. Kirke Kickingbird, "The American Indian Policy Review Commission: A Prospect for Future Change in Federal Indian Policy," *American Indian Law Review* 3 (1975): 245–48.

66. Hearings before the Subcommittee on Indian Affairs, Establishment of the American Indian Policy Review Commission, Ninety-Third Congress, first session, July 19–20, 1973, 20–22.

67. Ibid.

68. NTCA Board Meeting minutes, February 10, 1975, Series 2, Box 3, Folder 1, NTCA Papers.

69. The Menominees' status was indefinite. Termination had been imposed on the tribe in 1961, but President Nixon signed a restoration bill in 1973. At the time of the AIPRC, the Menominees were in the midst of the restoration process. The Tlingits, according to the NTCA, had been terminated by virtue of the Alaska Native Claims Settlement Act. The Quapaw and Cayuga-Seneca tribes were Oklahoma-based and therefore did not reside on reservations but on "tribal jurisdictional areas." See "Indian Group Tests Authority of Ada Deer," *Stevens Point (Wisc.) Journal*, May 24, 1975, 5; Bob Duke, "Indian Group Plans Ouster of Unrecognized Members," *El Paso Herald*, April 8, 1975, 12.

70. Denise Tessier, "Chino Scores Indian Policy Commission," *Albuquerque Journal*, May 25, 1975, 10.

71. William Youpee to Ben Reifel, May 28, 1975, Bradley H. Patterson Files, Box 5, Gerald R. Ford Presidential Papers, Gerald R. Ford Presidential Library, Grand Rapids, Mich. (hereafter cited as Ford Papers); "From Foreign Capitals: American Indian Policy Review Commission Selects Task Forces," *Akwesasne Notes* (N.Y.), August 31, 1975, 20; "Tribal Chairman's Association Protests Commission Selections," *Fort Apache Scout* (Ariz.), August 31, 1975, 3.

72. The case (Civil No. 75-803) was decided by a three-judge panel on February 19, 1976. On March 19, 1976, the NTCA's attorneys filed a "protective Notice of Appeal" with the U.S. Supreme Court. See Winston & Strawn file in Series 9, Box 31, NTCA Papers; Samuel R. Cook, "Indian Self-Determination: A Comparative Analysis of Executive and Congressional Approaches to Contemporary Federal Indian Policy" (M.A. thesis, University of Arizona, 1992), 131–32.

73. Paul R. Wieck, "Abourezk Striving Hard to Right Indian Wrongs," *Albuquerque Journal*, July 27, 1975, 13.

74. NTCA recommendations regarding the AIPRC, November 18, 1976, Series 10, Box 35, Folder 20, NTCA Papers.

75. William Youpee to tribal leaders, November 26, 1976, Series 10, Box 33, Folder 4, NTCA Papers.

76. Notes on Meeting with Rogers Morton, December 8, 1972.

Chapter 5. Backlash

1. Richard Nixon to NTCA Convention, November 21, 1973, Box 54, Bradley Patterson Papers, Richard M. Nixon Presidential Papers, Bradley M. Patterson Files, Richard M. Nixon Presidential Library, Yorba Linda, Calif. (hereafter cited as Nixon Papers).

2. "Official Predicts Backlash of Sentiment against Indian People," *Carolina Indian Voice*, September 13, 1974, 8–9.

3. Tassie Hanna, Sam Deloria, and Charles E. Trimble, "The Commission on State-Tribal Relations: Enduring Lessons in the Modern State-Tribal Relationship," *Tulsa Law Review* 47 (Spring 2002): 556–57.

4. "As Four Indians See It . . . ," *Minneapolis Star Tribune*, October 10, 1971, 23.

5. Ibid.

6. Hanna, Deloria, and Trimble, "Commission on State-Tribal Relations," 565.

7. In 1969, non-Indians paid $13.8 million in rents on produced goods valued at $109.3 million—about one-eighth of the value. The prevailing ratio for the rental of non-Indian lands, however, was one-third (around $36 million). See Sar A. Levitan and Barbara Hetrick, *Big Brother's Indian Programs—With Reservations* (New York: McGraw Hill, 1971), 133–36.

8. Thomas L. Kimball, the executive vice president of the National Wildlife Federation, makes this claim in the preface of C. Herb Williams and Walt Neubrech, *Indian Treaties—American Nightmare* (Seattle: Outdoor Empire, 1976), xii.

9. Rudolph C. Reyser, "Anti-Indian Movement on the Tribal Frontier," Occasional Paper #16, rev. ed., Center for World Indigenous Studies, June 1992; Zoltan Grossman, "Treaty Rights and Responding to Anti-Indian Activity, http://treaty.indigenousnative .org/anti-indian.html.

10. Hanna, Deloria, and Trimble, "Commission on State-Tribal Relations," 569.

11. Grossman, "Treaty Rights and Responding to Anti-Indian Activity."

12. "AIM Creates a Backlash," *Minneapolis Star*, March 20, 1973, 8.

13. Floyd Paxton, "Wounded Knee: A Pain Elsewhere," *Yakima (Wash.) Herald Republic*, May 22, 1973. This was a paid advertisement running under the heading "Who's Whose in America."

14. Grossman, "Treaty Rights and Responding to Anti-Indian Activity."

15. Joe Frazier, "American Indians Today Carrying on Their Struggles in Courtrooms and Congress," *Danville (Va.) Register*, April 11, 1976, 12C.

16. "Flathead Reservation Buzzes with Use Permit Disagreement," *The Missoulian* (Mont.), July 17, 1969, 15; "White Men Charge Rights Violated," *Billings (Mont.) Gazette*, June 19, 1969, 30; Ken Toole, *Drumming Up Resentment: The Anti-Indian Movement in Montana* (Helena: Montana Human Rights Network, 2000), 9–12.

17. MOD welcomed people "concerned with protecting and advancing the principles of the Declaration of Independence and the Constitutional rights of Montana citizens" and opposed any government distinction in civil or political rights on account of race, color, or national origin. See MOD pamphlet in Series 2, Box 3, Folder 6, National Tribal Chairmen's Association Records, 1971–1978, National Museum of the American Indian, Smithsonian Institution Archive Center, Suitland, Md. (hereafter cited as NTCA Papers).

18. Grossman, "Treaty Rights and Responding to Anti-Indian Activity"; Reyser, "Anti-Indian Movement on the Tribal Frontier"; ICERR pamphlet in Series 2, Box 3, Folder 6, NTCA Papers.

19. Lyn Gladstone, "Indian Backlash Group Outlines State Concerns," *Rapid City Journal* (S. Dak.), March 6, 1976, 1.

20. Confidential Memo to NR/Interior Branch, April 19, 1976, Box 54, Bradley H. Patterson Files, Gerald R. Ford Presidential Papers, Gerald R. Ford Presidential Library, Grand Rapids, Mich. (hereafter cited as Ford Papers); Howard Borgstrom, email to the author, January 22, 2019.

21. Confidential Memo to NR/Interior Branch, April 19, 1976.

22. Ibid.

23. Ibid.; Amanda J. Cobb, "Understanding Tribal Sovereignty: Definitions, Conceptualizations, and Interpretations," *American Studies* 46 (Fall/Winter 2005): 115–18.

24. Confidential Memo to NR/Interior Branch, April 19, 1976.

25. Richard LaCourse, "Covert White House Plan Sees Tribal Termination," *Confederated Umatilla Journal* 1, no. 7 (July 1976): 1, 3–5; "Memo Plans Indian Affairs Shake-Up," *Santa Fe New Mexican*, July 25, 1976, 21; Bill Donovan, "Memo Is Leaked on Plan to Close BIA," *Arizona Republic*, July 28, 1976, 25, B7.

26. Confidential Memo to NR/Interior Branch, April 19, 1976.

27. President Ford's remarks to Indian leaders, July 16, 1976, and related press clippings, Bradley H. Patterson Files, Ford Papers.

28. NTCA Board Meeting minutes, October 14, 1976, Series 2, Box 3, Folder 6, NTCA Papers.

29. Ibid.

30. Ibid.

31. Ibid.

32. NTCA Highlights, July 27, 1976, Series 10, Box 35, Folder 4, NTCA Papers.

33. NTCA resolution on Indian plank, May 14, 1976, Series 2, Box 3, Folder 5; NTCA Democratic Party Plank, May 1, 1976, Series 10, Box 33, Folder 3, NTCA Papers. Although both parties pledged to honor the government trust responsibilities, neither included the proposed NTCA Indian plank.

34. MOD Pamphlet.

35. NTCA Board Meeting minutes, October 14, 1976.

36. NTCA Report on Objective 10, undated, Series 13, Box 69, Folder 11, NTCA Papers.

37. Statement of Buffalo Tiger on backlash, November 2, 1977, Series 13, Box 68, Folder 15, NTCA Papers.

38. NTCA Report on Objective 10.

39. Ibid.

40. Proposal and Budget for Indian Anti-Backlash Film, October 1, 1977, Series 13, Box 67, Folder 8, NTCA Papers.

41. NTCA Resolution Seeking Help to Counter Backlash, December 17, 1976, Jimmy Carter Presidential Papers, Records of the Office of the Assistant for Public Liaison, Jane Wales, Indians: NTCA, 12/76 [O/A 4471], Jimmy Carter Presidential Library, Atlanta, Ga.

42. "Popularity vs. Integrity?" *Marshfield (Wisc.) News-Herald*, September 20, 1978, 4.

43. Ibid.; Alice Z. Cunee, "Supporting Indians No Longer Chic," *Lincoln (Neb.) Star*, October 2, 1977, 8.

44. Only by merging the jurisdiction of Indian Affairs with that of Public Lands into a single subcommittee was Udall able to entice Representative Teno Roncalio (D-Wyo.) to serve as chair. See Chuck Trimble, "95th Congress and Backlash Legislation," December 1, 1977, Series 13, Box 67, Folder 5, NTCA Papers.

45. Ibid.; Larry Light, "Backlash in Congress Seen as Indians Push Claims," *Congressional Quarterly Weekly Report*, December 2, 1978, 3388.

46. Light, "Backlash in Congress Seen as Indians Push Claims," 3385–88.

47. Ibid., 3387–88.

48. Odric Baker to NTCA Board, June 30, 1977; and Lucille Echohawk to Andrew Lawson, May 9, 1977, Series 13, Box 67, Folder 7, NTCA Papers.

49. Trimble, "95th Congress and Backlash Legislation."

50. Tanna Beebe to John Sylvester, August 19, 1977, Series 13, Box 67, Folder 6; Chip Herbst to William Youpee, August 25, 1977, Series 13, Box 69, Folder 1; Chuck Trimble to NCAI Executive Committee, November 8, 1977, Series 13, Box 67, Folder 5; NTCA to Tip O'Neill, November 3, 1977, Series 13, Box 68, Folder 13—all NTCA Papers.

51. Members included Sam Deloria, Paul Tafoya, Newton Lamar, Elmer Savilla, Wayne Ducheneaux, Chuck Trimble, and Fran Ayer. See Planning Meeting for Joint NTCA-NCAI Lobbying and Coordinating Committee, November 15, 1977, Series 13, Box 67, Folder 5, NTCA Papers.

52. Joint NTCA-NCAI Effort vs. Backlash, December 16, 1977, Series 13, Box 67, Folder 5; Planning Meeting for Joint NTCA-NCAI Lobbying and Coordinating Committee; Friends Committee on National Legislation, Highlighting Threats to Indian Rights, December 14, 1977, Series 13, Box 68, Folder 8, NTCA Papers.

53. Joint NTCA-NCAI Effort vs. Backlash.

54. United Effort Trust Status Report, Series 13, Box 70, Folder 1, NTCA Papers.

55. In letters to Joe Delacruz and Chuck Trimble, Winston & Strawn's Joseph S. Fontana denied the allegation but insisted that only the NTCA board—not Delacruz—possessed the authority to make decisions regarding the affairs, funds, and property of the association. See April letters, Series 13, Box 70, Folder 1, NTCA Papers.

56. It's unclear why Youpee did not attend. His wife was critically ill at the time, and he may have been attending to family issues. Another possibility is that the NTCA board had misgivings about the joint effort and Youpee was simply following instructions not to attend. That said, he was never enthusiastic about cooperating with NCAI—especially if NCAI was in a position of influence. If this was the case, his absence was in keeping with NTCA precedent.

57. According to the United Effort Trust Declaration, the NCAI Executive Council approved the joint effort on January 19, 1978, and the NTCA approved it at meetings held on January 16, 1978, and February 16–17, 1978. In a memorandum to the NTCA Board of Directors dated June 7, 1978, Winston & Strawn attorney John R. Keys Jr. stated that the two meetings "were not official meetings" at which a quorum was present. See Winston & Strawn memo, Series 13, Box 70, Folder 1, NTCA Papers.

58. The seven members included Joe Delacruz, Terald Goodwin, Calvin Isaac, Veronica Murdock, Rachel Nabahe, Paul Tafoya, and Mel Tonasket. See United Trust

Declaration and Report on March 21 meeting in Series 13, Box 70, Folder 1, NTCA Papers.

59. In a report titled "Congressional Opposition to Indian Tribes," a "core group" of five backlash congresspersons included Lloyd Meeds (D-Wash.), Jack Cunningham (R-Wash.), John Cohen (R-Maine), John Dingell (D-Mich.), William Walsh (R-N.Y.), and thirteen additional congresspersons who had cosponsored backlash legislation. The report also identified seven senators who could potentially sponsor backlash legislation: Henry Jackson (D-Wash.), Warren Magnuson (D-Wash.), Lee Metcalf (D-Mo.), John Melcher (D-Mo.), Carl Curtis (R-Neb.), Claiborne Pell (D-R.I.), and George McGovern (D-S. Dak.). Congressional Opposition to Indian Tribes, undated, Series 13, Box 67, Folder 5, NTCA Papers.

60. United Effort Trust Status Report; Hanna, Deloria, and Trimble, "Commission on State-Tribal Relations," 571–73, 575–78; UET Progress Report of July 21, 1978, Series 13, Box 70, Folder 1, NTCA Papers.

61. Hanna, Deloria, and Trimble, "Commission on State-Tribal Relations," 573–74; "Commission to Study Tribal, State Interactions," *Rapid City Journal* (S. Dak.), March 6, 1979, 2.

62. Garry J. Moes, "Value of Constant Communication between Tribes, Officials Stressed," *The Missoulian* (Mont.), May 29, 1980, 7.

63. Hanna, Deloria, and Trimble, "Commission on State-Tribal Relations," 589–97.

64. Other significant antibacklash organizations created at this time included the Navajo-led Native American Treaties and Rights Organization; New Mexicans for Tribal Development, led by former Oklahoma senator Fred Harris; and the National Coalition to Support Indian Treaties, which was funded by the Lutheran Church and the American Friends Service Committee.

65. Light, "Backlash in Congress Seen as Indians Push Claims," 3388; Larry Light, "Popularity of Indian Cause Wanes on Capitol Hill," *Messenger-Inquirer* (Owensboro, Ky.), December 3, 1978, 5A.

Chapter 6. The Reagan Revolution

1. George Pierre Castile, *Taking Charge: Native American Self-Determination and Federal Indian Policy, 1975–1993* (Tucson: University of Arizona Press, 2006), 17–30.

2. "Reagan's Son Says Dad Will Help Indians," *Sheboygan (Wisc.) Press*, October 18, 1980, 2; "Bump on the Head Reaffirms Reagan's Candidacy," *Arizona Republic* (Phoenix), March 24, 1980, 2.

3. Joseph S. Fontana to Wendell Chino, May 11, 1976 and John R. Keys to NTCA Board of Directors, June 7, 1978, Series 9, Box 31, Folder 1, National Tribal Chairmen's Association Records, 1971–1978, National Museum of the American Indian, Smithsonian Institution Archive Center, Suitland, Md. (hereafter cited as NTCA Papers).

4. NTCA Board Meeting Minutes, March 3, 1978, Series 2, Box 4, Folder 2, NTCA Papers.

5. "NTC Has Problems," *Southern Ute Drum* (Ignacio, Colo.), July 21, 1978, 6. Newspaper reports indicated that between seventy and one hundred tribal leaders attended—which was about half the usual attendance. Delacruz, it should be noted, was the chair

of the Quinault Nation of Washington. Moving the convention venue from Spokane to Minneapolis may have contributed to his position.

6. "Looking Out across the Prairie," *Sho-Ban News* (Fort Hall, Idaho), August 1, 1979, 5.

7. Marjorie Weeks Youpee died on February 19, 1979. See her obituary published in *Great Falls (Mont.) Tribune*, February 21, 1979, 17. Youpee would later be elected to the Fort Peck Tribal Council.

8. "Controversy Flares over Education Grant as NTCA Leaders Reveal Differences; Demand Termination of Executive Director," *Wassaja, The Indian Historian* 13 (September 1980): 26–29.

9. Obituary of Elmer M. "Sy" Savilla, *Yuma (Ariz.) Sun*, December 13, 2016; Terry Mikelson, "1975 Will Be Year of the Indian," *Yuma (Ariz.) Daily Sun*, January 5, 1975, 1; Vicky Taylor, "Quechans to Fight Yuman Pipeline Bill," *Yuma (Ariz.) Daily Sun*, August 6, 1975, 1; "Andrus Orders 25,000 Acres Restored to Quechan Indians' Reservation," Department of the Interior News Release, December 21, 1978.

10. Statement by the President, Indian Policy, January 24, 1983, Bush Presidential Records, Staff and Office Files, Counsel's Office, Jay S. Bybee Files, George H. W. Bush Presidential Library, College Station, Tex.; Dean Kotlowski, "From Backlash to Bingo: Ronald Reagan and Federal Indian Policy," *Pacific Historical Review* 77 (November 2008): 620–28.

11. Kenneth Black to Ronald Reagan, February 20, 1981, White House Staff and Office Files, Office of Intergovernmental Affairs, Rick Neal Files, OA 9726, NTCA-Correspondence and Memos, Ronald Reagan Presidential Papers, Ronald Reagan Presidential Library, Simi Valley, Calif. (hereafter cited as Reagan Papers).

12. Castile, *Taking Charge*, 52–53; Samuel R. Cook, "Ronald Reagan's Indian Policy in Retrospect: Economic Crisis and Political Irony," *Policy Studies Journal* 24 (Spring 1996): 15–16; *The American Indian World*, February 9, 1974, Records of the Office of the Assistant for Public Liaison; Jane Wales, Indians: NTCA, 12/76 [O/A 4471], Jimmy Carter Presidential Papers, Jimmy Carter Presidential Library and Museum, Atlanta, Ga.; C. Patrick Morris, "Termination by Accountants: The Reagan Indian Policy," *Policy Studies Journal* 16 (Summer 1988): 731–32.

13. Kenneth Black to Gregory Newell, March 17, 1981, OA 9726, NTCA-Correspondence and Memos, Reagan Papers.

14. "National Budget Cut Meeting by Tribes Slated," *Sho-Ban News* (Fort Hall, Idaho), April 29, 1981, 9; Mark Trahant, "Indian Organizations Call for Consultation of the Budget," *Sho-Ban News* (Fort Hall, Idaho), April 8, 1981, 1.

15. Report on National Tribal Governments Conference, May 6, 1981, and National Tribal Government's Conference Proposed Indian Policy for the Reagan Administration, May 7, 1981, OA 9726, NTCA-Correspondence and Memos, Reagan Papers.

16. Wendell Chino to Ronald Reagan, May 7, 1981, OA 9726, NTCA-Correspondence and Memos, Reagan Papers; A. O. Sulzberger Jr., "Indian Leaders Ask Watt to Quit," *New York Times*, May 9, 1981, 10.

17. Castile, *Taking Charge*, 54.

18. "Indians Demanding Watt Resignation," *Daily Oklahoman* (Oklahoma City), May 9, 1981, 98.

19. "White House Tribal Liaison, a Conservative Republican," *Sho-Ban News* (Fort Hall, Idaho), April 15, 1981, 13.

20. Elmer Savilla to Morton Blackwell, July 7, 1981, and July 16, 1981, OA 9726, NTCA-Correspondence and Memos, Reagan Papers.

21. NTCA Resolution calling for resignation of Watt, to restructure the BIA, and to protect Indian water rights, January 25, 1983, OA 9726, NTCA-Correspondence and Memos, Reagan Papers.

22. Jake Henshaw, "Indians Protest Cuts in Health Programs," *Argus-Leader* (Sioux Falls, S. Dak.), October 22, 1981, 10.

23. Morton Blackwell to Elmer Savilla, June 23, 1981, OA 9726, NTCA-Correspondence and Memos, Reagan Papers; Statement by the President, Indian Policy, January 24, 1983.

24. NTCA Resolution calling for resignation of Watt, to restructure the BIA, and to protect Indian water rights.

25. "Watt Apologizes to Indians for Any 'Hurt' from Socialism Remarks," *New York Times*, January 26, 1983, A13.

26. Steven R. Weisman, "Watt Quits Post; President Accepts with Reluctance," *New York Times*, October 10, 1983, 1.

27. Kotlowski, "From Backlash to Bingo," 624–26.

28. Fiscal Year 1984 Budget. Hearing before the Select Committee on Indian Affairs, U.S. Senate, Ninety-Eighth Congress, first session (February 23–25, 1983), ERIC No. ED238615. See https://archive.org/details/ERIC_ED238615/page/n1.

29. Ronald Reagan, "Inaugural Address," in *Reagan as President: Contemporary Views of the Man, His Politics, and His Policies*, ed. Paul Boyer (Chicago: Ivan R. Dee, 1990), 31–34; Kotlowski, "From Backlash to Bingo," 627–28. For an examination of George H. W. Bush's Indian policies, see Thomas A. Britten, "Prudence and Moderation: George H. W. Bush and Federal Indian Policy," *Indigenous Policy Journal* 29 (Spring 2018): 1–24.

30. "Interior Announces Change in BIA Organization," Department of the Interior News Release, February 19, 1982.

31. "Officers Criticize BIA head," *Kalispell (Mont.) Daily Inter Lake*, August 13, 1981, 9; "Tribes Will Have to Be More Accountable," *Kalispell (Mont.) Daily Inter Lake*, August 12, 1981, 2.

32. "Interior Announces Change in BIA Organization"; "Idaho Tribes Convene for Indian Quarterly Conference," *Sho-Ban News* (Fort Hall, Idaho), April 14, 1982, 8; "Reducing BIA's Role," *Arizona Republic* (Phoenix, Ariz.), February 20, 1982, 4.

33. "Tribal Leaders Meet with Watt," *Sho-Ban News* (Fort Hall, Idaho), February 3, 1982, 1.

34. "BIA Realignment Proposal Sent to Tribes for Review," Bureau of Indian Affairs News Release, May 6, 1982.

35. "Tribal Leaders Blast Federal Government," *New Mexican* (Santa Fe), May 11, 1983, 5.

36. *State of the American Indian Nations: 1983*, June 1, 1983, OA 9726, NTCA-Correspondence and Memos, Reagan Papers.

37. Ibid.

38. Ibid.

39. Ibid.

40. Ibid.

41. Ibid.

42. Ibid.

43. Ibid.

44. Ibid.

45. "Indian Leaders Rapping System," *Huntingdon (Penn.) Daily News*, June 2, 1983, 6; "Old Wounds: Indians Ask Action on Promise of Rights," *Indiana Gazette* (Penn.), June 2, 1983, 28.

46. "Martin Resigns Presidency of NTCA," *Indian Country Today*, July 20, 1983, 10.

47. "NTCA NCAI Outline Plan to Restructure BIA," *Indian Country Today*, July 20, 1983, 13; NTCA/NCIA Commission for Reorganizing BIA Requests Comments," *Sho-Ban News*, August 31, 1983, 18.

48. Ronald Reagan, Executive Order 12401—Presidential Commission on Indian Reservation Economies, The American Presidency Project, https://www.presidency.ucsb.edu/node/262331.

49. The commission comprised cochairs Bob Robertson (former NCIO executive director) and Ross Swimmer (principal chief of the Cherokee Nation), and Daniel Alex (Athabascan), Ted Bryant (Cherokee-Choctaw), Dr. Manuel H. Johnson (assistant secretary of the treasury), B. J. Kastler (former congressperson from Utah and oil company executive), David J. Matheson (Coeur d'Alene tribal chair), Neal McCabe (Chickasaw), and Walter B. McCay (Cherokee).

50. Reagan, Executive Order 12401

51. Robert Robertson and Ross O. Swimmer, Presidential Commission on Indian Reservation Economies, *Report and Recommendations to the President of the United States* (Washington, D.C.: Government Printing Office, 1984).

52. Ibid., 23–25.

53. Ibid., 27–61.

54. Adrian C. Louis, "Tribal Leaders Blast Presidential Commission," *Indian Country Today*, December 12, 1984, 1.

55. Ibid.; Elmer M. Savilla, "Chairmen's Association Calls for Emergency Conference," *Sho-Ban News* (Fort Hall, Idaho), December 19, 1984, 8.

56. Savilla, "Chairmen's Association Calls for Emergency Conference," 8; Louis, "Tribal Leaders Blast Presidential Commission," 1.

57. Louis, "Tribal Leaders Blast Presidential Commission," 1.

58. The initial vote was much closer—36 in favor and 18 opposed. Savilla then called for a second ballot "as a show of strength," and it passed 52-3. Several tribal leaders abstained pending feedback from their tribes. Pyramid Lake Paiute chair Wilfred Shaw stated that he had noted "no" because the NTCA represented only 187 of America's 492 tribes. See Wayne Melton, "Indians Reject Reagan Proposals," *Reno-Gazette Journal*, January 11, 1985, 28. The *New York Times* reported the vote tally as 84-18 to reject the commission's recommendations. See Iver Peterson, "Indians Resist Shift in Economic Goals Urged by U.S. Panel," *New York Times*, January 13, 1985, 1.

59. Joan Morrison, "Tribes Vote to Reject Commission Report," *Indian Country Today*, January 16, 1985, 1.

60. "Board Rejects Commission Report as Threat to Culture," *Sho-Ban News* (Fort Hall, Idaho), February 20, 1985, 15.

61. Ibid.

62. Robertson and Swimmer, *Report and Recommendations to the President of the United States*, 23, 66.

63. "Board Rejects Commission Report as Threat to Culture," 15.

64. Chris Brawley, "Reagan Picks Sooner for BIA Post," *Daily Oklahoman* (Oklahoma City), September 27, 1985, 1.

65. Lorna Thackeray, "Report on Indian Economies Blasted," *Billings (Mont.) Gazette*, October 22, 1985, 26.

66. "A Wise Choice," *Gallup Independent* (N.Mex.), December 11, 1973, 2.

67. "NTCA Official Says Indians Are Seeking Loans from Japanese Businessmen," *Sho-Ban News*, May 19, 1982, 7.

68. Elmer M. Savilla, "Forward into the Future: The Conclusion of a Fact/Fiction Story of How by 2075, American Indian Tribes Become Only a Dim Memory," http://eagle.indigenousnative.org/op0196.html.

Conclusion

1. Harlan McKosato, "Drums: Heartbeat of Mother Earth," *Native Peoples Magazine*, July/August 2009, 36.

2. "BIA Chief Receives Hostile Reception," *News from Indian Country*, September 10, 1986, 8; Peter B. Gallagher, "National Tribal Chairmen's Conference," *Seminole Tribune* (Hollywood, Fla.), August 11, 1986, 7.

3. "NCAI and NTCA to Lose BIA Direct Funding," *Indian Country Today*, February 26, 1986, 3; "NTCA Closes Office Doors," *Sho-Ban News* (Fort Hall, Idaho), February 19, 1987, 17.

4. The BIA financed a $175,000 NCAI program for information dissemination and policy analysis. See "NCAI Executive Council Meeting Held," *News from Indian Country*, March 31, 1986, 3.

5. "NTCA/NCIA Commission for Reorganizing BIA Requests Comments," *Sho-Ban News*, August 31, 1983, 18.

6. For example, see the ad in *Navajo Times* (Window Rock, Ariz.), March 26, 1984, 8.

7. Gallagher, "National Tribal Chairmen's Conference," 7.

8. "Raymond Field Named Executive Director of NTCA," *Indian Country Today*, August 21, 1985, 8.

9. "NTCA Closes Office Doors," 17.

10. Lynda Clause, "Going Belly Up: NTCA Closes Doors," *Indian Country Today*, February 11, 1987, 1.

11. Dean Chavers, "BIA Has 'Methods' for Destroying Leaders," *Sho-Ban News* (Fort Hall, Idaho), January 23, 1986, 7.

12. Charles Wilkinson, *Blood Struggle: The Rise of Modern Indian Nations* (New York: W. W. Norton & Co., 2005), 149.

13. Webster Two Hawk to NTCA Membership, September 30, 1972, Series 1, Box 5, Folder 2, NTCA Papers.

14. Jack Swanson, "Top Indians Meet on White Backlash," *Arizona Republic*, April 13, 1978, 9.

15. Elmer Savilla to Ronald Reagan, May 18, 1983, OA 9726, NTCA-Correspondence and Memos, Ronald Reagan Presidential Papers, Ronald Reagan Presidential Library, Simi Valley, Calif.

16. "Philip Morris Gives $10,000 to NTCA," *Indian Country Today*, November 26, 1986, 7.

17. Joane Nagle, *American Indian Ethnic Renewal: Red Power and the Resurgence of Identity and Culture* (New York: Oxford University Press, 1977), 177.

18. Brent L. Pickett, "Foucault and the Politics of Resistance," *Polity* 28 (Summer 1996): 447.

19. Vine Deloria Jr., *Behind the Trail of Broken Treaties: An Indian Declaration of Independence* (New York: Dell, 1974), 40–41; Deloria, "This Country Was a Lot Better Off When the Indians Were Running It," *New York Times*, March 8, 1970, 17; Robert Burnette and John Koster, *The Road to Wounded Knee* (New York: Bantam Books, 1974), 209.

20. Deloria, *Behind the Trail of Broken Treaties*, 282–84.

21. Ibid., 284–85.

22. NTCA Resolution 8/72–3, Box 54, Bradley Patterson Files, Nixon Papers; "Indians Want Revenue Sharing," *Honolulu Advertiser*, August 12, 1972, 2; Richard La Course, "What Revenue Sharing Law May Mean to Indians," *Gallup (N.Mex.) Independent*, September 14, 1972, 2.

23. Dennis Ickes to BIA, July 12, 1976, Box 6, Bradley H. Patterson Files, Gerald R. Ford Presidential Papers, Gerald R. Ford Presidential Library, Grand Rapids, Mich.

24. As quoted in Colin G. Calloway, *First Peoples: A Documentary Survey of American Indian History*, 4th ed. (New York: Bedford St. Martin's, 2012), 643; Sharon O'Brien, "Tribal Governments," *National Forum* 71 (Spring 1991): 18.

Epilogue

1. "Study of Constitution Focuses on Indian Rights," *Santa Fe New Mexican*, May 1, 1987, D-3.

2. Walter F. Naedele, "Indians Meeting on Constitution," *Philadelphia Inquirer*, October 11, 1987, 47.

3. Leah Lorber, "Senate Proposal to Transfer Programs to Tribes Rejected," *Albuquerque Journal*, January 22, 1990, 4; "Elimination of BIA Rejected," *Alamogordo News* (N.Mex.), January 22, 1990, 1, 12.

4. "Interior Secretary Lujan Invites Indian Tribal Leaders to National Conference to Strengthen Self-Determination Policy," Department of the Interior News Release, September 18, 1990; Susan Landon, "Albuquerque Indian Summit under Fire," *Albuquerque Journal*, September 26, 1990, 33.

5. Landon, "Albuquerque Indian Summit under Fire," 33.

6. Seth Mydans, "Indians Say U.S. Has Ignored Their Views in New Program," *Santa Fe New Mexican*, September 30, 1990, 3.

7. "Chino Rebukes Road-Closing Proposal, Calls Such a Demonstration Radicalism," *Roswell (N.Mex.) Daily Record*, February 4, 1998, B3.

Bibliography

Archival and Oral History Collections

Gerald R. Ford Presidential Papers, Bradley H. Patterson Files, Gerald R. Ford Presidential Library, Grand Rapids, Mich.

Jimmy Carter Presidential Papers, Records of the Office of the Assistant for Public Liaison, Jane Wales, Indians: NTCA, Jimmy Carter Presidential Library, Atlanta, Ga.

Julia B. Hansen Papers, Special Collections, University of Washington, Seattle, Wash.

National Council on Indian Opportunity Records, 1968–1974, Record Group 220, National Archives Building at College Park, Md.

National Museum of the American Indian Center Archive, Arrow Inc., and the American Indian Tribal Court Judges Records, 1949–1999. NMAI.AC.013. Accessed at http://nmai.si.edu/sites/1/files/archivecenter/AC013_arrow.html.

National Tribal Chairmen's Association Records, 1971–1978, National Museum of the American Indian, Smithsonian Institution Archive Center, Suitland, Md.

National Tribal Chairmen's Association Pierre, SD Constitutional Convention, MS 654–657. American Indian Research Project. University of South Dakota, Vermillion, S. Dak.

Northwest Tribal Oral History Interviews, 1963–1973, Western Washington University, Center for Pacific Northwest Studies, Bellingham, Wash.

Richard M. Nixon Presidential Papers, Bradley M. Patterson Files, Richard M. Nixon Presidential Library, Yorba Linda, Calif.

Ronald Reagan Presidential Papers, Ronald Reagan Presidential Library, Simi Valley, Calif.

Spiro T. Agnew Papers, Special Collections, University of Maryland Libraries, Hornbake Library, College Park, Md.

Government Documents

Executive Order No. 11399. Establishing the National Council on Indian Opportunity, March 6, 1968. The American Presidency Project, Accessed at https://www.presidency.ucsb.edu/documents/executive-order-11399-establishing-the-national-council-indian-opportunity.

Josephy, Alvin M. *The American Indian and the Bureau of Indian Affairs—1969: A Study with Recommendations*. February 11, 1969.

Lyon, Juana. *The Indian Elder, a Forgotten American. Final Report on the First National Indian Conference on Aging*. Phoenix, Ariz.: NTCA. June 15–17, 1976.

Nixon, Richard M. "Special Message to the Congress on Indian Affairs." July 8, 1970. The American Presidency Project. Accessed at https://www.presidency.ucsb.edu /documents/special-message-the-congress-indian-affairs.

Reagan, Ronald. Executive Order 12401. Presidential Commission on Indian Reservation Economies. The American Presidency Project, Accessed at https://www .presidency.ucsb.edu/documents/executive-order-12401-presidential-commission -indian-reservation-economies.

Robertson, Robert, and Ross Swimmer. Presidential Commission on Indian Reservation Economies. *Report and Recommendations to the President of the United States*. Washington, D.C.: Government Printing Office, 1984.

The Public Papers of the Presidents of the United States, Richard Nixon: 1971: Containing the Public Messages, Speeches, and Statements of the President. Washington, D.C.: Government Printing Office, 1972.

U.S. Census Bureau. *Decennial Census, 1970.*

U.S. Congress. American Indian Policy Review Commission. *American Indian Policy Review Commission Final Report*. May 17, 1977.

U.S. Congress. House. Subcommittee on Indian Affairs. *Indian Child Welfare Act of 1978*. Ninety-Fifth Congress, second session, February 5 and March 9, 1978.

———. Subcommittee on Indian Affairs. *Seizure of Bureau of Indian Affairs Headquarters*. Ninety-Second Congress, second session, December 4–5, 1972.

———. Subcommittee on Indian Affairs and Public Lands. *Federal Recognition of Indian Tribes*. Ninety-Fifth Congress, second session, August 10, 1978.

U.S. Congress. Senate. Select Committee on Indian Affairs. *Fiscal Year 1984 Budget*. Ninety-Eighth Congress, first session, February 23–25, 1983.

———. Subcommittee on Administrative Practice and Procedure. *Federal Protection of Indian Resources*. Ninety-Second Congress, first session, January 3, 1972.

———. Subcommittee on Indian Affairs. *Establishment of the American Indian Policy Review Commission*. Ninety-Third Congress, first session, July 19–20, 1973.

Books, Articles, Theses, Dissertations, and Addresses

James, Lenada, et al. "Activism and Red Power." In *Indian Self Rule: First-Hand Accounts of Indian White Relations from Roosevelt to Reagan,* edited by Kenneth R. Philip, 228–42.. Logan: Utah State University Press, 1995.

American Friends Service Committee. *Uncommon Controversy: Fishing Rights of the Muckleshoot, Puyallup, and Nisqually Indians*. Seattle: University of Washington Press, 1970.

Banks, Dennis, with Richard Erdoes. *Ojibwa Warrior: Dennis Banks and the Rise of the American Indian Movement*. Norman: University of Oklahoma Press, 2005.

Barsh, Russel L., and James Youngblood Henderson. *The Road: Indian Tribes and Political Liberty*. Berkeley: University of California Press, 1980.

Bellecourt, Clyde. *The Thunder before the Storm: The Autobiography of Clyde Bellecourt as Told to Jon Lurie*. St. Paul: Minnesota Historical Society Press, 2016.

Berkhofer, Robert F. *The White Man's Indian: Images of the American Indian from Columbus to The Present*. New York: Vintage, 1979.

Biolosi, Thomas. "The IRA and the Politics of Acculturation: The Sioux Case." *American Anthropologist* 87 (September 1985): 656–59.

———. *Organizing the Lakota: The Political Economy of the New Deal on the Pine Ridge and Rosebud Reservations.* Tucson: University of Arizona Press, 1988.

Britten, Thomas A. *American Indians in World War I: At Home and at War.* Albuquerque: University of New Mexico Press, 1997.

———. *The National Council on Indian Opportunity: Quiet Champion of Self-Determination.* Albuquerque: University of New Mexico Press, 2014.

———. "Prudence and Moderation: George H. W. Bush and Federal Indian Policy." *Indigenous Policy Journal* 29 (Spring 2018): 1–24.

———. "Urban American Indian Centers in the Late 1960s–1970s: An Examination of Their Function and Purpose." *Indigenous Policy Journal* 27 (Winter 2017): 1–18.

Bruyneel, Kevin. *The Third Space of Sovereignty: The Postcolonial Period of U.S. Indigenous Relations,* Minneapolis: University of Minnesota Press, 2007.

Buffalohead, W. Roger. "Self-Rule in the Past and the Future: An Overview." In *Indian Self Rule: First-Hand Accounts of Indian-White Relations from Roosevelt to Reagan,* edited by Kenneth R. Philip, 260–77. Logan: Utah State University Press, 1986

Burnette, Robert. *The Tortured Americans.* Englewood Cliffs, N.J.: Prentice Hall, 1971.

Burnette, Robert, and John Koster. *The Road to Wounded Knee.* New York: Bantam Books, 1974.

Calliou, Brian. "The Culture of Leadership: North American Indigenous Leadership in a Changing Economy." In *Indigenous Peoples and the Modern State,* edited by Duane Champagne, Karen Jo Torjesen, and Susan Steiner, 47–68. New York: Alta Mira, 2005.

Calloway, Colin G. *First Peoples: A Documentary Survey of American Indian History.* 4th ed. New York: Bedford St. Martin's, 2012.

Cash, Joseph H. "Louis Rooks Bruce, 1969–73." In *The Commissioners of Indian Affairs, 1824–1977,* edited by Robert M. Kvasnicka and Herman J. Viola, 333–40. Lincoln: University of Nebraska Press, 1979.

Castile, George Pierre. *Taking Charge: Native American Self-Determination and Federal Indian Policy, 1975–1993.* Tucson: University of Arizona Press, 2006.

———. *To Show Heart: Native American Self-Determination and Federal Indian Policy, 1960–1975.* Tucson: University of Arizona Press, 1998.

Chaves, Mark, Laura Stephens, and Joseph Galaskiewicz. "Does Government Funding Suppress Nonprofits' Political Activity?" *Sociological Review* 69 (April 2004): 292–316.

Churchill, Ward. *Perversions of Justice: Indigenous Peoples and Angloamerican Law.* San Francisco: City Lights, 2003.

Clarkin, Thomas. *Federal Indian Policy in the Kennedy and Johnson Administrations, 1961–1969.* Albuquerque: University of New Mexico Press, 2001.

Clow, Richmond L. "The Indian Reorganization Act and the Loss of Tribal Sovereignty: Constitutions on the Rosebud and Pine Ridge Reservations." *Great Plains Quarterly* 7 (Spring 1987): 125–34.

Cobb, Amanda J. "Understanding Tribal Sovereignty: Definitions, Conceptualizations, and Interpretations." *American Studies* 46 (Fall/Winter 2005): 115–32.

Cobb, Daniel M. *Native American Activism in Cold War America: The Struggle for Sovereignty.* Lawrence: University of Kansas Press, 2008.

———. "Philosophy of an Indian War: Indian Community Action in the Johnson Administration's War on Indian Poverty, 1964–1968." *American Indian Culture and Research Journal* 22 (1998): 71–102.

Cobb, Daniel M., and Loretta Fowler, eds. *Beyond Red Power: American Indian Politics and Activism since 1900.* Santa Fe, N.Mex.: School for Advanced Research Press, 2007.

Coffey, Wallace, and Rebecca Tsosie. "Rethinking Tribal Sovereignty Doctrine: Cultural Sovereignty and the Collective Future of Indian Nations." *Stanford Law and Policy Review* 12 (Spring 2001): 191–221.

Cohen, Felix S. *On the Drafting of Tribal Constitutions.* Edited by David W. Wilkins. Norman: University of Oklahoma Press, 2006.

"Community Action: Main Features of the Program." *Congressional Digest* 47 (February 1, 1968): 36–40, 64.

"Controversy Flares over Education Grant as NTCA Leaders Reveal Differences; Demand Termination of Executive Director." *Wassaja, The Indian Historian* 13 (September 1980): 26–29.

Cook, Samuel R. "Indian Self-Determination: A Comparative Analysis of Executive and Congressional Approaches to Contemporary Federal Indian Policy." M.A. thesis, University of Arizona, 1992.

———. "Ronald Reagan's Indian Policy in Retrospect: Economic Crisis and Political Irony." *Policy Studies Journal* 24 (Spring 1996): 11–27.

Cornell, Stephen. "The New Indian Politics." *Wilson Quarterly* 10 (New Year's 1986): 113–31.

———. *Return of the Native: American Indian Political Resurgence.* New York: Oxford University Press, 1990.

Cowger, Thomas W. *The National Congress of American Indians: The Founding Years.* Lincoln: University of Nebraska Press, 2001.

Coy, Patrick G. Coy, and Tim Hedeen. "A Stage Model of Social Movement Co-Optation: Community Mediation in the United States." *Sociological Quarterly* 46 (Summer 2005): 405–35.

Deloria, Vine, Jr.. *Behind the Trail of Broken Treaties: An Indian Declaration of Independence.* New York: Dell, 1974.

———. *Behind the Trail of Broken Treaties: An Indian Declaration of Independence.* Austin: University of Texas Press, 1985.

———. *Custer Died for Your Sins: An Indian Manifesto.* Norman: University of Oklahoma Press, 1969.

———. "Intellectual Self-Determination and Sovereignty: Looking at the Windmills in Our Minds." *Wicazo Sa Review* 13 (Spring 1998): 25–31.

Dorris, Michael A. "The Grass Still Grows, the Rivers Still Flow: Contemporary Native Americans." *Daedalus* 110 (Spring 1981): 43–69.

Edmunds, R. David. *American Indian Leaders: Studies in Diversity.* Lincoln: University of Nebraska Press, 1980.

Evans, Laura E. "Expertise and Scale of Conflict: Governments as Advocates in American Indian Politics." *American Political Science Review* 105 (November 2011): 663–82.

Fixico, Donald. *Termination and Relocation: Federal Indian Policy, 1945–1960.* Albuquerque: University of New Mexico Press, 1986.

———. *The Urban Indian Experience in America*. Albuquerque: University of New Mexico Press, 2000.

Forbes, Jack D. *Native Americans and Nixon: Presidential Politics and Minority Self-Determination, 1969–1972*. Los Angeles: UCLA American Indian Studies Center, 1981.

Fleming Mather, Mary E. "The Duke Had a Word for It: Local-Level Competition between Tribals and Non-Tribals." In *Political Anthropology: The State of the Art*, edited by S. Lee Seaton and Henri M. Claessen, 121–48. New York: Mouton, 1979.

Gamson, William A. "Reflections on 'The Strategy of Social Protest.'" *Sociological Forum* 4 (September 1989): 455–67.

Goldberg-Ambrose, Carole. "Of Native Americans and Tribal Members: The Impact of Law on Indian Group Life," *Law and Society Review* 28 (December 1994): 1123–48.

Gross, Michael P. "Indian Self-Determination and Tribal Sovereignty: An Analysis of Recent Federal Indian Policy." *Texas Law Review* 56 (1978): 1195–244.

Grossman, Zoltan. "Treaty Rights and Responding to Anti-Indian Activity." The Midwest Treaty Network. Accessed at http://treaty.indigenousnative.org/anti-indian.html.

Hanna, Tassie, Sam Deloria, and Charles E. Trimble. "The Commission on State-Tribal Relations: Enduring Lessons in the Modern State-Tribal Relationship." *Tulsa Law Review* 47 (Spring 2002): 553–97.

Hauptman, Laurence M. *The Iroquois and the New Deal*. Syracuse, N.Y.: Syracuse University Press, 1981.

Henry, Jeanette, and Rupert Casto. "Who Is an Indian?" *Wassaja* 13 (June 1980): 15–20.

Hertzberg, Hazel W. "Indian Rights Movement, 1887–1973." In *Handbook of North American Indians*, vol. 4, edited by Wilcomb E. Washburn, 305–23. Washington, D.C.: Smithsonian Institution, 1988.

Holm, Tom. "Indian Concepts of Authority and the Crisis in Tribal Government." *Social Science Journal* 19 (July 1982): 59–71.

Iverson, Peter. "Peter MacDonald." In *American Indian Tribal Leaders: Studies in Diversity*, edited by R. David Edmondson, 222–38. Lincoln: University of Nebraska Press, 1980.

Kalt, Joseph P., and Joseph W. Singer. "Myths and Realities of Tribal Sovereignty: The Law and Economics of Indian Self-Rule." *Harvard University Native Issues Research Symposium* (March 2004): 1–48.

Kelly, Lawrence C. "The Indian Reorganization Act: The Dream and the Reality." *Pacific Historical Review* 44 (August 1975): 291–312.

Kickingbird, Kirke. "The American Indian Policy Review Commission: A Prospect for Future Change in Federal Indian Policy." *American Indian Law Review* 3 (1975): 243–53.

Kipp, Woody. *The Trail of a Blackfeet Activist*. Lincoln: University of Nebraska Press, 2004.

Kotlowski, Dean. "From Backlash to Bingo: Ronald Reagan and Federal Indian Policy." *Pacific Historical Review* 77 (November 2008): 617–52.

———. *Nixon's Civil Rights: Politics, Principle, and Policy*. Cambridge, Mass.: Harvard University Press, 2002.

Lagace, Naithan, and Niigaanwewidam James Sinclair. "The White Paper, 1969." Canadian Encyclopedia. Revised November 12, 2015. Accessed at http://www.thecanadianencyclopedia.ca/en/article/the-white-paper-1969.

Larabee, Eunice. "Health Education." In *Indian Education Confronts the Seventies,* edited by Vine Deloria Jr., 153–68. Washington, D.C.: Office of Education, Department of Health, Education, and Welfare, 1974.

Levitan, Sar A., and Barbara Hetrick. *Big Brother's Indian Programs—With Reservations.* New York: McGraw Hill, 1971.

Long, J. Anthony, Leroy Little Bear, and Menno Boldt. "Federal Indian Policy and Indian Self-Government in Canada: An Analysis of a Current Proposal." *Canadian Public Policy* 8 (Spring 1982): 189–99.

Lujan, Carol Chiago, and Gordon Adams. "U.S. Colonization of Indian Justice Systems: A Brief History." *Wicazo Sa Review* 19 (Autumn 2004): 9–23.

Lurie, Nancy Oestrech. "The Voice of the American Indian: Report on the American Indian Chicago Conference." *Current Anthropology* 2 (December 1961): 478–500.

Mann, Henrietta. "Earth Mother and Prayerful Children: Sacred Sites and Religious Freedom." In *Native Voices: American Indian Identity and Resistance,* edited by Richard Grounds, George E. Tinker, and David E. Wilkins, 194–208. Lawrence: University of Kansas Press, 2003.

Marger, Martin N. "Social Movement Organizations and Response to Environmental Change: The NAACP, 1960–1973." *Social Problems* 32 (October 1984): 16–30.

Maynor Lowery, Malinda. *Lumbee Indians in the Jim Crow South: Race Identity and the Making of a Nation.* Chapel Hill: University of North Carolina Press, 2010.

———. "Telling Our Own Stories: Lumbee History and the Federal Acknowledgment Process." *American Indian Quarterly* 33 (Fall 2009): 499–522.

McClellan, E. Fletcher. "The Politics of American Indian Self-Determination, 1958–1975: The Indian Self-Determination and Education Assistance Act of 1975." Ph.D. diss., University of Tennessee, 1988.

McLeod, Martha. "Keeping the Circle Strong: Learning about Native American Leadership." *Tribal College Journal of American Indian Higher Education* 13 (Summer 2002): 10–12.

McKosato, Harlan. "Drums: Heartbeat of Mother Earth." *Native Peoples Magazine* 22 (July/August 2009): 36–40.

Meriam, Lewis, et al. *The Problem of Indian Administration.* Washington, D.C.: Brookings Institution, 1928.

Miller, David, et al. *The History of the Assiniboine and Sioux Tribes of the Fort Peck Indian Reservation: 1600–2012.* Poplar, Mont.: Fort Peck Community College, 2012.

Miller, Mark Edwin. *Claiming Tribal Identity: The Five Tribes and the Politics of Federal Acknowledgment.* Norman: University of Oklahoma Press, 2013.

———. *Forgotten Tribes: Unrecognized Indians and the Federal Acknowledgment Process.* Lincoln: University of Nebraska Press, 2004.

Monette, Richard A. "Sovereignty and Survival: The Status of Indian Tribes under American Law Is a Key to Their Cultural Existence." *ABA Journal* 86 (March 2000): 64–65.

Montanaro, Laura. "The Democratic Legitimacy of Self-Appointed Representatives." *Journal of Politics* 74 (October 2012): 1094–107.

Morris, C. Patrick. "Termination by Accountants: The Reagan Indian Policy." *Policy Studies Journal* 16 (Summer 1988): 731–50.

Morris, Glenn T. "International Law and Politics: Toward a Right to Self-Determination for Indigenous Peoples." In *Native American Sovereignty*, edited by John Wunder, 323–55. New York: Routledge, 1999.

Mosely, Jennifer E. "Keeping the Lights On: How Government Funding Concerns Drive the Advocacy Agendas of Nonprofit Homeless Service Providers." *Journal of Public Administration Research and Theory* 22 (2012): 841–66.

Moynihan, Daniel P. *The Politics of a Guaranteed Income: The Nixon Administration and the Family Assistance Plan*. New York: Random House, 1973.

Nickeson, Steve. "The Structure of the Bureau of Indian Affairs." *Law and Contemporary Problems* 40 (Winter 1976): 61–76.

Nownes, Anthony J. *Interest Groups in American Politics: Pressure and Power*. New York: Routledge, 2013.

O'Brien, Sharon. "Tribal Governments." *National Forum* 71 (Spring 1991): 18.

Officer, James E. "The American Indian and Federal Policy." In *The American Indian in Urban Society*, edited by Jack O. Waddell and O. Michael Watson, 8–65. New York: University Press of America, 1984.

Ornstein, Norman J., and Shirley Elder. *Interest Groups, Lobbying and Policymaking*. Washington, D.C.: Congressional Quarterly Press, 1978.

Pacheco, Michael M. "Finality in Indian Tribunal Decisions: Respecting Our Brothers' Vision." *American Indian Law Review* 16 (1991): 119–66.

Padget, Cindy D. "The Lost Indians of the Lost Colony: A Critical Legal Study of the Lumbee Indians of North Carolina." *American Indian Law Review* 21 (1997): 392–400.

Philip, Kenneth R., ed. *Indian Self-Rule: First-Hand Accounts of Indian White Relations from Roosevelt to Reagan*. Logan: Utah State University Press, 1995.

Philpott, Daniel. "Sovereignty." The Stanford Encyclopedia of Philosophy Archive (Summer 2016 edition). Revised March 25, 2016. Accessed at https://plato.stanford.edu/archives/sum2016/entries/sovereignty/.

Pickett, Brent L. "Foucault and the Politics of Resistance." *Polity* 28 (Summer 1996): 445–66.

Reagan, Ronald. "Inaugural Address." In *Reagan as President: Contemporary Views of the Man, His Politics, and His Policies*, edited by Paul Boyer, 31–33. Chicago: Ivan R. Dee, 1990.

Rehfeld, Andrew. "Towards a General Theory of Political Representation." *Journal of Politics* 68 (February 2006): 1–21.

Reinhardt, Akim D. *Ruling Pine Ridge: Oglala Lakota Politics from the IRA to Wounded Knee*. Lubbock: Texas Tech University Press, 2007.

Rey-Bear, Daniel I. S. J., and Matthew L. M. J. Fletcher. "We Need Protection from Our Protectors: The Nature, Issues, and Future of the Federal Trust Responsibility to Indians." *Michigan Journal of Environmental and Administrative Law* 6 (2017): 397–461.

Reyser, Rudolph C. "Anti-Indian Movement on the Tribal Frontier." Occasional Paper #16, revised edition, *Center for World Indigenous Studies* (June 1992): 1–14.

Rosier, Paul C. *Serving Their Country: American Indian Politics and Patriotism in the Twentieth Century*. Cambridge, Mass.: Harvard University Press, 2009.

Salamon, Lester M. ed. *The State of Non-Profit America*. Washington, D.C.: Brookings Institution Press, 2002.

Savilla, Elmer M. "Forward into the Future: The Conclusion of a Fact/Fiction Story of How by 2075, American Indian Tribes Become Only a Dim Memory." *America's Eagle*, January 1996, http://eagle.indigenousnative.org/op0196.html.

Sclar, Lee J. "Participation of Off-Reservation Indians in Programs of the Bureau of Indian Affairs and the Indian Health Service." *Montana Law Review* 33 (Summer 1972): 191–232.

Selznick, Philip. *TVA and the Grass Roots: A Study in the Sociology of Formal Organization*. Berkeley: University of California Press, 1949.

Senese, Guy B. *Self-Determination and the Social Education of Native Americans*. New York: Praeger, 1991.

Shreve, Bradley G. "'From Time Immemorial': The Fish-In Movement and the Rise of Intertribal Activism." *Pacific Historical Review* 78 (August 2009): 403–34.

———. *Red Power Rising: The National Indian Youth Council and the Origins of Native Activism*. Norman: University of Oklahoma Press, 2011.

Smith, Paul Chaat, and Robert Allen Warrior. *Like a Hurricane: The Indian Movement from Alcatraz to Wounded Knee*. New York: New Press, 1996.

Smith, Steven R., and Michael Lipsky. *Nonprofits for Hire: The Welfare State in the Age of Contracting*. Cambridge, Mass.: Harvard University Press, 1995.

Stotik, Jeffrey, Thomas E. Shriver, and Sherry Cable. "Social Control and Movement Outcome: The Case of AIM." *Sociological Forces* 27 (February 1994): 53–66.

Strommer, Geoffrey D., and Stephen D. Osborne. "The History, Status, and Future of Tribal Self-Governance under the Indian Self-Determination and Education Assistance Act." *American Indian Law Review* 39 (2015): 1–75.

Stubben, Jerry D. *Native Americans and Political Participation*. Santa Barbara, Calif.: ABC-CLIO, 2006.

Taylor, Graham D. *The New Deal and American Indian Tribalism*. Lincoln: University of Nebraska Press, 1980.

Toole, Ken. *Drumming Up Resentment: The Anti-Indian Movement in Montana*. Helena: Montana Human Rights Network, 2000.

Trahant, Mark. *The Last Great Battle of the Indian Wars*. Fort Hall, Idaho: Cedars Group, 2010.

Trimble, Charles. "The Betrayal of Sergeant Crazy Horse." Manataka American Indian Council. October 2011.

———. *Iyeska*. Indianapolis: Dog Ear Publishing, 2012.

———. "NCAI Made It through Rocky Era." Keynote Address to the NCAI. October 14, 2009. https://www.indianz.com/News/2009/10/21/charles_trimble_ncai_made_it _t.asp.

Troutman, John. "The Citizenship of Dance: Politics of Music among the Lakota, 1900–1924." In *Beyond Red Power: American Indian Politics and Activism since 1900*, edited by Daniel M. Cobb and Loretta Fowler, 91–108. Santa Fe: School for Advanced Research Press, 2007.

Tyler, S. Lyman. *A History of Indian Policy*. Washington, D.C.: Department of the Interior, 1973.

Warner, Linda Sue, and Keith Grint. "American Indian Ways of Leading and Knowing." *Leadership* 2 (May 2006): 225–44.

Washburn, Wilcomb W. "A Fifty-Year Perspective on the Indian Reorganization Act." *American Anthropologist* 16 (June 1984): 279–89.

———. "Legitimate Indian Leaders." *Wilson Quarterly* 10 (Autumn 1986): 173–74.

Werhan, Keith. "The Sovereignty of Indian Tribes." *Notre Dame Lawyer* 54 (October 1978): 5–25.

Wilkins, David E. *American Indian Politics and the American Political System.* New York: Rowman and Littlefield, 2002.

———. "Breaking into the Intergovernmental Matrix: The Lumbee Tribe's Efforts to Secure Federal Acknowledgment." *Publius* 23 (Autumn 1993): 123–42.

Wilkins, David E., and Sheryl Lightfoot. "Oaths of Office in Tribal Constitutions: Swearing Allegiance, but to Whom?" *American Indian Quarterly* 32 (Fall 2008): 389–411.

Wilkinson, Charles. *Blood Struggle: The Rise of Modern Indian Nations.* New York: W. W. Norton, 2005.

Williams, C. Herb, and Walt Neubrech. *Indian Treaties—American Nightmare.* Seattle: Outdoor Empire, 1976.

Interviews and Correspondence

Borgstrom, Howard. Email to the author, January 27, 2019.

Deloria, Philip S. Email to the author, March 16, 2018.

———. Email to the author, March 17, 2018.

Robertson, Bob. Interview with the author, Smithfield, Va., August 18, 2007.

Skye, Clarence. Phone interview with the author, February 12, 2018.

———. Phone interview with the author, August 14, 2018.

Trimble, Charles. Email to the author, May 22, 2018.

———. Interview with the author, Omaha, Neb., March 2, 2018.

Index